SEARCHING FOR RAYMOND

Anglicanism, Spiritualism, and Bereavement between the Two World Wars

RENE KOLLAR

LEXINGTON BOOKS
Lanham • Boulder • New York • Oxford

BF
1275
.C5
K65
2000

LEXINGTON BOOKS

Published in the United States of America
by Lexington Books
4720 Boston Way, Lanham, Maryland 20706

12 Hid's Copse Road
Cumnor Hill, Oxford OX2 9JJ, England

Copyright © 2000 by Lexington Books

All rights reserved. No part of this publication may be reproduced,
stored in a retrieval system, or transmitted in any form or by any
means, electronic, mechanical, photocopying, recording, or otherwise,
without the prior permission of the publisher.

British Library Cataloguing in Publication Information Available

Library of Congress Cataloging-in-Publication Data

Kollar, Rene.
　Searching for Raymond : Anglicanism, spiritualism, and bereavement between
the two world wars / Rene Kollar.
　　p. cm.
　Includes bibliographical references and index.
　ISBN 0-7391-0161-7 (cloth : alk. paper)
　　1. Spiritualism—Great Britain—History—20th century. 2. Church of England
Doctrines—History—20th century. I. Title.

BF1275.C5 K65 2000
261.5'13—dc21   00-42814

Printed in the United States of America

∞™ The paper used in this publication meets the minimum requirements of American
National Standard for Information Sciences—Permanence of Paper for Printed Library
Materials, ANSI/NISO Z39.48–1992.

To the students of Saint Vincent College

Contents

Introduction		ix
Chapter 1	The Great War: The Relationship between Spiritualism and Christianity	1
Chapter 2	The Anglican Church and the Question of Spiritualism after the Great War: The 1920 Lambeth Conference	33
Chapter 3	Psychical Studies, the Crisis of Faith, and the Anglican Church: Spiritualism and Religion during the 1930s	77
Chapter 4	The Archbishop's Committee on Spiritualism: The 1939 Report of the Committee to the Archbishop of Canterbury	107
Chapter 5	The 1940 Bishops' Meeting: Actions and Reactions	139
Appendix 1	Resolutions of the 1920 Lambeth Conference	155
Appendix 2	Conclusions of the Majority	157
Appendix 3	Minority Report	165
Bibliography		175
Index		183
About the Author		189

Introduction

David Lodge's character in *Paradise News*, Bernard Walsh, is a former priest, an agnostic theologian who teaches at St. John's College in South Rummidge, and a person terribly insecure about his sexuality and inexperience in love. After a comic escapade in sunny Hawaii, where Bernard re-unites his father and his dying aunt and falls in love with the wise and caring Yolande, Lodge's hero turns back to the clouds and cold of his college. Bernard admits that he is a horrible teacher. His first lecture in the new term addresses the question of eschatology, and he begins by debunking some traditional beliefs.

> But the concepts and images of this next world which have come down to us in Christian teaching no longer have any credibility for thoughtful, educated men and women. The very idea of an afterlife for individual human beings has been regarded with scepticism and embarrassment—or silently ignored—by nearly every major twentieth-century theologian.[1]

After painfully struggling through this lecture, Bernard Walsh ends the subject with an impromptu joke, which shocks one of the nuns in the lecture hall. Bernard Walsh's introductory lecture, however, contains one mistake. Throughout the twentieth century, numerous Anglicans had taken the idea of life after death very seriously.

In 1939, the archbishop of Canterbury, C. G. Lang, established a committee to discuss the relationship, if any, between spiritualism and the traditional teachings of the Anglican Church. With the horrific experiences of the Great War still clearly in the minds of many Britons, a number of Anglicans freely embraced the claims of spiritualism to help them cope with the losses resulting from that conflict. Not only did the doctrines of Anglicanism, some believed, fail to meet the psychological and spiritual needs of the bereaved, but churchmen and members of the laity also argued that spiritualism did not necessarily stand in opposition to the beliefs and teachings of their church. After several months of deliberation and listening to the testimony of both friendly and hostile witnesses, the Archbishop's Committee on Spiritualism wrote a report which was rather favorable to the claims of spiritualism and even argued that spiritualism might indeed complement Anglicanism and help Christians searching for meaning in their lives, especially those who were experiencing difficulties accepting the death of a friend or relative. The findings of this committee, however, were not made public until 1979.

Using the deliberations of the 1920 Lambeth Conference and then the Report of the Archbishop's Committee on Spiritualism as an expression or barometer of Anglican beliefs and attitudes on the subject, this book explores the position of the Anglican Church toward spiritualism and the increasing popularity of psychical studies within church circles during the early years of the twentieth century. The Great War and the enormous loss of life associated with it helped to ensure the growth of spiritualism. Commenting on a disturbance he experienced in England after the war, Robert Graves commented, "There were thousands of mothers like her, getting in touch with their dead sons by various spiritualistic means."[2] Consequently, spiritualism moved from the fringes of acceptability and began to occupy an important position in the lives of many Anglicans. It became fashionable; it became popular; and more importantly spiritualism helped those many Christians struggling to come to terms with the personal sorrows caused by the war. In a way, many religions, either openly or through nuance, offer to their adherents plausible explanations for disasters and also a series of rituals or practices which attempt to control or subdue the forces of nature, thus offering a modicum of protection to the believer. In this anthropological sense, therefore, such religions do possess a "magical" element or component.[3] In the mind of some Anglicans, their church failed to address the sorrow, grief, and anxiety occasioned by the staggering casualty lists of the war. Without the benefit of a belief in purgatory, a strong commitment to prayers for the dead, or a clear conception of the communion of saints, all expressed in Roman Catholic theology, many Anglicans turned to spiritualism for consolation and support following the war. Many embraced spiritualism as a surrogate or substitute religion. It offered the bereaved Christian those consoling and "magical" elements which many believed Anglicanism had abandoned during the Reformation.

The Anglican attitudes toward spiritualism during and after the Great War, the chaos and destruction of the war and the consequences for traditional religious beliefs, as well as the campaign waged by members of the church, authors, scientists, and spiritualists for official ecclesiastical recognition and the acceptance of spiritualism, all set the stage for the establishment of the Archbishop's Committee on Spiritualism in 1939. This book ends with a brief chapter which describes the unsuccessful attempts by the supporters of spiritualism to have the report published and thus vindicate the position of spiritualism within traditional Anglicanism and Christianity in general.

Spiritualism and groups of individuals dedicated to psychic research had existed in England long before the outbreak of the Great War, and several books admirably sketch the growth and development of spiritualism from the middle of the nineteenth century through the opening decades of the new century.[4] While I do not want to explore the same ground already surveyed by more competent authorities, some background information is needed to place spiritualism within the context of nineteenth- and twentieth-century Christianity, especially the pastoral demands the Great War placed on the Anglican Church, which eventually led to the formation of the Archbishop's Committee on Spiritualism. In the first place, the apparent triumph of rationalism, science, and the arguments of Charles Darwin meant that religion, like all other realms of thought, would come under the microscope of scientific methodology. "Spiritualism arose from the need that was felt to apply scientific methods to the solution of some problems that had previously been thought to be the exclusive province of religion."[5] A major tenet of all Christian denominations, the belief in a life after death, soon became the object of these early spiritualists, who now eagerly brought to their holy quest the methods of science.

One authority, Janet Oppenheim, emphasizes another aspect of Victorian society. While correctly pointing out that "the Victorian age was a period of religious uncertainty," she then argues that the "Victorians themselves were fully aware that the place of religion in the cultural fabric of their times was scarcely secure."[6] "In an effort to counter that insecurity, to calm their fears, and to seek answers where contemporary churches were ambiguous, thousands of British men and women in the Victorian and Edwardian eras turned to spiritualism and psychical research." Mediums, publications specializing in topics dealing with spiritualism, and numerous dedicated groups and societies contributed to the popularity of spiritualist claims. The atmosphere of "religious perplexity and tension was not, of course, coincidental."[7]

Although examples of psychic phenomena can be found throughout history and in the sacred writings of the Judeo-Christian tradition, the "established Churches, however, have been very loath to have much to do with the practitioners of the psychic."[8] At the official level, the churches have always regarded the existence of individuals possessing paranormal gifts "coolly at best, and normally with disfavour." Nonetheless, spiritualism flourished during the nineteenth and early twentieth centuries and quickly became identified with religion "because there is a close connection in the human mind (at least in the west in the modern period) between the concept of personal survival in an afterlife and man's relationship with ultimate reality—with the non-empirical which is the basis of religion."[9] According to some, moreover, spiritualism should not be regarded as a religious novelty: "Religious spiritualists seem to have held from the first the view that psychic phenomena not only supported the claims of religion but were at the basis of all religious beliefs, and that consequently spiritualism was not a new religion but the ground of all religion."[10]

According to Geoffrey Nelson, "Christian Spiritualists saw in the evidence of psychic phenomena proof which would dispel the doubt cast on the miraculous elements within Christianity by the development of science." And most spiritualist societies and organizations began to view themselves as churches, although attempts to merge Christian spiritualists into a federation eventually failed. "In proclaiming the existence and activity of spirit agencies throughout the universe, spiritualists were articulating a fundamentally religious point of view."[11] If science and rationalism posed some serious threats to orthodox Christianity, the new creed of materialism, a constant theme in 1920 Lambeth Conference discussions and other Anglican documents of the early twentieth century, also had to be resisted. Spiritualists could always be counted to be in the vanguard of this opposition.

"Indeed, materialism was widely perceived as the archvillain of the age. With its partner atheism, the alarmists moaned, it uprooted churches, made a mockery of morality, undermined social sanctions, and sapped the very foundations of western society and culture." According to Professor Oppenheim, "That, in fact, became the special task of the spiritualists in Victorian and Edwardian Britain: to deplore and combat the materialism that they perceived as all too rampant in their time." One must recognize, therefore, the close connection which some people saw between spiritualism and traditional Christian beliefs, although there were some areas of contention and conflict. Spiritualism attempted to fill the voids in traditional religions created by the modernizing trends of nineteenth century Britain, offering "a path away from uncompromising materialism when secularist zeal faltered as well as a buttress for faith when Christian optimism sagged."[12]

Some churchmen, however, felt uncomfortable about spiritualism and believed that it posed a serious threat to traditional Christianity. Some English clerics and church officials even described spiritualism as a diabolical and evil practice. During the nineteenth century, the Anglican Church saw no real or urgent need to embrace Spiritualism as an ally. "Officially, the Church of England . . . had no choice but to turn its back on spiritualism as doctrinally unacceptable, morally hazardous, and socially demeaning."[13] Not all Anglicans saw a chasm between their faith and psychic happenings; some Anglican clerics "chose to explore for themselves the borderland between life and death." The same tension which colored the relationship between the priest and the medieval wizard and between faith and superstition in pre-Reformation Roman Catholic England also existed to some extent between modern spiritualism and orthodox Anglicanism. As long as the claims of spiritualism did not openly challenge or confront the teachings of the Anglican Church, it could be conveniently ignored. But another avenue soon appeared for Anglicans who were interested in the beliefs of spiritualism.

> Psychical research, however, with its attempt to maintain neutrality on the crucial theological issues at stake, did not involve such compromises; the Society for Psychical Research, with its prestigious social and intellectual

Introduction xiii

status, was the perfect home for Anglicans who were uneasy over spiritualism, but deeply concerned to learn if there was, after all, "something in it."[14]

"So it was that a group of friends, mainly Cambridge philosophers and scientists, formed the Society for Psychical Research in 1882. The scientific optimism of late Victorianism was in full flood, and psychical research was part of the attempt to apply rigid scientific criteria to human experience."[15] According to Michael Perry, "the Church was happier with psychical research than with Spiritualism, and there has been a smattering of Christians active in the field ever since." The *Proceedings* (vol. 1) of the SPR defined the subject matter of psychical research as "that large group of debatable phenomena designated by such terms as mesmeric, psychical and spiritualistic."[16] Committees undertook investigation of the following subjects: "the nature and the extent of any influence which may be exerted by one mind upon another"; a study of hypnotism, mesmeric trances, clairvoyance, and associated phenomena; "a critical revision of Reichenbach's[17] researches with certain organisms called 'sensitive', and an enquiry whether such organisms possess any power of perception beyond a highly exalted sensibility of the recognized sensory organs"; an investigation of reports of apparitions at death or the haunting of houses; investigation of "psychical phenomena commonly called spiritualistic"; and the collection of material dealing with the history of these areas.[18]

The worthwhile and valuable committee work and the areas of investigation, however, were not as important as the method which the SPR championed. Volume 1 of the *Proceedings* pointed out that "the aim of the Society will be to approach these various problems without prejudice or prepossession of any kind, and in the same spirit of exact and unimpassioned enquiry which has enabled science to solve so many problems, once not less obscure nor less hotly debated." The membership of the SPR grew steadily throughout the twentieth century because of its insistence on objectivity, scientific methods, and its successes in exposing frauds and charlatans. Because of the number of casualties of the Great War and the increasing public interest in questions dealing with survival after death, the membership of the SPR increased greatly. In the discussions and deliberations of the Anglican Church following the war dealing with the relationship between spiritualism and Christianity, the work and reputation of the SPR figured greatly.

It was undoubtedly the horrors of the Great War and those long, unforeseen death lists which not only drew more people into the ranks of spiritualism but also forced the Anglican Church to finally come to terms with the relationship or the possibility of a connection between spiritualism and traditional Christianity. This book will attempt to explore the questions which confronted many Anglicans after the end of the war. Were the doctrines and teachings of the Anglican Church adequate to offer explanations and comfort to the bereaved? Was the theological inheritance of the Reformation and Puritanism, which emphasized rugged individualism, ill-equipped to handle the misery caused by the war? Was something lacking in the Anglican view of the afterlife which forced people into the arms of spiritualism? Did spiritualism, consequently, become a surrogate or substitute religion for some Anglicans? How did the Great War bring the Anglican Church to address seriously spiritualism? What were the factors and who were the leading individuals who eventually forced the archbishop of Canterbury, C. G. Lang, to form a committee to study the relationship between spiritualism and Christianity? Did the committee's report adequately address this issue? Why did the Anglican Church refuse to publish the findings of this report immediately?

First the 1920 Lambeth Conference and then the Archbishop's Committee on Spiritualism wrestled with the relationship between spiritualism and Christianity, and the findings of these discussions of churchmen help to illuminate the challenging and sometimes complementary connection between the two beliefs. A modern authority and Anglican cleric wrote in 1984: "I believe that a paranormal experience, or reflection on the paranormal experiences of others, can similarly be an avenue to a transcendent realization which can point us towards belief in God."[19] Explaining to his readers why he was a Christian parapsychologist, Michael Perry concluded with the following words: "My overall world view is one in which my Christian faith and the discoveries of psychic studies come together in a convergent way. Faith, reason, and evidence have produced their subtle amalgam." His statement would have certainly appealed to those Anglicans who tried to come to terms with the destruction of the Great War and who eventually found in spiritualism some consolation.[20]

My interest in this subject, not my usual field of research within English religious history, was sparked by an article appearing in the Roman Catholic publication *The Tablet*, which drew attention to the work of the Archbishop's Committee on Spiritualism and the fact that the report had not been made public until 1979. Curiosity, and not the search for great historical truths, drove me to investigate more. My latent interest in and appreciation of anthropology, especially aspects dealing with organized religion, became a second contributing factor which pushed me down the path to a study of spiritualism and psychical studies. Keith Thomas's *Religion and the Decline of Magic* made a great impact on me when I was a graduate student. The relation between magic, in the anthropological sense, and Christianity has always intrigued me, as the relation between spiritualism and Christianity most certainly interested the generation after the 1914-18 war. The book, with one exception, deals exclusively with Anglican attitudes toward spiritualism; views of other religious bodies in Great Britain lie outside the scope of this work.

The Proceedings of the 1920 Lambeth Conference and the Lang Papers, which deal with the background and the appointment of the Archbishop's Committee, are both located at Lambeth Palace Library and provide the basis for this study. The papers of the individual members of Archbishop Lang's committee and the witnesses do not shed additional light on the workings of the group: some have been lost and others do not mention the work or deliberations of the committee. The failure to locate the papers of Bishop Francis Underhill, the chairman of the committee, proved especially disappointing. Libraries in America and Great Britain provided the secondary sources, and the large collection of spiritualist literature, pamphlets, and newspapers in the London area proved invaluable. The British Library and the Society for Psychical Research proved to be a treasure trove for my research. I would like to thank Lambeth Palace Library for permission to publish the Majority and Minority Reports of the Archbishop's Committee on Spiritualism and to quote from the proceedings of the Lambeth Conferences and the Bishops' Meetings papers.

Canon Michael Perry, former sub-dean of Durham Cathedral and editor of the *Christian Parapsychologist*, helped and encouraged me in the early stages of my research, introduced me to the journal which he edits, and sent relevant material to me in America. The monks of Ealing Abbey, London, graciously offered me hospitality and invaluable friendship during my stays in London. Several faculty development grants from Saint Vincent College and Saint Vincent Seminary, Latrobe, Pennsylvania, permitted me to cross the Atlantic numerous times to search out information. One particular grant financed the purchase of a powerbook, which brought me out of the confines of a scriptorium into the modern world of research. This modern quill has made the writing and editing less burdensome. Finally, Archabbot Paul Maher, OSB, the former superior of Saint Vincent Archabbey, and Archabbot Douglas R. Nowicki, OSB, the current superior, allowed me the time away from the monastery to complete my work. As always, my thanks to those special students who struggle to keep me young in spirit and outlook.

RK
March 2000

Notes

1. D. Lodge, *Paradise News* (London: Penguin Books, 1992), 352.
2. R. Graves, *Goodbye to All That* (London: Penguin Books, 1960), 192.
3. See K. Thomas, *Religion and the Decline of Magic: Studies in Popular Belief in Sixteenth and Seventeenth Century England* (London: Weidenfeld & Nicolson, 1971).
4. For a good general history of Spiritualism and psychic research, see the following: R. Brandon, *The Spiritualists: The Passion for the Occult in the Nineteenth and Twentieth Centuries* (New York: Prometheus Books, 1984); R. Haynes, *The Society for Psychical Research, 1882-1982* (London: MacDonald, 1982); B. Inglis, *Science and Parascience: A History of the Paranormal, 1914-1939* (London: Hodder & Stoughton, 1984); G. Nelson, *Spiritualism and Society* (New York: Schocken Books, 1969); J.

Oppenheim, *The Other World: Spiritualism and Psychical Research in England, 1850-1914* (Cambridge: Cambridge University Press, 1985); and W. H. Salter, *The Society for Psychical Research: An Outline of Its History* (London: Society for Psychical Research, 1970). For contemporary studies of the relationship between Christianity and spiritualism, see E. Garth Moore, *Try the Spirits: Christianity and Psychical Research* (New York: Oxford University Press, 1977); *Survival: A Reconsideration: The Sixteenth Frederic W. H. Myers Memorial Lecture* (London: Society for Psychical Research, 1966); and M. Perry, *Psychic Studies: A Christian's View* (Wellingborough, Northamptonshire: Aquarian, 1984).

    5. G. Nelson, *Spiritualism and Society*, 136.
    6. J. Oppenheim, *The Other World*, 1.
    7. Ibid., 59.
    8. M. Perry, *Psychic Studies*, 7.
    9. G. Nelson, *Spiritualism and Society*, 137.
    10. Ibid., 145.
    11. J. Oppenheim, *The Other World*, 61.
    12. Ibid., 62.
    13. Ibid., 68.
    14. Ibid., 81.
    15. M. Perry, *Psychic Studies*, 8-9.
    16. Quoted in W. H. Salter, *The Society for Psychical Research: An Outline of Its History*, 13. This short pamphlet contains a brief outline of the various groups and organizations which predated the formation of the SPR and also a short biographical sketch of the leading personalities involved in its early history. Salter chronicles the work of the SPR from its beginnings up to the decade of the 1960s. A short but valuable bibliography, in addition to publications by the SPR, is also included.
    17. According to the society's history, "Baron von Reichenbach was a distinguished chemist and metallurgist, who claimed to have discovered that some persons could see lights near the poles of magnets" 14.
    18. Ibid., 13.
    19. M. Perry, *Psychic Studies*, 48.
    20. Ibid., 64.

Chapter One

The Great War: The Relationship between Spiritualism and Christianity

On 14 September 1915, Raymond, the youngest son of Sir Oliver Lodge, was killed in the Ypres campaign. Father and son had been very close. Prior to this tragedy, Sir Oliver, a leading figure in the Society for Psychical Research, had already become well acquainted with several mediums, and after he received the sad news from the front, some of them began to claim that they had already established contact with the dead son.[1] Skeptical at first, both Lord and Lady Lodge eventually became believers after several sittings with a professional medium, Mrs. Osborne Leonard. One year later in 1916, Sir Oliver published his book, *Raymond: Or Life and Death*,[2] "in which he reported on messages received from his son who had been killed in France . . . His book had a tremendous impact."[3] Sir Oliver possessed both outstanding scientific and academic credentials, and people thus took his views on spiritualism seriously. But on the other hand, he stood with numerous other people who had lost relatives and friends during the Great War and who also searched for ways to assuage their grief. The war had brought incalculable sorrow and suffering into the lives of all classes of Britons, and a large number turned to spiritualism for answers and consolation.

At the beginning of the conflict, most people believed that the war effort in Europe would be both swift and glorious, but the reports from the trenches and the death lists quickly changed the enthusiasm and unbridled patriotism into horror. The unbelievable number of casualties literally shattered the lives of individuals and families and destroyed an entire generation of young, promising, and bright people. Including the Irish losses, a recent study estimated British deaths during the Great War at 772,000.[4] On the first day of the Battle of the Somme, for example, 20,000 English soldiers died. The death toll for the Second World War, approximately 200,000, seems small by comparison. Additional statistics for the Great War painfully tell the tale of suffering and sorrow.

> Altogether, some six million men from the United Kingdom fought during the First World War, so that roughly one in eight were killed (to say nothing of a further one and a half million who were disabled). And when broken down, the figures become even more extraordinary. Of the men who were aged 20-24 in 1914, death came to 30.58 per cent, and of those aged 13-19, the figure was 28.15 per cent which, as Rosalind Mitchison notes, "meant grief and shock for almost every family in the country."[5]

"Oxford University's roll of honour contained 14,561 names; of these, 2,680 were killed or died of wounds or sickness. Trinity College, Cambridge, lost over 600 of its former undergraduates . . . Across the nation as a whole nine per cent of all British men under 45 were killed."[6] Death from another cause also terrorized the country in the last stages of the Great War. "An epidemic of influenza spread across the world. Starting apparently in the Near East, it reached central Europe in August, and England in October. Something like three quarters of the population were struck down . . . All told, some 150,000 English people died of influenza in the winter of 1918-19."[7]

But it was the magnitude of the senseless casualties on the Continent which caused the anxiety and touched people spiritually and psychologically. "Between 1914 and 1918 families were suddenly forced to deal with vast numbers of violent and unnatural deaths of adult sons, as though they were the norm."[8] Moreover, "the Great War combined and far exceeded all those forms of violent, unnatural, and premature death which the Victorians had been unable to resolve effectively even within the conventional Christian framework." According to David Cannadine, "the impact of the First World War on attitudes to death . . . was profound for at least a generation; and that inter-war Britain was probably more obsessed with death than any other period in modern history."[9] Death did not discriminate between social classes: "For once again, it was both 'the castle of the rich and the cottage of the lowly' that the angel of death visited in these years."[10] The greatest proportion of the deaths, however, did come from the country's elite, and the public schools and Oxbridge felt the loss significantly. Professor Cannadine skillfully describes other devastating effects of the war: the horrors of trench life, direct experience of the carnage, and the witnessing of friends and comrades cut to pieces, which certainly left deep psychological scars on the tender psyches of the survivors, and finally the intense sense of bereavement felt by those who received the sad news of a death in England. Some turned to literature for an outlet, and numerous poems and short stories told of the anxieties, despair, and destruction associated with the deaths on the Western Front.[11] Others, naturally, sought comfort in the words of the Anglican Church.

The Church of England certainly did not abandon its flock during the Great War and, moreover, a number of its leaders and theologians began to address the issues being brought into relief by the war, namely, the apparent inability of Anglicanism to help its faithful to cope with the death or deaths of loved ones. The church responded enthusiastically to the war effort, and in a show of patriotism and dedication, chaplains rushed to the Western Front to minister to the religious needs of the troops. Throughout the country, churchmen wrote pamphlets, books, and newspaper columns which dealt with the problems of wartime. Anxious people in the parishes throughout Great Britain heard their clergymen speaking on all aspects associated with the conflict in Europe. A mixture of patriotism and religion colored these sermons. The leadership of the Anglican Church, moreover, did not shrink from nor neglect responsibility, and members of the clergy began to address questions dealing with the war. "It is right that men should expect from the Christian pulpit a vision and a leadership," a preface to a collection of sermons preached by prominent churchmen declared, and "in the tremendous world-debate of the War, the Church of Christ should have some relevant—even some final—word to utter."[12]

As the Primate of the Anglican Church, the archbishop of Canterbury, Randall Davidson, was the one to whom people looked for religious leadership and guidance. Preaching at All Hallows, Barking-by-the-Tower, on All Souls Day in 1914, Archbishop Davidson began with an appeal to patriotic emotions: "while England is throbbing with excitement and our streets echo to the tramp of armed men, and great camps for the first time in our history bring into our green fields and country lanes a new kind of life, and with it some new kinds of peril."[13] He mentioned the sacrifices of the soldiers and also drew attention to the "self-offerings" experienced by England's mothers and daughters "—for the women, after all, feel it most and suffer most."[14] The archbishop also recognized that "the shadow of bereavement has fallen, [and] there goes up, spoken or unspoken, a bewildered cry, or at least the sigh of a bewildered and wondering heart."[15] Davidson recommended to those suffering through the grief of a death a quiet and firm resignation and faith in God.

> Bewilderment does not mean unbelief. I see no lack of faith or of courage. Rather the quiet Christian courage of fathers and mothers and sisters who have lost the very light of their eyes, or the simple, loyal bravery of quiet young wives who have been widowed at a stroke, sends one to one's knees before God in reverent recognition that to those, His children, He is indeed a very present help in trouble.

On 3 January 1915, Archbishop Davidson preached at St. Paul's Cathedral, and he again made reference to the importance of one's faith in times of trouble. Noting the sorrow that had blanketed the land, the archbishop praised "the bright face of mother, or elder sister, or young wife, self-controlled and keen with the background of anxious stress or poignant sorrow behind the smile, but with the 'peace, which passeth understanding.'"[16]

The Right Rev. Arthur F. Winnington-Ingram, the bishop of London, also wrote and preached frequently throughout the course of the Great War on issues and questions arising from the conflict on the Continent. He argued against those Christians who believed that the war was a punishment for the country's past sins, and he expressed his conviction that England's armies fought for a righteous and just cause. The bishop did not avoid mentioning the pessimism and sorrow occasioned by those long and terrible death lists. In 1916, he opened a sermon by telling his listeners that "in the first view the year opens with nothing but clouds and thick darkness."[17] "Not only is the night of war still upon us," he continued, "but there is not even a streak of dawn." A pall of grief and sorrow had suddenly descended upon Great Britain. "The trenches are hell; London is becoming a city of mourners."[18] Speaking at Hammersmith Parish Church, the bishop of London announced, "Here we are in a world of death."[19] But what advice did this prolific prelate give to the thousands of grieving people throughout the land?

He tried to offer comfort to those who had personally experienced the death of a loved one by assuring them that soldiers killed in battle received the supreme and ultimate reward in heaven. "I believe that not only will CHRIST welcome them as comrades in arms," the bishop preached at St. Martin in the Fields, "but over every one who dies in this war with his face towards the foe, if he dies in CHRIST, will be said those words: 'This is My beloved son . . . This is My beloved son, in whom I am well pleased.'"[20] He believed that death was a passing phenomenon, and attempted to link patriotism with religion. The brave and the pure of heart would inherit peace and happiness greater than anything experienced on earth. In addition to this attempt of the bishop of London at consolation, moreover, "a relatively small number of clergymen stated that no matter what kind of life he [the soldier] had led in the past, the man who died for England would stand 'cleansed from the stain of sin, crowned and triumphant, looking unto Jesus in the unveiled splendour of Paradise.'"[21]

Bishop Winnington-Ingram offered other words of comfort. "Then, again, it is the duty of the Church in the war," he wrote in 1918, "to keep very bright the hope of the other life."[22] The tears of the sorrowful and mournful could be wiped away by what Winnington-Ingram termed, "a bright view of death."[23] "We have not risen to the spirit of our responsibilities, of our glorious privileges, if we have not in some way, however simple, brought home this bright view of death to the nation in the war, if we have not shown that death is not the ultimate calamity and the end of all." At the parish church in Islington, for example, he spoke on the theme, "Heaviness may endure for a night, but joy cometh in the morning." "We have not sufficiently preached the Gospel of Hope to the mourners," he pointed out, and "if you and I are to preach a message of hope to the nation, we must go back to a much brighter view of death than we now have in the Church."[24]

During this period of trial or heaviness, the confused or perplexed Christian must cling to one's Christian faith and persevere. "We are working for the great morning," Winnington-Ingram told a parish audience, "and we must not lose our faith in the night"[25] of doubt, anxiety, and grief. God never allowed evil and destruction ultimately to triumph. Consequently, a spirit of hope should animate the life of a Christian during the uncertain climate of the war. This spirit, the bishop argued, "requires only faith in God, faith in God which first produces penitence, then inspires action, then draws out sacrifice, and then breathes fortitude into the soul."[26] For the bishop of London, the war had indeed produced much suffering and bereavement throughout the country, and he did not dismiss these emotions lightly. To help people cope with their losses, he offered the traditional religious virtues of faith, hope, and perseverance. It appears, however, that this episcopal advice did not satisfy the needs of some Anglicans.

William Ralph Inge, the dean of St. Paul's, also addressed the problems caused by the Great War. A productive writer, especially in the newspaper columns, the dean wrote comments that reached the ears of many Christians. Like others, he did not attempt to diminish the horrors of the war: "We may be reduced to great distress and poverty; and we are likely to lose thousands or tens of thousands of gallant lives. Each death of a brave soldier means agonising distress to one English home . . . for in a great war all classes are levelled."[27] Distress and sorrow had indeed become a common experience. "To hundreds of thousands of English people this longing has come with a poignant intensity through bereavement caused by this war," Dean Inge pointed out, especially that "lives so young and fresh and full of promise . . . should be suddenly cut short, seems an indictment against God's goodness, unless death is but the gate into a higher and more blessed life."[28]

Inge recognized the problem facing the church. Anglicanism had an obligation to minister pastorally to people in need, and during the war it did not turn its back on the faithful, but apparently much was lacking in the approach taken and solutions offered. "And so the bereaved looked in vain for comfort to their spiritual guides," he maintained, and they did not receive any satisfaction. Consequently, some poor souls embraced spiritualism, and the Anglican Church must come to terms with this dangerous trend. Searching frantically for answers, these individuals "have gone back to the old discredited, barbarous superstitions of necromancy and so-called spiritualism." Inge vigorously assailed and condemned the claims of spiritualism: "These sham sciences, which the Church has discountenanced from the first, these companion sciences of astrology, witchcraft, and other mischievous delusions, have once more stalked out into the light of day, and are unsettling the reasons of hundreds." The pretensions of spiritualism pale before the true and authentic claims of the Christian creed. But, he queried, what should the Anglican Church do for those individuals whose "loving hearts that cling to them [superstitions] are very sore"?

Dean Inge took a conservative Anglican approach to anguish and personal distress. Growth and spiritual maturity could take place through suffering; in the face of disasters the faithful Christian should adopt the attitude of Job. Believing that suffering was "a divine thing" and "an essential part not only of the discipline of life for the erring and weak, but even more, part of the royal prerogative of life for those whom God calls to follow most closely in His own footsteps,"[29] he called for a new attitude toward and an appreciation of suffering. A strong faith in human immortality would help the pain and bereavement, and thus "they are constantly borne with a patience and resignation which we recognise as morally beautiful." Moreover, "Christianity teaches plainly that every temporal evil may be transmuted into an instrument of spiritual good."[30] People should, therefore, joyfully embrace the cross of Jesus, since one's bereavement might be part of a mysterious and divine grand plan in which one is "called upon to advance the Kingdom of God more by what we bear than by what we do."[31] A Christian reached his or her perfection by a patient and stoic acceptance of suffering. This necessarily presupposed a strong and personal faith, and Dean Inge's advice for those who "walk through the valley of the shadow of death" came from accepted Anglican theology: "Keep your faith and hope strong, as our forefathers did one hundred years ago."[32]

The words, prescriptions, and thoughts of traditional Anglicanism did not appeal to all, especially some of the English troops at the Western Front who faced death daily. "Death was always present, confronted not only in battle but also in no man's land and in the trenches themselves. Soldiers used unburied corpses as support for their guns and as markers to find their way in the trenches; they sometimes took off those boots of fallen soldiers that were in better condition than their own."[33] The claims of spiritualism and beliefs in the supernatural, however, did pervade the thoughts and actions of some of the soldiers in the trenches. Consequently, "a host of spiritualist images, stories, and legends proliferated during the conflict among the British, as among all other, troops."[34] Winter points out that a popular art, such as pictures of saints or the figure of Jesus Christ associated with the battlefield and "a brisk business in religious bric-a-brac," existed among all the armies on the Western Front. Dean Inge also did not fail to recognize this tendency of the troops. "Soldiers are always prone both to fatalism and to superstition; many of our men are said to have carried amulets with them into action."[35]

> Almost from the beginning, tales of unusual happenings which purported to prove that supernatural forces had intervened in the earthly conflict were circulated by word of mouth and in the press. Cases of churches completely destroyed save for an ancient relic or picture of Jesus, wayside crosses which

stood unscathed at shell-swept crossroads, and the alleged appearances of Joan of Arc, were discussed with the utmost gravity even by educated persons.[36]

The stories and the legends of the soldiers "were important in deepening popular spiritualism, in that they added the prestige of the Tommy and the weight of his experience to those who lived within or on the fringes of the spiritualist community." One tale, the Angels of the Mons, achieved a particular status.

In September 1914, the author Arthur Machen wrote a short piece for the *Evening News* which described how Agincourt bowmen appeared on the horizon to defend the retreating British at the battle of the Mons.[37] Machen later described the appeal of this story for the beleaguered troops: "First of all, all ages and nations have cherished the thought that spiritual hosts may come to the help of earthly arms, that gods and heroes and saints have descended from their high immortal places to fight for their worshippers and clients."[38] After its publication in the newspaper, the legend became extremely popular. Witnesses came forward and testified that they certainly saw "something" protecting the British, and numerous variations of Machen's story were reported: in one version St. George appeared; in another, a cloud interceded and defended the English; and finally, bodies of dead Germans were found on the battlefield riddled with arrows! Machen's own explanation for the popularity and success of the tale among the war-weary English sounds similar to the reaction of spiritualism against the materialism of the age.

> But, taking the affair as it stands at present, how is it that a nation plunged in materialism of the grossest kind has accepted idle rumours and gossip of the supernatural as certain truth? The answer is contained in the question: it is precisely because our whole atmosphere is materialist that we are ready to credit anything—save the truth.[39]

In addition to Machen's description of the miraculous rescue by that "tremendous host" under the command of "St. George [who] had brought his Agincourt Bowmen to help the English,"[40] the same author also recounted several other stories told by soldiers detailing alleged interventions by supernatural forces. But it was the belief in the Angels of the Mons which caught the imagination. "*The Real Angels of the Mons* (1915), a pamphlet by the Rev. A. A. Boddy, was published with the permission of the Official Censor as an aid to recruiting."[41] When Herbert Hensley Henson preached a sermon on 25 July 1915 in Westminster Abbey during which he referred to the Angels of Mons in a skeptical tone, he later revealed that his remarks "drew down on me a number of protests, some very angrily expressed, and some written 'more in sorrow than in anger.'"[42]

A strong belief in an afterlife, not surprisingly, also spoke strongly to many of the soldiers who faced death on a daily basis, and numerous testimonies from the front testified to this. According to the words of an infantry officer, for example, "The young have a vague instinct that somehow, somewhere, life *as we know it,* goes on."[43] A Royal Army Medical Corps (RAMC) captain speaking for his comrades pointed out that "the life beyond the grave is very widely believed in, though in a vague way." One journal, the *Occult Review*, published the texts of communications between the living and the dead soldiers. And the English public became acquainted with other similar stories, such as the revelations of a Bournemouth soldier recently killed in action[44] and the communications between "Roger" and his father.[45] Gloom and distress dominated the lives of many Britons. Painfully calling to mind the death of Edward, Vera Brittain remarked in *Testament of Youth*: "It lasted so long, perhaps, because I decided in the first few weeks after his loss that nothing would ever really console me for Edward's death or make his memory less poignant; and in this I was quite correct, for nothing ever has."[46] She also expressed a feeling common to many of her contemporaries who had to face a personal loss:

> During this period, one or two sympathetic friends wrote earnestly to me of the experimental compensations of spiritualism. As always in wartime, the long casualty list has created throughout England a terrible interest in the idea of personal survival, and many wives and mothers had turned to *séances* and mediums in the hope of finding some indication, however elusive, of a future reunion "beyond the sun."

Bereavement and the attempts to deal with death became more intense throughout Great Britain after the victory in 1918. In a sense, "Britain became a nation of bereaved."[47] People tried to cope in several ways. David Cannadine notes, for example, the construction of war memorials throughout the countryside, the introduction of Armistice Day, which quickly evolved into an national ritual celebrated annually, and "the massive proliferation of interest in spiritualism."[48] "In the case of spiritualism, the upsurge of popular interest in the years immediately after 1918 was quite remarkable." The war confirmed for many that spiritualism, popular in some circles of British life from the mid-nineteenth century, might offer consolation to those suffering a personal loss. "The 1914-18 conflict certainly did not create these modes of thought, but neither did the war discredit or destroy them," J. M. Winter argues, and the "bereaved—and they numbered in the millions—needed all the help they could get. The magical and mythical realm flared up at a time of mass death and destruction to help illuminate a world darkened by the catastrophe that today we call the Great War."[49] Consequently, the number of people who sought shelter in spiritualist organizations began to increase.

The membership of the Society for Psychical Research, for example, increased significantly after the war. In 1920, the peak year, "403 full members and 902 associates" belonged to the SPR.[50] But membership began to decrease in that year due to the policy of the organization which suspended the election of new associate members because the one guinea subscription did not cover administrative costs. The Society for Psychical Research continued to keep the country informed of its work, and during 1934 members presented talks on the BBC dealing with the activities of the organization. The membership rolls of another group, the Spiritualists' National Union, also increased following the Great War.[51] "By 1919, there were already 309 societies affiliated to the SNU, exactly double the pre-war figure."[52] A number of factors contributed to the popularity of spiritualism following the horrors of the war.

The writings and lectures of significant people helped to turn the thoughts of many to spiritualism. Sir Oliver Lodge, nationally recognized scientist, member and president of the Society for Psychical Research, became one of the most important and influential evangelists for the claims of spiritualism.[53] "He was a pillar of the Society for Psychical Research, publishing in its journals learned articles both on spiritualist phenomena and on the physics of wireless telegraphy."[54] Even before his son was killed in France, Sir Oliver began to write about psychical research in addition to his establish works on physics. In 1909, he published *The Survival of Man*, "revealing that his experience with mediums had led him to accept the evidence for life after death."[55] "The truth as I am learning to regard it is that incarnate and discarnate humanity is all one family," Sir Oliver wrote in 1917, and "that the screen between the materialised and the immaterial variety is of a sensory and material and temporary order, and that communication through the veil is even now occasionally possible."[56] In an article discussing the relationship between ether, matter, and the soul, he prophesied that "the obscure communications and strange movements which are now studied or experienced in spiritualistic circles . . . will gradually take their place in the orderly scheme of recognised science."[57] Moreover, Lodge ended,

> ultimately the subject will emerge from its dark and difficult period—a period clouded with traces of superstition and obstructed by well-meant but antiquated prejudice—and familiar intercourse across the veil or gulf of death will become sufficiently common to prove an untold blessing to the human race.

More controversial was the publication in 1916 of Sir Oliver's book, *Raymond*. Overcome with grief and sorrow due to the death of his son, Raymond, at Ypres in September 1915, Lodge and his wife began to attend séances conducted by the medium Mrs. Osborne Leonard, and in "the following weeks the Lodge family—father, mother, and at least two of the eleven children—continued the sessions and built up a detailed picture of Raymond's life in what they called 'Summerland.'"[58] These communications provided the material for Sir Oliver's description of his son's existence in the afterlife. In the opening pages of the book, the interested reader encountered the following words which explained Sir Oliver's intentions:

> It is not without hesitation that I have ventured thus to obtrude family affairs. I should not have done so were it not that the amount of premature and unnatural bereavement at the present time is so appalling that the pain caused by exposing one's own sorrow and its alleviation, to possible scoffers, becomes almost negligible in view of the service which it is legitimate to hope may thus be rendered to mourners, if they can derive comfort by learning that communication across the gulf is possible.[59]

The power of the book's appeal was that it showed "the dead themselves attempting to reach the living in order both to help them cope with the pain of bereavement and to help establish the truth of the spiritualist message."[60] *Raymond* quickly became very popular and spoke to the needs of many people, and it went through several printings before the war ended. Sir Oliver's book, however, did receive some nasty comments. "But, as may be imagined, it did not have an easy critical ride. A great many reviews were hostile or jocular. It was banned from the shelves of Aberdeen Public Library. Some clergymen thought the whole thing was a Satanic delusion."[61] But Sir Oliver and *Raymond* correctly gauged the temperament of the English and their struggles to come to terms with the dead.

Sir Oliver Lodge also tried to make the connection between spiritualism and Christianity. He admitted that traditional Christianity and professional theologians had expressed some justifiable objections to the claims of spiritualism, but some of the criticism, however, flowed from ignorance and prejudice. In one essay, Sir Oliver was to comment on the relationship between spiritualism and Christianity, "the higher and more mystical and ancient form carried on by a highly developed organization, namely, the Church in its broadest sense."[62] After cautioning the reader to avoid seeking after anything of lasting importance or infallible proofs in human endeavors, such as a book, a church or a medium, he pointed out that "psychical research is primarily an inquiry; and as such has no creed."[63] Throughout the pages of sacred and holy writings, one encounters numerous examples of psychical phenomena such as "supernormal communications. But the possibility has never been fully recognized, and has not widely been made use of as a comfort to the bereaved and as a means of obtaining initial information about the conditions of a future state."[64] Moreover, he believed that some spiritualists had been repelled and disgusted not by the essential message of Christian teaching but by its doctrines and dogmas.

The Christian, Lodge argued, should not quickly dismiss or discard the beliefs of spiritualism. Moreover, the pages of the Bible, the foundation of Christianity, contained numerous examples of psychical activities, "and which for certain purposes regards spiritual enquiry through human intermediaries as not only possible but commendable."[65] Sir Oliver also recognized important pastoral implications for the Christian churches and believed that psychical happenings or experiences which "were common in old times are still feasible." Calling to mind the bereavement and sorrow caused by the Great War, he pointed out "that if they are rationally and reverently conducted they bring comfort and consolation . . . They convey a certainty of present hope and guidance, and a hope of further beneficent activities in the future." In the addendum to the tenth edition of *Raymond*, published in 1918, he wrote that "the main purpose of a book like this is to help to bring comfort to bereaved persons, especially to those who have been bereaved by war."[66] Consequently, Sir Oliver gave a favorable judgment concerning the relationship of spiritualism to Christianity: "But, so far as I am entitled to form an opinion, there is nothing in the Spiritualistic creed, at least as above formulated, which is alien to the Christian faith."[67]

Just as Lodge shifted some of his interests from the arena of experimental science to the exploration of the realm of the supernatural, the man behind Sherlock Holmes moved from the world of literature to the realm of spiritualism.[68] Like Sir Oliver, Sir Arthur Conan Doyle touched the needs and emotions of a number of people and offered spiritualism as an antidote to their grief. Other similarities also existed between the two men. Both lost sons in the Great War and both published books about spiritualism. The second volume of *The History of Spiritualism*, which Sir Arthur dedicated to Lodge, sounds similar to thoughts expressed in *Raymond*:

> If for a moment the author may strike a personal note he would say that, while his own loss had no effect upon his views, the sight of a world which was distraught with sorrow, and which was eagerly asking for help and knowledge, did certainly affect his mind and cause him to understand that these psychic studies, which he had so long pursued, were of immense practical importance and could no longer be regarded as a mere intellectual hobby or fascinating pursuit of a novel research.[69]

Sir Arthur pursued the cause of spiritualism in an active and dedicated manner: during the 1920s he took to the road and traveled throughout the world preaching the benefits of the gospel of spiritualism. He correctly recognized the impact of the Great War on the recent upsurge in the popularity of spiritualism. "The shock of the war," he wrote, "was meant to rouse us to mental and moral earnestness, to give us the courage to tear away venerable shames, and to force the human race to realise and use the vast new revelation which has been so clearly stated and so abundantly proved, for all who will examine the statements with proofs with an open mind."[70] "In the presence of an agonized world, hearing every day of the deaths of the flower of our race in the first promise of their unfulfilled youth, seeing around one the wives and mothers who had no conception whither their loved ones had gone to," he began to recognize the importance of spiritualism as "a call of hope and of guidance to the human race at the time of its deepest affliction."[71] In his *History of Spiritualism*, Sir Arthur, like other observers of contemporary England, sadly noted that "the deaths occurring in almost every family in the land brought a sudden and concentrated interest in life after death."[72] People, he pointed out, "not only asked the question, 'If a man die shall he live again?' but they eagerly sought to know if communication was possible with the dear ones they had lost." These individuals, moreover, "sought for 'the touch of the vanished hand, and the sound of the voice that is still.'"

In addition to drawing the close connection between the war and spiritualism, the bereavement of many Britons, and the hidden treasures of spiritualism, Conan Doyle, along with other committed spiritualists,[73] attempted to bring out the positive relationship between traditional Christianity and spiritualism, and he spent the rest of his life trying to demonstrate the similarities between psychical phenomena and Christian thought and beliefs. In 1918, Sir Arthur wrote *The New Revelation* in which he argued that the Great War was religious in nature. "Conan Doyle's intention was to reveal the religious importance of spiritualism and to provide a personal testimony which would be comprehensible to the masses."[74] Sir Arthur had rejected Roman Catholicism as a youth and thus "sought for a theistic system of belief which would accommodate the principle of the survival of bodily death. Spiritualism offered him this with its non-sectarian approach and insistence upon the provable existence on an afterlife."[75]

"Spiritualism is a system of thought and knowledge which can be reconciled with any religion," he wrote, and the "basic facts are the continuity of personality and the power of communication after death."[76] Moreover, characteristics of spiritualism seem to have been present in the development of Judeo-Christian thought. In the Bible, he wrote in *The Vital Message*, "the foundation of our present religious thought, we have bound together the living and the dead, and the dead have tainted the living."[77] Although Conan Doyle disapproved of much contained in the Old Testament, such as its prohibitions against spiritualistic activities and its concept of a wrathful and vengeful God, he looked favorably on the books of the New Testament. Sir Arthur interpreted the life and ministry of Jesus Christ in terms of "a messenger from the 'other world' . . . [whose] life on earth had an importance and he left behind him an example which might be matched by others should they wish to emulate him."[78] Jesus effectively used His psychical powers, "not sporadic miraculous things . . . produced according to law—a law common to all who had the knowledge, but pushed to its furthest point by so exceptional a being,"[79] to preach and spread His message.

Jesus, moreover, chose the apostles because of their psychic powers; "they were all psychic." Sir Arthur also gave the miraculous activities of Jesus a similar interpretation: "All of the Christ's miracles fit themselves very readily into the different categories of psychic phenomena as we know them."[80] In addition to the apostles, those who followed after Jesus also shared fully in psychic powers. Conan Doyle believed that the gifts of the Holy Spirit associated with Pentecost, for example, were "various types of spiritual manifestation."[81] And Paul's letter to the Corinthians "enumerates almost every psychic faculty which is known to modern spiritualists." Sir Arthur also persistently argued that the early Christian communities and the wide scope of patristic literature demonstrates an appreciation of what the twentieth century might categorize or identify as modern spiritualism. "The Early Christian Church," he pointed out, "was saturated with Spiritualism, and they seem to pay no attention to those Old Testament prohibitions which were meant to keep those powers only for the use and profit of the priesthood."[82] Absent so long in Christianity because the "worldly man" had bested the "spiritual man," a new appreciation of psychical powers was close at hand. "We believe that the spiritual man will in the near future be recognized as the precious thing he is, and that he, the man of soul rather than the man of brain will be the leader."[83]

During the 1920s and 1930s, therefore, Sir Arthur argued for the compatibility of biblical Christianity and spiritualism. In some instances, however, he spoke in a hostile manner against the failures and hollowness of traditional Christian beliefs and practices. "While its [spiritualism] teachings would deeply modify conventional Christianity," Sir Arthur wrote, "the modifications would be rather in the direction of explanation and development than of contradiction."[84] This would result in "the reform of the decadent Christianity of today, its simplification, its purification, and its reinforcement by the facts of spirit communion and the clear knowledge of what lies beyond the exit-door of death."[85] Writing earlier, he warned that "Christianity must change or must perish."[86] "The apathy and ignorance concerning this spiritual knowledge which is shown among many of the leaders of religion is hard to understand," he noted, and "it is a source of weakness for the Churches which turn away from that spiritual help and inspiration which God's new revelation brings with it."[87]

Traditional religion, consequently, received a firm scolding from Sir Arthur. Spiritualism offered an healthy alternative to "that faith which has in the past planted a dozen different signposts to point in as many different directions."[88] In his new world vision, all religions would enjoy equal footing and status, traditional theological questions would disappear, and those many confusing doctrines and dogmas, such as those dealing with Christ's divinity or the virgin birth, would disappear, and people would "follow their own high teachers on a common path of morality, and forget all that antagonism which has made religion a curse rather than a blessing to the world."[89] In fact, Conan Doyle maintained, too much emphasis had been placed on the death of Jesus by theologians. "In my opinion," he wrote," far too much stress has been laid upon Christ's death, and far too little upon His life. That was where the true grandeur and true lesson lay."[90] A new Christology would necessarily develop, and Sir Arthur's vision ran counter to accepted Christian views:

> If the human race had earnestly centred upon that [the positive aspects of Jesus' earthly life] instead of losing itself in vain dreams of vicarious sacri-

fices and imaginary falls, with all the mystical and contentious philosophy which has centred round the subject, how very different the level of human culture and happiness would be to-day.[91]

Moreover, wars, conflicts, and feuds "would have been at least minimized, if not avoided, had the bare example of Christ's life been adopted as the standard of conduct and religion."[92]

In Sir Arthur's view, the alleged inability of the Christian churches to offer succor and comfort to those who had suffered losses because of the Great War unfortunately demonstrated the weaknesses of twentieth-century English religion. People searched for meaning and answers but found little consolation. Spiritualism, however, gave the bereaved something positive: "Why should we fear our dear ones' death if we can be so near to them afterwards?"[93] According to Conan Doyle, "where the séance is used for the purpose of satisfying ourselves as to the conditions of those whom we have lost, or of giving comfort to those who crave for a word from beyond, then it is, indeed, a blessed gift from God to be used with moderation and with thankfulness."[94] On the other hand, it appeared that Christianity had unwittingly forsaken its adherents in their hour of need. Sounding very similar to the arguments in *Religion and the Decline of Magic* by Keith Thomas, Sir Arthur argued that unfortunately "Protestantism abolished the old saints, many of whom no doubt may have well deserved such abolition, but they placed nothing in their stead."[95] That "magical" dimension of religion which enabled people to cope better with the hardships of reality had been expunged. Conan Doyle naturally saw the ramifications for the faithful. "The old idea that a Francis Assisi, or a Vincent de Paul was near us, taking an interest in our actions, and ready to respond to an appeal seems to me to bring actual religion into our everyday life in a very practical and intimate way." In *The New Revelation*, he sketched his picture of a Christian England comfortable with spiritualism.

> If such a view of Christianity were generally accepted, and if it were enforced by assurance and demonstration from the New Revelation which is coming to us from the other side, then we should have a creed which would unite the churches, which might be reconciled to science, which might defy all attacks, and which might carry the Christian Faith on for an indefinite period.[96]

Traditional religions, including Anglicanism, must consequently come to terms with spiritualism and recognize the beneficial and positive aspects of its teachings. With reference to a person's grief and the inability of modern Christianity to respond adequately to bereavement, Sir Arthur Conan Doyle offered the following as a remedy:

> We have great gifts to bring the world. We have deep comfort for suffering humanity and a vision of indescribable happiness for those whose present

lives are drab and gray. We can remove the fear of death, we can give solace to the mourner, and we can lay down a firm and definite path amid all the quagmires of the creeds, avoiding irrational faith upon the one side and barren negation upon the other. It is upon this path that we are pioneers of the human race.[97]

The death and destruction of the Great War had indeed produced immeasurable personal sufferings and tragedies. Family and friends in England had to struggle to cope with the loss of loved ones. Many believed that Christianity was ill-equipped to help these individuals who searched for answers and consolation.[98] Spiritualism, however, did offer a peaceful haven and a possible way for the bereaved to heal their wounds; some even began to advertise spiritualism as a new and vital religion. It did contain, many argued, elements and beliefs compatible with traditional Christian religions. Implicit in the new popularity of spiritualism and the efforts to present it as a viable religious system was a critique of twentieth-century Christianity. Anglicanism, as the established or state church, naturally came under close scrutiny by friend and foe alike. And some asked difficult questions. Did the Anglican Church effectively minister to its faithful, both the soldier and non-combatant, during the war? Did the Great War reveal serious deficiencies and weaknesses in the structure and teachings of the church? And more importantly, were the doctrines of the Anglican Church ill-equipped and insufficient to comfort and console its faithful who had experienced the sorrows of death? Had the church lost ground to spiritualism?

The Anglican Church entered August 1914 experiencing a declining membership in church attendance, at least in the towns. This trend had already started in the last decade of the nineteenth century.[99] "It cannot be doubted that there was a serious increase in these years in that part of the population which had lost all real sense of connection with the Church of England," Adrian Hastings notes, and the "Church's penumbra, its larger and looser constituency, was steadily shrinking, and as it did so the Church itself was declining in national significance." However, the war also demonstrated another shortcoming in the Anglican spiritual fabric in addition to decreasing numbers: "doctrinally, and therefore pastorally, the ministry of the Church of England to the dying and the bereaved was confused."[100] The old Anglican doctrines about heaven, hell, death, to name a few beliefs, had been successfully challenged and replaced by the liberalism and materialism associated with mid-Victorian England. But the transformation had started centuries earlier. Writing during the war, one individual "believed the war would bring back a more definite doctrine of the Communion of Saints. He believed that Protestantism had 'little comfort to give to mourners, for it has been so sadly silent regarding the fate of our dead.'"[101]

The Reformers of the sixteenth century consciously criticized and then did away with those Roman Catholic beliefs and practices which they maintained were superstitious or tinged with "magic." Authentic religion must find its anchor or basis in sacred Scripture. One's individual faith in God replaced reliance on good works. A loyal Christian must confront his or her God directly. Men and women now had to endure the harsh realities of life in this vale of tears, including death, without the help or assistance which Roman Catholics still retained. In the pages of the 1552 *Book of Common Prayer*, one read that "the dead were no longer with us. They could neither be spoken to nor even about, in any way that affected their well-being."[102] According to Eamon Duffy, "The dead had gone beyond the reach of human contact, even of human prayer. . . . The service [the 1552 *Book of Common Prayer* funeral service] was no longer a rite of intercession on behalf of the dead, but an exhortation to faith on the part of the living."

The Reformers had abolished the superstitious Roman belief in Purgatory, that comforting alternative between the cut-and-dried eternal punishment in hell or the everlasting reward in heaven. They believed that the "Romish Doctrine concerning Purgatory, Pardons, Worshipping and Adoration, as well of Images as of Reliques, and also invocation of Saints, is a fond thing vainly invented, and grounded upon no warranty of Scripture, but rather repugnant to the Word of God."[103] According to a modern commentary, the Reformers "rejected the Roman idea of purgatory out of hand, on the grounds that God's free gift of eternal justification here and now, through faith in Christ alone and without works, rules out all need to expiate one's own sins after death."[104] Moreover, they "held that Christians, made perfect at death, go straight to enjoy a fellowship with God in Christ into which penal and corrective inflictions do not enter."[105] A corollary of the rejection of a belief in purgatory, however, had far reaching implications for the spiritual life of the new state church: their "condemnation of prayers and masses for the dead . . . [was] linked with their assumption of the decisiveness of this life for determining one's future and their observation that prayer for the dead in Christ is nowhere prescribed in the Bible."[106]

What was the proper relationship between the living and the departed? Could one in good conscience pray for the repose of the dead? Because of perceived widespread abuses within Roman Catholic practices,[107] which some characterized as crude, the "Reformers mostly condemned any form of Prayer for the Departed."[108] Sixteenth-century Anglican theologians "rejected prayers for the dead as inexpedient if not unlawful as such."[109] However, an undercurrent of thought and practice continued to exist which quietly recognized the benefits in the prayerful remembrance and commemoration of the departed souls. It was the Oxford Movement in the nineteenth century with its "great stress on the centrality of the Eucharist and the reality of the Communion of the Saints, [which] inevitably led to a desire for a fuller commemoration of the departed." But the move to adopt such prayers for general use in the Church of England did not gain much support until the outbreak of the war. "The events of the First World War," the report of the Archbishop's Commission on Christian Doctrine pointed out in 1971, "marked a decisive point in this development, and since that time prayers for the dead have been widely used among Anglicans."[110]

Anglicans who had experienced the death of a family member or a friend naturally turned to prayers for the dead in search for consolation. Large-scale bereavement brought back a practice banished at the Reformation. "In 1914 public prayer for the dead was uncommon in the Church of England; by the end of the war it had become widespread."[111] In November 1914, the archbishop of Canterbury, Randall Davidson, preached a sermon which contained the following reference to prayers for the dead:

> But surely now there is place for a gentler recognition of the instinctive, the natural, the loyal craving of the bereaved, and the abuses of the chantry system and the extravagances of Tetzel need not now, nearly four centuries afterwards, thwart or hinder the reverent, the absolutely trustful prayer of a wounded spirit who feels it natural and helpful to pray for him whom we shall not greet on earth again, but who, in his Father's loving keeping, still lives, and, as we may surely believe, still grows from strength to strength in truer purity and in deepened reverence and love.[112]

The Anglo-Catholic party, not surprisingly, welcomed this growing recognition of the efficacy of prayers for the dead; the Evangelical or Protestant party within Anglicanism decried this trend as a unfortunate departure from Scripture and a dangerous drift to Romanism.

Closely related to a belief in the afterlife and the question of the relationship between the living and the dead is the doctrine of the Communion of Saints, the spiritual union which exists between all Christians, living or dead, and Jesus Christ. Many Anglicans living during the twentieth century also came to believe that the doctrine of the communion of the saints, which had the potential of offering great solace and comfort to the bereaved or grief-stricken Christian, had become too confused and too obtuse to have much positive effect. Some, therefore, felt abandoned by their church in their time of bereavement and, to the chagrin of some ecclesiastical officials, began to embrace spiritualism. "They turned to the Spiritualists who offered knowledge and not mere belief, and who claimed to provide them with communication with their dead."[113] And some Anglicans attacked this trend. The influential dean of St. Paul's, W. R. Inge, described spiritualism in the columns of the press as "an outburst of purile superstition which carries us back to the mentality of barbarians."[114] Lord Halifax, Dick Sheppard, and the bishop of London, Winnington-Ingram, all spoke out and denounced spiritualism. In spite of the critiques of spiritualism and its claims by Anglican clerics, its popularity did not abate. The same dean of St. Paul's who described spiritualism as uncivilized had to acknowledge its successes. In 1926, W. R. Inge wrote that "at home there was a great outbreak of necromancy and spiritualism, which was supported by a few well-known men whose names gave authority to the movement."[115] He also correctly identified the reasons behind its popularity. "These men were themselves suffering from bereavement, and a large number of sorrowing parents and widows followed them in a pathetic endeavour to establish, by various forms of occultism, communion with the spirits of those whom they had dearly loved." Because of the magnitude of the war time casualties and the obvious effect it had on the faithful and because of the apparent successes of spiritualism in addressing these issues and offering consolation, it became apparent that Anglicanism had to re-think or at least articulate more clearly its views on death, the afterlife, and the relationship of the church to these pastoral issues.

As a young theologian, William Temple[116] began to write and theologize on important issues concerning eschatology and the position of the Anglican Church in regard to life after death. From his youth, when his first biographer noted that he asked his father, Frederick, the archbishop of Canterbury, "whether he did not agree that the doctrine of the Communion of Saints was sadly neglected in the Church,"[117] through his tenure as headmaster at Repton School (1910-14), vicar at St. James', Piccadilly, and eventually to his position on the episcopal bench as bishop of Manchester (1921), archbishop of York (1929), and finally as archbishop of Canterbury, William Temple wrote on the subjects of death, the afterlife, and the communion of saints. During the 1939-45 war, for example, he composed comforting letters from Lambeth Palace to bereaved people seeking episcopal advice about spiritualism and psychic phenomena. "His approach to theology, derived from the liberal outlook common in the universities in the early years of the twentieth century," his entry in the *Dictionary of National Biography* notes, "stressed a theology of Incarnation rather than of Redemption, and his Christo-centric metaphysic was out of line with the dogmatic theology to which the younger thinkers were calling their contemporaries to return."[118]

As headmaster of Repton School in Derby, he delivered a series of sermons in the school's chapel dealing with subjects which he would develop later throughout his career. On 5 November 1911, for example, Temple preached on the communion of saints, a topic which had fascinated him from youth, and began by proclaiming: "It is an integral part of the Creed; it is not something which a few peculiarly constituted people may believe in if they are so disposed; it is something accounted by the Church as real and as vital as the Catholic Church or the Forgiveness of Sins."[119] Death, he told the boys, "makes no division in that society; those who still follow Christ on earth and those whose service is in whatever sphere may be appointed for us after this life is over, are still members of one fellowship." Christ knitted "all generation of believers" together into one body or communion. This doctrine of the communion of saints, moreover, offered the hope of consolation to those, deeply troubled by sorrow and grief, who tended to despair.

One year later in March 1912, the headmaster addressed the school on the topic of death and resurrection in a memorial service for a member of Repton School who had recently died. Recognizing the troubles and hardships of earthly life, Temple told the students that the "gloom of life is always due either to our forgetfulness of God or to the sense that God has forgotten us."[120] The resurrection of Jesus Christ, however, offered the ultimate antidote for the curse of desolation and pessimism. "The Resurrection of Christ is the reversal of tragedy," Temple emphasized, and the "joy of this faith is intoxicating."[121] He then touched on the topic of untimely death and tried to offer his young listeners some consolation. Death did indeed signal an end, but it also inaugurated "the beginning of energy, of strength, of power."[122] The gateway to the proper Christian acceptance of death could be found in an appreciation of the communion of saints.

> But even this separation is not the real truth of the matter. The living and the dead alike stand in the presence of God; and when we become conscious of His presence, we find the presence also of all the fellowship of the departed, so that, as we are lifted in heart and mind into God's presence at our Communion Service, it is with the company of heaven that we laud and magnify His Name.[123]

Because of his associations with Oxford University and Repton School, his pastoral involvement at St. James' in central London, and his theological interests, William Temple could not avoid speaking out on the consequences of the Great War, especially the deep sorrow caused by the large number of deaths on the religious tenor of the country. Commenting on the forces which separated people, he believed that death "is the chief of them, and with the severing power of death the world is grimly familiar to-day."[124] The death of friends or family members became the price the country had to pay for its victory in the war. In a sermon at Westminster Abbey in May 1920, Temple told the congregation that "we know the sorrow of those whose sons or husbands are called to serve their country admidst the perils of war,"[125] and in another sermon, entitled "Triumphant Sacrifice," preached at Rugby School soon after the war, he pointed out that "nowhere has the bitterness of the war been more keenly felt than at Schools . . . [and] nowhere has the splendour of its heroism shone with brighter light."[126] "But here, as at all other great Schools in England, we stand at a place made sacred for ever by the steady stream of boys who, throughout the war, went forth to danger and endurance without shrinking and without parade."[127]

Temple recognized the problems which Anglicanism had to address and then answer. Early in the war, he pointed out that the "spiritual life of men is not limited to this planet, and the fulfillment of the Church's task can never be here alone."[128] "Every consideration of serious importance intensifies the urgency of the moral demand for at least the possibility of life after the death of the body," Temple wrote in *Nature, God and Man*, but "there has never been a period in which there was so little positive belief in this, or indeed so widespread an absence of concern for the whole subject."[129] He believed that it was not the idea nor notion of immortality, but rather the manner in which it had been customarily articulated and presented to members of the Anglican Church. Consequently, he pointed out, some turned to spiritualism for needed consolation. According to Temple, "it is worth while for Christians to mark carefully the different methods by which contemporary spiritualism and historic revelation seek to afford the same assurance"[130] of life after death. "Spiritualism," unlike Christianity, he argued, "offers direct communication with the departed apart from any reference to the moral and spiritual attainment either of the departed soul or of the person in this world who seeks such converse." Spiritualism, however, diverted one's attention away from the divine to things human. Spiritualism tended to be self-centred; Christianity worked to turn people "away from self till they centre their lives on God, because that alone is their true welfare."[131]

But what was an appropriate balm for the pain caused by the death of a loved one? Written before the end of the war, *Mens Creatrix* emphasized that "death is not the end of the individual life is guaranteed by the Christian revelation of the love of God."[132] Moreover, he drew attention to the fact that "there is already a Communion of Saints, a fellowship of the living and the departed." Temple continually returned to the reality of the doctrine of the communion of saints in his writings.

> And the core of the doctrine is this: Man is not immortal by nature or of right; but he is capable of immortality and there is offered to him resurrection from the dead and life eternal if he will receive it from God and on God's terms. There is nothing arbitrary in that offer or in those terms, for God is perfect Wisdom and perfect Love. But Man, the creature and helpless sinner, cannot attain to eternal life unless he gives himself to God, the Creator, Redeemer, Sanctifier, and receives from Him both worthiness for life eternal and with that worthiness eternal life—for indeed that worthiness and that life are not two things, but one.[133]

The "blessed dead . . . with us are members of the one great fellowship, the Fellowship or Communion of Saints."[134] A proper understanding and acceptance of the doctrine of the communion of saints offered the believer consolation when confronted with death. "They are not lost to us. In their closer union with God we find them once more in the degree in which our own souls attain to unity with Him."[135] His words to the lads at Rugby, however, sounded more tangible: "The good comradeship, the high purpose, the close sympathy, the ringing laughter—all that we have loved in them is ours still and shall be ours for ever in the Communion of Saints, the Fellowship of the Followers of Jesus, who also died in youth for the sake of the Kingdom that He served."[136]

In the decade after the Great War, William Temple attempted to clarify the teachings of the Anglican Church concerning death and the question of the afterlife. His sermons and writings reveal that he was responding to the pastoral needs of the faithful who had lost someone during the war. And Temple struggled to give them some answers or guidance to help them during the difficult time of bereavement. He restated the traditional Anglican beliefs on eschatology, and emphasized the doctrine of the communion of the saints as a source of comfort or consolation. Temple recognized the challenges of spiritualism for the minds and souls of grieving Anglicans, but he confidently dismissed it as a self-centered attempt which turned people away from the divine. But did William Temple's answers and suggestions really touch and address the needs of the bereaved? Did the methods and language of traditional theology, as many spiritualists contended, fail to reach people? Was there another Christian approach which might more effectively and more powerfully speak to and comfort those who were trying to cope with the death of a loved one?

Some Anglican clerics began to study seriously the relationship between spiritualism and Christianity.[137] Others gave their own testimonies of psychical experiences. One cleric, for example, mentioned the growing number of so-called "spiritualist churches," revealed that he had personally experienced psychic phenomena, and urged the Christian churches not to characterize spiritualism as fraudulent or trendy. "The Spiritualist movement is a challenge to the Church to recover the full Christian teaching about the future life," he wrote, because the "traditional dogmas of heaven and hell have entirely lost their hold upon thinking people."[138] "Why? Because the forms in which they are clothed do not in any way fit the inner realities." The same author, moreover, proposed a plan:

> The spirit of the time seeks for an understanding and a fuller *rapprochement* between the Churches themselves. But the further question of recovering for the Christian Church any forgotten Christian truths which others, not professedly Christian, have discovered, and in which they rejoice, is one of not less importance.[139]

In *The History of Spiritualism*, Sir Arthur Conan Doyle attempted to "see to what degree Spiritualism and psychical research tend to induce or to strengthen religious beliefs," and he believed that "there is one class beyond all others who should be able to talk with authority on the religious tendencies of Spiritualism, [and] it is the clergy."[140] Consequently, his history of the movement also contained the testimonies of many clerics who supported the religious dimensions of spiritualism and saw the benefits spiritualism could bring to Christianity.

One Anglican cleric, in particular, promoted spiritualism especially for Christianity in general and for the searching believer in particular. In 1909, the

Rev. Charles Tweedale, the vicar of Weston in Yorkshire, took up the pen and began to write. After some general introductory remarks, his book, *Man's Survival after Death*,[141] presented numerous examples from sacred Scripture, human experiences of psychic happenings, and finally the strong conclusions from modern science in support of spiritualism. Tweedale quickly found fault with the state of contemporary Anglicanism: "In these days, following upon hundreds of years of preaching and exegesis, Christianity, as usually expounded and understood, is more a moral and ethical system for the regulation of conduct, than a teaching to inspire one . . . with the reality and imminence of life after death."[142] A person's conduct in this world, although important, had unfortunately eclipsed the resurrection and the belief in life after death.

His influential book, therefore, argued for the restoration of "the sense of the reality and imminence of the life of the world to come."[143] Tweedale did not miss the pastoral implications of this necessary shift in theology. Anglicanism had certainly failed to offer comfort and succor to the bereaved. "My fervent desire . . . is to bring the joy of the resurrection to those who either do not possess it, or see it so dimly and afar off that it affords no real consolation to the mind, but leaves them a prey to doubt and uncertainty."[144] Christ's mission on earth focused on the transformation of sorrow into joy, and Christianity must work to recapture this ideal. Realizing that many would scoff at his thoughts, Tweedale vigorously defended his views against all critics. "They of this school, who profess and call themselves Christians, have to explain on what grounds of evidence they accept the accounts of similar things in the Gospels."[145] Psychic phenomena or happenings, moreover, did not come from evil demons or spirits.

Responding to the alleged inability of the Established Church to meet the needs of the faithful during the Great War, some Anglicans organized groups to promote the benefits of spiritualism. In the decade after the war, the Rev. Charles Tweedale established the Society of Communion. Founded for spiritualists in the Church of England, this "society insisted on the acceptance of the doctrine of the divinity of Christ and existed mainly to encourage psychic study among Anglicans."[146] In a pamphlet which he distributed to all bishops attending the 1920 Lambeth Conference,[147] he noted that the Christian churches were currently "completely out of all conscious objective touch with the spirit world . . . Their attitude is such as to completely cut them off from those good or holy spiritual manifestations which were the privilege and constant experience of the early Christian Church."[148] Like other supporters of the benefits of spiritualism, Tweedale pointed out the close connection between spiritualist activities, the ministry of Jesus Christ, and the life of the early Christian communities: "The external witness of apparitions, voices, visions and various physical phenomena was also constantly in evidence in the lives of the Apostles and the members of the early Church."[149]

After attacking the accepted Anglican teaching on the resurrection of the body, which was based on "an imperfect understanding of the phenomena," namely, the church's belief that communication between the living and the dead had ceased to exist in modern times, Tweedale offered his own interpretation of the doctrine of the communion of the saints.

> It is evident from the above consideration that the Communion of the Saints must consist largely of communion with the "dead." Communion means fellowship, mutual intercourse. There can be no effective fellowship and mutual intercourse without communication. Psychic phenomena constitute the only effective and recognizable means of this communion with the dead and with the Spirit-world.[150]

Manifestations of departed spirits were not, he argued, linked with the occult or the devil, nor would those people who experienced psychic happenings be plagued with insanity or madness. In fact, a proper knowledge of psychical phenomena provided an essential key for the understanding of the Bible.

Tweedale's main objective, however, was to call the Anglican Church to task for its neglect of the rich and hallowed religious traditions such as spiritualism possessed. "Just so long as the Church of these days excludes from her evidence the external objective witness of the spirit, she will be like a person deprived of the use of a limb, and will remain crippled and helpless," he maintained. "Let the Church take her courage in both hands, and claim her ancient gifts."[151] Tweedale wanted the church to reformulate the doctrine of the communion of the saints along the lines of the spiritualist belief in communication with the departed, and he even suggested that the Anglican Church seriously consider the establishment of a "School of the Prophets." The twentieth century must not repeat the tragedy which zealous churchmen had committed in the unfortunate condemnation of Galileo. Moreover, spiritualism could easily become a powerful "weapon against materialism, and such a confirmation of the central fact of Christianity."[152]

This campaign which emphasized the religious aspects of spiritualism also received some valuable help and support outside of clerical circles. "A small group of Christian spiritualists, led by Mrs St Clair Stobart, felt that the ultimate aim should be to persuade the Christian churches of the essential Christianity of Spiritualism, and to show that the teachings of Spiritualism were in no way contrary to those of Christianity."[153] Both the Christian churches and spiritualism should recognize their essential similarities. In May 1935, the Confraternity of Clergy, Ministers, and Spiritualists was founded to advertise and promote these views. Mrs. M. A. St. Clair Stobart served as the chairman of this organization. "Mrs. Stobart was to make a valiant effort in her books to remind her co-religious that the Bible, upon which they based their faith, was packed with psychical phenomena and spirit interventions."[154]

Mrs. St. Clair Stobart did not use cautious or soft language in her critique of contemporary Christianity. The Christian churches, including Anglicanism, had failed because they "still insist upon a crude materialism in doctrines, rituals, and foundational beliefs, and still consider it dangerous to admit their congregations to the reality of the spirit-life, to the true communion of Saints, which remains a dead letter of a lifeless creed."[155] In addition to this dogged insistence on doctrine and ritual, which did not adequately address the needs of modern men and women, she argued that Christianity had traditionally attacked and criticized spiritualism either out of ignorance or jealousy.

> The Churches crudely assume that for thousands of years—until the Christian era—mankind remained in spiritual darkness, unable to establish any relationship with God, and denied all knowledge of those great basic truths without which Man could never have oriented himself in the Universe, namely: the existence of a Universal Intelligence or God, the three fold nature of man, body, soul, and spirit . . . and Immortality.[156]

Moreover, she pointed out, the "Christian Churches have . . . lost all sense of historic proportion and of historic continuity." And consequently, "they almost assume that the religious history of mankind began with the Crucifixion."[157] Religion had to readjust or modify its emphasis. "By concentrating unduly on the Death and the Crucifixion, the Churches thus mistake the means for the end, for these were only the preliminary to the crowning of Christ's mission, which was to prove, by His Resurrection and Ascension, the truth of a future life for all men."[158]

The Anglican Church had to shoulder the blame for both the mistakes of the past and the contemporary misunderstandings of spiritualism. The cornerstone of Anglicanism, the *Book of Common Prayer*, came in for severe criticism from St. Clair Stobart. Drawing attention "to some of the offending features in the book which is regarded as the official text-book of Anglican Christian teaching,"[159] she singled out especially the pessimism and lack of joy at the church's burial services, the teachings concerning the nature of God and the future life, the "vengeful" and "wrathful" descriptions of God, and the emphasis given to the resurrection of the body.[160] Mrs. St. Clair Stobart also mentioned other doctrines which sounded an "equally unreal and repugnant note," such as vicarious atonement, predestination and election, and the Christian interpretation of miracles.

In addition to doctrinal difficulties or shortcomings, the Anglican Church also came up short in its ministry to the faithful. Because of the alleged sterility of its teachings and the inadequacies of the *Book of Common Prayer*, Anglicanism could not effectively and positively address the sorrow and bereavement which pervaded the church during the 1920s. England had experienced a decline in church attendance and the candidates for holy orders had also decreased, and she identified the root cause as the lack of Anglican pastoral zeal. "And if we would regain the consolation and assurance of immortality which was once within the gift of the Churches to bestow, it is our duty to try and discover where lies the failure of the clergy to convey that which was once so freely given and received."[161] The sad experiences and personal distresses of the Great War should have taught the Anglican Church important lessons. "What had happened to our million men who were snatched from us in the full glory of manhood?"[162] Her answer was damning: "the Churches remained silent. They gave no help." Consequently, St. Clair Stobart maintained, some Anglicans embraced spiritualism. "The Nation's heart was at a breaking point . . . [and] the heart of the people turned to God,—it went back to the religion which for many centuries before the Christian era, had assuaged the griefs, and soothed the sorrows of mankind."

But she did not just cast stones at the Established Church; she also devoted much of her writing to building a bridge between Anglicanism and spiritualism. Both enjoyed a common ground in sacred Scripture. The Old Testament held special significance for her. According to St. Clair Stobart, "the value of the Old Testament lies . . . not at all in its moral teaching but in its psychic bearing on life in general."[163] Both parts of the Bible, however, were storehouses "of psychic stories, of episodes which though formerly denominated miracles, were to-day explicable by laws of that science, psychic science."[164] The Bible, therefore, most certainly gave its sanction and approbation to spiritualism. Because the Bible was firmly based on psychical evidence, her reasoning went, and because the church took its authority from sacred Scripture, the Anglican Church could not logically condemn spiritualism. Moreover, she believed, spiritualism could perform a great service by reinterpreting the Bible, and thus give needed hope to people by making the message of Scripture more meaningful and acceptable.[165]

She begged the church authorities not to dismiss lightly the claims of spiritualism and to study the benefits which might accrue to Christianity if spiritualism were taken seriously. If the church would, for example, interpret miracles in the light of psychical science, "the Christian story would find its true place in the magic chain of historic revelations, and the world would recognize in the Christian Faith a presentation of cosmic truths whose acceptance is essential for the spiritual welfare of mankind."[166] Moreover, Mrs. St. Clair Stobart believed that aspects of spiritualism would revive and give life to "the dry bones of a moribund religion which has lost the Spiritualism on which it was originally based."[167] Throughout the decade of the 1930s and into the 1940s, she continued to preach her gospel which mixed the beliefs of spiritualism with the doctrines of Christianity. St. Clair Stobart never ceased from urging the Anglican Church to explore the richness of spiritualism, and when it appeared that the church might give spiritualism a serious hearing in the late 1930s, she vigorously urged churchmen to seize this golden opportunity.

The years following the armistice in 1918, consequently, did experience significant and drastic alterations at all levels of English society, even in the realm of religion. The Anglican Church had to adapt or modify its message to meet this new climate. According to one prediction, "It is certain that when the war is over . . . there will be great and far-reaching changes . . . in the whole structure of the national and international life of Christendom."[168] One area of increasing popularity which Anglicanism could no longer avoid or neglect was the question of spiritualism and its relationship to traditional Christianity.

Notes

1. B. Inglis, *Science and Parascience: A History of the Paranormal, 1914-1939*, 50.

2. O. Lodge, *Raymond: Or Life and Death: With Examples of the Evidence for Survival of Memory and Affection after Death* (London: Methuen, 1916). By November 1918, the tenth edition with an addendum had been published.

3. G. Nelson, *Spiritualism and Society*, 157.

4. J. M. Winter, *The Great War and the British People* (Cambridge: Harvard University Press, 1986), 67.

5. D. Cannadine, "War and Death, Grief and Mourning in Modern Britain," in *Mirrors of Mortality*, ed. J. Whaley. *Studies in the Social History of Death* (New York: St. Martin's Press, 1981), 197. For the statistics of the Great War and how they compared with other recent European wars, see George L. Mosse, *Fallen Soldiers: Reshaping the Memory of the World Wars* (New York: Oxford University Press, 1990). A recent article also explores the question of the wounded soldiers: S. Koven, "Remembering and Dismemberment: Crippled Children, Wounded Soldiers, and the Great War in Great Britain," *The American Historical Review* 99 (October 1994): 1167-1202.

6. A. Wilkinson, *The Church of England and the First World War* (London: SPCK, 1978), 171-72. For the position of the Free Churches and how they reacted to the challenges of the Great War, see A. Wilkinson, *Dissent or Conform: War, Peace, and the English Churches, 1900-1945* (London: SCM, 1986).

7. A. J. P. Taylor, *English History, 1914-1945* (Oxford: Clarendon Press, 1965), 112.

8. P. Jalland, *Death in the Victorian Family* (Oxford: Oxford University Press, 1996), 373.

9. D. Cannadine, "War and Death, Grief and Mourning in Modern Britain," 189.

10. Ibid., 198.

11. See P. Fussell, *The Great War and Modern Memory* (New York: Oxford University Press, 1975).

12. B. Mathews, ed., prologue to *Christ and the World at War: Sermons Preached in War-Time* (London: James Clarke, 1917), vi.

13. R. Davidson, "The Church's Opportunity," in *War and Christianity* (London: Jarrold, 1914), 7.

14. Ibid., 8.

15. Ibid., 9.

16. R. Davidson, "The Peace of God," in *The Testing of a Nation* (London: Macmillan, 1919), 20.
17. A. F. Winnington-Ingram, "The Conditions of Victory," in *Christ and the World at War*, 132.
18. A. F. Winnington-Ingram, "Heaviness and Joy," in *The Church in Time of War* (London: Wells Gardner, Darton, 1915), 226.
19. A. F. Winnington-Ingram, "The Way Everlasting," in *The Church in Time of War*, 243.
20. A. F. Winnington-Ingram, "Bearing the Cross," in *The Church in Time of War*, 212.
21. A. Marrin, "The Church of England in the First World War" (Ph.D. diss., Columbia University, 1968), 226.
22. A. F. Winnington-Ingram, *Rays of Dawn* (Milwaukee: Morehouse Publishing, 1918), 14.
23. Ibid., 15.
24. A. F. Winnington-Ingram, "Heaviness and Joy," in *The Church in Time of War*, 234.
25. Ibid., 241.
26. A. F. Winnington-Ingram, "The Conditions of Victory," in *Christ and the World at War*, 137.
27. W. R. Inge, "Perfect through Suffering," in *War and Christianity*, 16.
28. W. R. Inge, "Risen with Christ," in *Christ and the World at War*, 87-88.
29. W. R. Inge, "Perfect through Suffering," in *War and Christianity*, 12.
30. Ibid., 13.
31. Ibid., 14.
32. Ibid., 17.
33. George L. Mosse, *Fallen Soldiers: Reshaping the Memory of the World Wars*, 5.
34. J. M. Winter, "Spiritualism and the First World War," in *Religion and Irreligion in Victorian Society: Essays in Honor of R. K. Webb,* ed. R. W. Davis, and R. J. Helmstadter (New York: Routledge, 1992), 191.
35. W. R. Inge, *Lay Thoughts of a Dean* (New York: G. P. Putnam's Sons, 1926), 304.
36. A. Marrin, "The Church of England in the First World War," 125.
37. A. Machen, *The Angels of the Mons: The Bowmen and Other Legends of the War* (Freeport, N.Y.: Books for Libraries Press, 1972). In addition to the story of the bowmen, the author also supplies a lengthy introduction and several other legends associated with the war.
38. Ibid., 6.
39. Ibid., 19-20.
40. Ibid., 31
41. A. Marrin, *The Church of England in the First World War*, 126.
42. H. H. Henson, *Retrospect of an Unimportant Life,* vol. 1 (London: Oxford University Press, 1942), 181.
43. M. Moynihan, ed., *God on Our Side* (London: Secker & Warburg, 1983), 217.
44. E. W. Oaten, *"That Reminds Me": A Medley of Personal Psychic Experiences* (Manchester: Two Worlds Publishing, 1938), 12. This book is a collection of psychical experiences which appeared in the columns of the newspaper, *Two Worlds*, edited by Oaten.

45. R. Wilkinson, "'The War Has Made Me Think!' A Personal and Plain Statement of Fact," *London Magazine* 39 (1918): 118-20.
46. V. Brittain, *Testament of Youth* (London: Virgo Press, 1993), 445.
47. G. Nelson, *Spiritualism and Society*, 155.
48. D. Cannadine, "War and Death, Grief and Mourning in Modern Britain," 219.
49. J. M. Winter, "Spiritualism and the First World War," 197.
50. W. H. Salter, *The Society for Psychical Research: An Outline of Its History*, 39.
51. In 1891 the Spiritualists National Federation (SNF) was established. Forty-two spiritualist societies affiliated with this organization immediately. In order to gain legal recognition, the SNF, after much debate, was transformed into the Spiritualists' National Union (SNU) in 1902. See G. Nelson, *Spiritualism and Society*, 125-27; and J. Oppenheim, *The Other World: Spiritualism and Psychical Research in England, 1859-1914*, 52.
52. D. Cannadine, "War and Death, Grief and Mourning in Modern Britain," 229.
53. See O. Lodge, *Past Years: An Autobiography* (London: Hodder & Stoughton, 1931); W. P. Jolly, *Sir Oliver Lodge* (London: Constable, 1974).
54. J. M. Winter, "Spiritualism and the First World War," 188.
55. B. Inglis, *Science and Parascience*, 49.
56. O. Lodge, "The Scientific World and Dr. Mercier: A Reply," *Hibbert Journal* 16 (1917): 131.
57. O. Lodge, "Ether, Matter, and the Soul," *Hibbert Journal* 17 (1919): 260.
58. J. M. Winter, "Spiritualism and the First World War," 189.
59. O. Lodge, *Raymond*, vii-viii.
60. J. M. Winter, "Spiritualism and the First World War," 189.
61. R. Brandon, *The Spiritualists*, 218.
62. O. Lodge, "Christianity and Spiritualism," in *Life after Death according to Christianity and Spiritualism*, ed. J. Marchant (London: Cassell, 1925), 156-57.
63. Ibid., 163.
64. Ibid., 164.
65. O. Lodge, introduction to M. A. St. Clair Stobart, *Ancient Lights of the Bible, the Church, and Psychic Science: An Attempt to Restore the Ancient Lights of the Bible and the Church* (London: Kegan Paul, Trench, Trubner, 1923), xv.
66. O. Lodge, *Raymond* [1918 edition], ix.
67. O. Lodge, "Christianity and Spiritualism," 171.
68. K. Jones, *Conan Doyle and the Spirits: The Spiritualist Career of Sir Arthur Conan Doyle* (Wellingborough, Northamptonshire: Aquarian), 1989.
69. Arthur Conan Doyle, *The History of Spiritualism*, vol. 2 (London: Cassell, 1926), 226.
70. Arthur Conan Doyle, *The Vital Message* (London: Hodder & Stoughton, 1919), 17.
71. Arthur Conan Doyle, *The New Revelation* (London: Hodder & Stoughton, 1918), 49.
72. Arthur Conan Doyle, *The History of Spiritualism*, 2:225.
73. A large number of sincere and interested people began to speak and write on the positive relationship of spiritualism and Christianity. They generally followed the lines also put forth by Sir Arthur. For an example of this literature, see two books by S.

de Brath: *Psychical Research Science and Religion* (London: Methuen, 1925); and *The Religion of the Spirit* (London: Rider, 1927).

74. K. Jones, *Conan Doyle and the Spirits*, 118.
75. Ibid., 119.
76. Arthur Conan Doyle, *The History of Spiritualism*, 2:246.
77. Arthur Conan Doyle, *The Vital Message*, 21-22.
78. K. Jones, *Conan Doyle and the Spirits*, 120.
79. Arthur Conan Doyle, *The Early Christian Church and Modern Spiritualism* (London: Psychic Bookshop and Library, 1925), 5.
80. Ibid., 6.
81. Ibid., 8.
82. Arthur Conan Doyle, *The New Revelation*, 80.
83. Ibid., 11.
84. Arthur Conan Doyle, *The History of Spiritualism*, 2:262.
85. Arthur Conan Doyle, *The Vital Message*, 17.
86. Arthur Conan Doyle, *The New Revelation*, 70.
87. Arthur Conan Doyle, *An Open Letter to Those of My Generation* (London: Psychic Press, 1929), 7.
88. Arthur Conan Doyle, *Psychic Experiences* (London: G. P. Putnam's Sons, 1925), 116. Sir Arthur's unorthodox religious views drew criticisms from many quarters. See the following works: J. Boyd, *The New Spiritualism: Is It from Heaven or Hell? A Sober Examination of Sir Arthur Conan Doyle* (London: Pickering & Inglis, 1920); D. Forster, *The Vital Choice: Endor or Calvary? A Reply to Sir A. Conan Doyle's "The New Revelation"* (London: Morgan & Scott, 1919); and *Spiritualism and Life and Death: Addresses Delivered in Reply to Sir Arthur Conan Doyle by Mr. James Boyd and Mr. J. T. Mawson* (London: The Central Bible Trust Depot, 1920).
89. Ibid., 115.
90. Arthur Conan Doyle, *The New Revelation*, 73.
91. Arthur Conan Doyle, *The Vital Message*, 27.
92. Ibid., 28.
93. Arthur Conan Doyle, *Psychic Experiences*, 114.
94. Arthur Conan Doyle, *The Vital Message*, 117-18.
95. Arthur Conan Doyle, *Pheneas Speaks: Direct Spirit Communications in the Family Circle* (London: Psychic Press, 1927), 9-10.
96. Arthur Conan Doyle, *The New Revelation*, 75-76.
97. Arthur Conan Doyle, *The Early Christian Church and Modern Spiritualism*, 12.
98. For a bibliography dealing with the relationship of the war to religion, see M. Bradshaw, comp., *The War and Religion: A Preliminary Bibliography of Material in English Prior to January 1, 1919* (New York: Association Press, 1919).
99. A. Hastings, *A History of English Christianity, 1920-1985* (London: Fount Paperbacks, 1986), 35.
100. A. Wilkinson, *The Church of England and the First World War*, 175. See also A. Marrin, *The Last Crusade: The Church of England in the First World War* (Durham, N.C.: Duke University Press, 1974).
101. Quoted in A. Wilkinson, *The Church of England and the First World War*, 175.

102. E. Duffy, *The Stripping of the Altars: Traditional Religion in England, c. 1400-c. 1580* (New Haven: Yale University Press, 1992), 475.
103. *Book of Common Prayer*, Articles of Religion, Article XXII.
104. *Prayer and the Departed: A Report of the Archbishops' Commission on Christian Doctrine* (London: SPCK, 1971), 35.
105. Ibid., 35-36.
106. Ibid., 36.
107. For a list of arguments against prayers for the dead, see *Prayer and the Departed*, 22-24.
108. *Doctrine in the Church of England (1938): The Report of the Commission on Christian Doctrine Appointed by the Archbishops of Canterbury and York* (London: SPCK, 1938), 215.
109. *Prayer and the Departed*, 36.
110. Ibid.
111. A. Wilkinson, *The Church of England and the First World War*, 176.
112. Quoted in A. Wilkinson, *The Church of England and the First World War*, 176.
113. G. Nelson, *Spiritualism and Society*, 156.
114. Quoted in B. Inglis, *Science and Parascience*, 70.
115. W. R. Inge, *Lay Thoughts of a Dean*, 304.
116. For biographies of William Temple, see F. A. Iremonger, *William Temple Archbishop of Canterbury: His Life and Letters* (London: Oxford University Press, 1948); and J. Kent, *William Temple* (Cambridge: Cambridge University Press, 1992).
117. F. A. Iremonger, *William Temple, Archbishop of Canterbury*, 18.
118. *Dictionary of National Biography 1941-1950*, 873.
119. W. Temple, "The Communion of Saints," in *Repton School Sermons: Studies in the Religion of the Incarnation* (London: Macmillan, 1913), 185.
120. W. Temple, "Death and Resurrection," in *Repton School Sermons*, 247-48.
121. Ibid., 249.
122. Ibid., 250.
123. Ibid., 251.
124. W. Temple, "The Secret of Peace," in *Fellowship with God* (London: Macmillan, 1920), 10.
125. W. Temple, "More Than Conquerors," in *Fellowship with God*, 179.
126. W. Temple, "Triumphant Sacrifice," in *Fellowship with God*, 200.
127. Ibid., 199.
128. W. Temple, *Church and Nature: The Bishop Paddock Lectures for 1914-15* (London: Macmillan, 1915), 30.
129. W. Temple, *Nature, Man and God: Being the Gifford Lectures Delivered in the University of Glasgow in the Academic Years, 1932-1933 and 1933-1934* (London: Macmillan, 1934), 453.
130. W. Temple, "All Saints' Day," in *Fellowship with God*, 73.
131. Ibid., 74.
132. W. Temple, *Mens Creatrix: An Essay* (London: Macmillan, 1949), 349.
133. W. Temple, *Nature, Man, and God*, 472.
134. W. Temple, "All Saints' Day," in *Fellowship with God*, 77-78.
135. W. Temple, "More Than Conquerors," in *Fellowship with God*, 180.

136. W. Temple, "Triumphant Sacrifice," in *Fellowship with God*, 200-201.
137. For example, see B. H. Streeter et al., *Immortality: An Essay in Discovery* (New York: Macmillan, 1917). The subtitle to this collection of essays is entitled "Co-ordinating Scientific, Psychical, and Biblical Research."
138. F. C. Spurr, "Christianity and Spiritualism," in *Life after Death*, ed. J. Marchant, 153.
139. Ibid., 139.
140. A. C. Doyle, *The History of Spiritualism*, 2:262-63.
141. C. Tweedale, *Man's Survival after Death or the Other Side of Life in the Light of Human Experience and Modern Research* (London: Grant Richards, 1909).
142. Ibid., 16.
143. Ibid., 18.
144. Ibid., 15.
145. Ibid., 257-58.
146. G. Nelson, *Spiritualism and Society*, 160.
147. See chapter 2 for an extended discussion of the 1920 Lambeth Conference and the positions of the Anglican bishops concerning spiritualism.
148. C. L. Tweedale, *Present Day Spirit Phenomena and the Churches: The Modern Religious Position* (St. Louis: Progressive Thinker Publishing, 1933), 2.
149. Ibid., 3.
150. Ibid., 10.
151. Ibid., 24.
152. Ibid., 4. Some people, however, criticized the positions taken by the Rev. C. Tweedale. Mrs. M. le F. Shepherd, for example, found fault with his beliefs on the resurrection of the body, revelation, and his interpretations of sacred Scripture. Spiritualism also received a strong condemnation. "Does Mr. Tweedale suggest that the religious life, with its Christ-love, its self-sacrificing labours and profound spiritual impulses, be exchanged for the gibberings of 'trance mediums,' the revelations of 'clairvoyants,' the miracles of so-called 'healers,' 'spirit photographers,' 'materializing mediums,' and all that may be called the Hurly-Burly of Spiritualism as distinct from the progress of the Soul?" M. le F. Shepherd, *Religion after the War: A Reply to the Rev. Chas. Tweedale, Vicar of Weston, Yorks.* (London: Church Army Press, 1917), 8.
153. G. Nelson, *Spiritualism and Society*, 160. For the life of A. M. St. Clair Stobart, see her autobiography: *Miracles and Adventures: An Autobiography* (London: Rider, 1935). Pages 366-75 discuss the history of her involvement in spiritualism.
154. B. Inglis, *Science and Parascience*, 70.
155. M. A. St. Clair Stobart, *Ancient Lights*, 4.
156. M. A. St. Clair Stobart, *Torchbearers of Spiritualism* (London: George Allen Unwin, 1925), 7.
157. Ibid., 6.
158. M. A. St. Clair Stobart, *Ancient Lights*, 13.
159. M. A. St. Clair Stobart, *The Prayer Book X-Rayed* (London: Psychic Press, 1939), 1.
160. Ibid., 1-12.
161. M. A. St. Clair Stobart, *The Apocrypha Reviewed by a Spiritualist* (London: Kegan Paul, Trench, Trubner, 1930), 3.
162. M. A. St. Clair Stobart, *The Either-Or of Spiritualism* (London: Rider, 1928), 196.

163. M. A. St. Clair Stobart, *Ancient Lights*, 27.
164. M. A. St. Clair Stobart, *Miracles and Adventures*, 368.
165. M. A. St. Clair Stobart, *Psychic Bible Stories for Young and Old* (London: Wright & Brown, 1933). In addition to many others, some of her favorite Old Testament stories included Joseph, Moses, Gideon, Samuel, David, Elijah, Elisha, Daniel, and Jonah. In the New Testament, she emphasized the stories of the woman at the well, the transfiguration, the resurrection, and the appearances of Jesus after the crucifixion.
166. M. A. St. Clair Stobart, *The Either-Or of Spiritualism*, 3.
167. M. A. St. Clair Stobart, *Miracles and Adventures*, 371.
168. D. S. Cairns, ed., *The Army and Religion: An Enquiry and Its Bearing upon the Religious Life of the Nation* (London: Macmillan, 1919), xxiii.

Chapter Two

The Anglican Church and the Question of Spiritualism after the Great War: The 1920 Lambeth Conference

During the Great War, the armies of both sides destroyed the landscape of Continental Europe and severely damaged the economic health of both the victor and the vanquished. Moreover, the people killed and wounded far exceeded any rational prediction made early in 1914. England did not suffer the physical devastation that the other countries on the Continent experienced, but another more valuable resource, the number of the youth who represented the hope for a better future, had been dramatically depleted. And the country mourned. An entire generation of the "best and the brightest" had suffered and died on the Western Front; the members elected to the new Parliament after the armistice were old men who looked to the past rather than the future. During the next decade the country tried to reconcile the enormous human tragedy with the crown of victory.

The personal losses of many English men and women, however, could not be measured by hard and cold statistics. Many found it difficult to find comfort or consolation in traditional Anglicanism, and some eventually turned to spiritualism for support. Even during the course of the war, the Anglican Church had recognized some of its weaknesses or shortcomings in respect to bereavement. With reference to the National Mission of Repentance and Hope, a committee established by Archbishop Randall Davidson noted that "five subjects in the life of the Church and nation stood out with obvious claim for our rehandling."[1] One area of concern was worship. The military chaplains who sat as members of the archbishop's committee wrote that "contact with all and sundry of British manhood has revealed the crying need of a simple form of devotion."[2] These three chaplains serving with the British Expeditionary Force noted that in their view, the soldiers at the front had problems with the manner in which religious services were conducted in England prior to the outbreak of the war. They warned that if Anglican liturgies continued "without a generally accepted and loved popular devotion which corrects what is lacking in present forms and litanies put out by authority," for example, no mention of the communion of saints, "increasing resort to Roman systems of devotion (the Rosary, Reservation and Benediction) will be likely to follow."[3] Consequently, the committee "wishes to see a more adequate provision made in the Prayer Book to guide and satisfy the widespread desire for Prayers for the Dead."[4]

Others, however, continued to cope with their sorrow and bereavement within the fabric of the Anglican Church, and a few sought the answers to their questions and their soul-searchings from the archbishop of Canterbury, Randall Davidson. In August 1919, for example, Mr. Charles Dawbarn, a member of the press, wrote to Archbishop Davidson and enclosed a proof of an interview he recently had with Sir Arthur Conan Doyle, and he indicated that he planned to publish it in the *Daily Chronicle*. "It will be seen," Dawbarn told the archbishop, "that Sir Arthur blames the Church for cold comfort administered to those who mourn their dead and declares that windy words and dogmatic assertions prevail in the pulpit."[5] The writer of this letter asked Davidson for an interview, "which would put the case of Christianity in regard to Spiritualism." He reminded the archbishop that the bishop of London, Arthur Foley Winnington-Ingram, had recently denounced spiritualism at a memorial service in Hyde Park, claiming it "was leading many away." What position did the archbishop of Canterbury hold on the subject? According to Mr. Dawbarn, "It is certainly true that . . . members in England and Scotland are flocking to the banners of Spiritualism [and] that about every month books come from the press filled with 'evidence' of communication with the departed."

The bishop of London, A. F. Winnington-Ingram, had conducted a memorial service on 27 July in the nation's capital to commemorate the "memory of those who have fallen in the war."[6] The Metropolitan Divisional Council of the National Federation of Discharged and Demobilized Sailors and Soldiers had arranged the event. According to *The Times*, "in addition to the 50,000 ex-service men who assembled on the Victoria Embankment and marched in procession to the Park, thousands of people were present." The bishop of London, no friend of spiritualism, addressed the grief experienced by many of those present. "He said that those who had lost loved ones in the war might be comforted by the fact that they had died in a noble cause and that they were with them in spirit." Bishop Winnington-Ingram told the audience of a mother who had experienced the psychical presence of her son when she received the sad news of his death. The bishop suggested that these "visions were only very seldom vouchsafed and faith did not depend upon them, but they enforced what they were promised, and that was that their son, their husband, friend, or comrade was the same person five minutes after death as he was before." But spiritualism also came under attack by the bishop. He "advised them, however, to have nothing to do with those attempted communications with the dead," and Bishop Winnington-Ingram "believed that it was a sin to seek to know what we could not know." According to the bishop of London, let "Sir Oliver Lodge and Sir Conan Doyle do what they like, but do not let the ordinary mourner spend his hours in trying to get into communication with the dead." In light of these critical remarks, Dawbarn keenly wanted the archbishop of Canterbury's reactions.

Without waiting for a reply from Lambeth Palace, Charles Dawbarn wrote to Archbishop Davidson the day following his initial letter. Determined to have a meeting with the archbishop, he again drew attention to the text of the interview with Sir Arthur Conan Doyle in an attempt to lure the archbishop into talking with him. "For apart from the attacks of the Spiritualists," he informed Davidson, "many now in England attack openly the Church for what they consider its lukewarm and non-committal attitude towards many subjects of the day, and this conversation would give me the occasion to rectify assertions and suggestions of this sort."[7] This ploy did not work. The archbishop's secretary responded in a short, clear, and decisive manner: "The Archbishop of Canterbury has throughout the whole of his episcopate consistently declined to give 'interviews' to representatives of the Press on matters of public discussion."[8]

The interview with Sir Arthur Conan Doyle, however, appeared two days later in the columns of the *Daily Chronicle* without any words of clarification or rebuttal from the archbishop of Canterbury. Charles Dawbarn's article, "The Challenge of Spiritualism: Does It Confirm the Christian Doctrine of Immortality?" introduced Sir Arthur as "the immortal literary figure. . . . Sure we are that nothing but sincerity and a desire to serve humanity lies at the bottom of his missionary efforts for spiritualism."[9] The author then drew the attention of the reader to the central message of the article and noted that spiritualism constituted a "challenge to the Churches, which has not been disregarded." He made reference to the words of Bishop Winnington-Ingram at the recent Hyde Park meeting, "many have been led astray." This statement by the bishop of London, consequently, became the occasion which led to the newspaper interview with Sir Arthur.

"How strange," observed Sir Arthur Conan Doyle, "that the Church should attack us for confirming its own doctrine of immortality, its basic creed, in fact." Sir Arthur then pointed out the fact that in the past societies tended at first to dismiss or scoff at new discoveries or findings. Later, however, they received unconditional and enthusiastic endorsement. "I expect that the same thing will happen now: the world will accept Spiritualism, but under another name." "If we were worldly wise," he continued, "I have no doubt that we could help the acceptance of our doctrine by calling it psychic-religion or some other term." Sir Arthur did concede that "spiritualism, like charity, has covered a multitude of sins in the past, and has been besmirched by rogues and fools." After Conan Doyle described some of his own experiences which led him to accept spiritualism as a creed and way of life, Lady Doyle, also present at the interview, gave her thoughts on the matter to the *Daily Chronicle*.

Lady Doyle emphasized the "comforting results of the new faith" and told Mr. Dawbarn that spiritualism had "brought great happiness into her own life, just as it has brought happiness to thousands, able now to communicate with their departed." One should nor fear or dread death; "death is like passing into the next room, where are gathered our familiars." Like many others who suffered a tragedy during the Great War, a personal loss led Lady Doyle to an appreciation of the benefits of spiritualism: "It was the death of my brother at Mons that brought me to believe in Spiritualism." After trying to cope with this tragedy, the interviewer was told, she succeeded in establishing communication with the spirit of her deceased brother. This testimony of Lady Doyle tried to offer the comfort and hope to many Christians which traditional Anglicanism apparently failed to communicate. "The knowledge that we can speak with those who have passed over," she maintained, "has been of the greatest consolation to mourners, to those who are broken hearted at the loss of a dear husband or son killed in the war." Spiritualism, therefore, successfully helped thousands of people devastated by the horrors and deaths of the last war, and consequently their "life has been rendered full of hope and happiness."

Sir Arthur then broke in and began to comment on the inadequacy or inability of contemporary English Christianity to offer needed support to the faithful looking for answers or succor. "The Churches have failed in the present crisis," he strongly declared, and the bereaved "get cold comfort from ordinary religion, and so seek after Spiritualism." In a scathing and sarcastic fashion, he attacked the churches and argued that "sermons are full of windy words and dogmatic assertions." Conan Doyle told the *Daily Chronicle* that the English have not become irreligious, but they "have outgrown this presentment of religion." However, there was a remedy at hand. He maintained that spiritualism offered an escape from the snares of materialism and those modern systems of thought, especially natural sciences, which demanded empirical proof. Influential and learned people had already embraced the creeds of spiritualism. According to Sir Arthur, scientists, "at least 50 professors at seats of learning," and many "clergymen are adherents [of spiritualism] in spite of the bishop of London's injunction." Moreover, spiritualism was a proper religion. According to Lady Doyle, "It is an eminently practical religion for one feels that a cross word or action may retard one's progress in the Beyond." Sir Arthur also pointed out that "it is a religion that approaches that of the Early Christian Church." "Christ was the great Psychic," he reasoned, "and His disciples . . . were chosen because they were psychic." Quoting the First Letter of John, Sir Arthur told the readers of the *Daily Chronicle* "to try the spirits if they be of God." Even the sittings take on the ambiance of a church service. They should be held in "a reverent and religious atmosphere . . . [and] begin with a hymn and a prayer."

The day following the publication of the interview with Conan Doyle and his wife, the persistent Charles Dawbarn again approached Archbishop Randall Davidson and tried to elicit some comments from him. He tactfully began by accepting the logic behind the archbishop's policy of refusing interviews on certain topics, "but with the authority and backing of the greatest official of the Church to state what is exactly the Church's view in relation to this great question of spiritualism, which . . . is causing profound agitation in the country" any statement or clarification from Lambeth Palace would certainly clarify the issue for many people.[10] The thoughts of the archbishop of Canterbury on the subject would certainly help many troubled Anglicans. Dawbarn continued to push for an interview for his newspaper, arguing that the subject of spiritualism and its relationship to Christianity was "not a question of sensation but a question much more vital to the Church." He even tried to shame the archbishop into action and told him that the Anglican Church should be "eager and active to set at rest any doubts that may be in the unlearned mind as to her attitude upon this and other 'burning' topics of the day."

Archbishop Davidson's response to Charles Dawbarn's invitation acknowledged his earlier requests for an interview, but Davidson still remained firm in his refusal. "I do not find it right or wise to use newspaper interviews as a means of saying what I have to say on those very important subjects."[11] The archbishop told Dawbarn that he had read the recent interview with the Doyles in the *Daily Chronicle* and noted that "there is much in what Sir Arthur Conan Doyle says in the printed interview which I should emphatically challenge." Davidson questioned, for example, Sir Arthur's contention that spiritualism enjoyed the support from scientific circles; this conflicted with the archbishop's personal knowledge on the subject. But Davidson directed his strongest critique against Doyle's views about the inability of the Anglican Church to address seriously the claims of spiritualism:

> I do not contend that the Church has said all that she ought to say or might say on this most difficult subject but the opinions which Sir Arthur challenges and comments upon . . . are opinions very different from those which are entertained I think by most of the large number of thoughtful Churchmen who look at this wholly mysterious question with very different sentiments from those with which he credits us.

Some elements within the Anglican Church, however, did not shy away from discussing the relationship between spiritualism and Christianity in a public forum. Meeting in Leicester in 1919, members of the Church Congress[12] heard a number of addresses and listened to a series of discussions on one topic in particular, namely, the Christian doctrine of the future life with special reference to spiritualism. On 14 October 1919, the Right Rev. Frank Theodore Woods, the bishop of Peterborough, gave his presidential address to the assembly. He drew attention to the recent war and the apparent weaknesses and failings of contemporary Christianity, and argued that Anglicanism needed a living theology. "We suspected this before the war," Bishop Woods stated, and "now we know it for certain."[13] The teaching of the church "has been all too often quite inadequate when measured either by the New Testament revelation or by the needs of modern men." Consequently, the bishop continued, "This is one reason why cults as Christian Science, Theosophy and Spiritualism enjoy an increasing popularity. They attempt to state in terms which are modern and living and practical, the fact of God and man's relation to Him."[14] Naturally, the bereaved man and woman and those Anglicans seeking answers "will accept guidance from those who offer it most speedily and most simply."

The Very Rev. William Ralph Inge, the dean of St. Paul's and a persistent critic of spiritualism, presented the first paper, which dealt with the Christian doctrine of the future life. He began by telling the assembly that belief in eternal life had suffered in the decades before the Great War, but the casualties from the Continent had suddenly and drastically changed the outlook of many Christians. One consequence was the growth of popularity in spiritualism. "I am sure I need not warn you against the pitiable revival of necromancy in which many desolate and bleeding hearts have sought a spurious satisfaction," the dean concluded his address, and "if this kind of after-life were true, it would indeed be a melancholy postponement or negation of all that we hope and believe about our blessed dead."[15] After another presentation which emphasized the evil influences of materialism, the increasing popularity of prayers for the dead, and the appreciation of the doctrine of the communion of the saints, several papers specifically addressed the question of spiritualism.

The dean of Manchester, the Very Rev. W. S. Swayne, skillfully identified the key points of the issue in question, namely, the Great War and the bereavement and sorrow caused by the deaths. "It is in no way surprising that one of the results of the enormous and distressing loss of life in the Great War has been a considerable development in the practice of spiritualism," he began his address.[16]

> Sudden and grievous bereavement has come to many who have either never professed the Christian faith, or have no sure hold of that faith, and they have turned readily to those who have assured them that they can give them positive proof of the survival of those whom they love, and sometimes can put them in actual communication with their friends.

The church's "hesitations and timidity" to preach the doctrines of immortality and the communion of the saints contributed to the popularity of spiritualism, which he described "as fraud, and, as some would urge, nauseous fraud."[17]

Some areas of psychic experience or happenings needed to be explored by skilled and trained investigators, but from the Christian point of view "the whole subject is settled by quoting passages from the Old Testament condemning those who have familiar spirits, or ordering the capital penalty in the case of a witch." But Dean Swayne returned again to the culpability of the Anglican Church. "It remains to be considered whether we and our brethren of the Free Churches are not in some measure responsible for the modern vogue of spiritualism by the silence we have observed in our public services with regard to the relations between the Church on earth and the Church beyond the veil."[18] The absence of prayers for the departed, a practice of the primitive church which the Reformers unfortunately abolished, had created a "defective" communion service. The Burial Office of the Anglican Church, he argued, "though solemn and not without dignity, is cold."[19] He presented the following solution: "let us restore intercessions for the departed to their rightful place in our devotions both public and private." "It is probable," the dean concluded, "that spiritualism has come in to fill a void in the current teaching and practice of the church."

After another presentation which traced the history of spiritualism and condemned some of the actions of the Reformers, who "strove to erect an adamantine barrier between the living and the dead,"[20] several members of the Church Congress offered their statements on the position papers and on spiritualism in general. One expressed an openness of mind to some psychic phenomena, another offered a theological critique based on the writings of St. Paul, and a third emphasized the importance of the communion of saints. The response of the Rev. T. L. Lomax, Vicar of Ferryhill, Durham, savaged spiritualism. After expressing his "solemn disapproval of spiritualism," he pointed out that "necromancy, that is, dealing with the dead, is forbidden in the Scriptures. It is wrong."[21] The remarks from a Brighton clergymen addressed the pastoral problems associated with spiritualism, and he suggested that the church should establish a list of competent speakers whom the parish clergy could consult about spiritualism. The last cleric on the agenda maintained that it would be inappropriate to condemn all investigations or studies of psychic phenomena, urged the church to clarify its teachings about life after death, and also believed that each diocese should have an expert or an authority to handle problems dealing with spiritualism.

Following these discussions, the president of the Church Congress introduced the Rev. J. A. V. Magee, vicar of St. Mark's in London, and remarked that "the discussion should not be the final word, but that the final word should be spoken by a selected speaker who should bring all the threads together."[22] "Spiritualism, like the spirits," Magee began, "is in the air." Magee went on to describe the popularity which spiritualism enjoyed, not as a passing fad or trend but as "a passion." One could, naturally, number charlatans among the ranks of spiritualism, but on the other hand, its members also included professors and other individuals who honestly and sincerely explored its claims. He singled out, for example, Sir Arthur Conan Doyle for special attention: he "is moving from city to city, casting out common sense and ministering to popular crazes." The Rev. J. A. V. Magee's talk to the members of the Leicester Church Congress then addressed the dishonesty and perils some associated with spiritualism.

First of all, Magee used a few examples to demonstrate "that there is a vast amount of fraud in the whole thing."[23] Second, he questioned the contributions of the Society for Psychical Research in the area of psychical phenomena, pointing out that "it is amazingly how little of any real value has come through to us despite all the efforts of that eminent Society for Psychical Research and all the efforts that are being made to-day." To make his point more convincing, the speaker listed a series of examples to illustrate his contention that communications with the departed spirits about the conditions of the life after death were valueless. More importantly, he argued, spiritualism presented a "grave peril to countless parishioners of our own up and down this land, and it is a peril which we dare not ignore." Again, he mentioned Conan Doyle's name. "We want here and to-day to challenge Sir Arthur Conan Doyle to deny if he will and if he dare that this thing [spiritualism] involves grave peril to mental, moral, and spiritual health." Magee attributed the danger to the vulnerability of the "sub-conscious mind" and the ways in which practices associated with spiritualism could do it harm. "In the abnormal conditions of the séance, of hypnotism, and so on, the conscious intelligence which keeps it in order is surrendered and that sub-conscious mind is lain open to any suggestion for good or for evil that may come to it from outside."[24] According to his logic, this could injure one's mental health and even produce insanity.

What then, Magee asked his audience, could the Anglican Church do to protect the faithful? "In the first place the Church can give you, not communications which are doubtful, but communion which is certain." He then went on to explain this statement. "The Church can tell you that there are voices from the unseen but that they come . . . through those sacramental channels which have been the means of communication from Christ's day until now."[25] By this, the Rev. J. A. V. Magee meant the belief in the communion of saints: "the Church can speak to you of the saints on whom you can call to help you in this earthly pilgrimage."[26] He proclaimed this position as "the Church's spiritualism." Magee ended his statement to the Church Congress with a direct challenge to the archbishop of Canterbury, Randall Davidson, who was in attendance at the meeting. "I would ask if it be possible," he began, "that some committee might be appointed to investigate these matters from the Christian standpoint, that the Church should have her society for psychical research, based on the foundations of the faith and yet not unwilling to study each psychic movement as it comes before her." Consequently,

I would humbly ask that as a result of this debate we may have a Christian Committee for psychical research, and it may be by the providence of God, we shall help those who have sought the unseen on dangerous and devious by-paths, to find within the borders of the Catholic Church the peace for which they long.

Magee's words, and especially his proposal for the establishment of a committee to investigate the claims of spiritualism in the context of Christianity, did not fall on deaf ears. Archbishop Randall Davidson rose and gave a response. Davidson told the audience that he did not intend to comment on the substance of Magee's "eloquent speech," but the archbishop wanted to say something about the responsibility of the Anglican Church to study the question of spiritualism which Magee had addressed. The archbishop announced that spiritualism "is one of the subjects which is to be considered when the Lambeth Conference of Bishops meets next year." Davidson also promised that when the bishops of the Anglican Communion gathered "first in committee, then in conference as a whole, they shall have before them what are already in preparation—the results of inquiry by our best men and our best women who have knowledge, experience and thought on this great subject."

Sir Oliver Lodge, however, did not like the manner in which the Church Congress handled the subject of spiritualism, and he expressed his discomfort in the pages of the *Hibbert Journal*. "The recent Church Congress at Leicester attracted considerable attention," he began his critique, "partly because it dealt with a live subject—the question of human survival, whether there could be any proof of it, and what future existence would be like."[27] Some of the comments about spiritualism, he complained, were "jocular," and this "treatment of human destiny illustrates the distance the clergy have travelled from mediaeval eschatology, or even from that which prevailed half a century ago, when hell was held over the laity as a terrible and authoritative threat."[28] Lodge defended the right of all people to search for truth, and argued that the church, founded on faith, could not view the question of spiritualism from an objective and unbiased point of view. However, "if ministers of religion really open their minds to the evidence, if they examine the proofs carefully and without prejudice, they will surely be guided in the direction of the truth."[29] After taking issue with several of the reports in the papers and statements critical of spiritualism, Sir Oliver ended his unfavorable evaluation of the Leicester Church Congress:

The spirit of the inquisition is not yet dead. If communication is feasible, no Church has a right to forbid it, any more than it forbids an emigrant in a new country to make use of such means of correspondence with those at home as the progress of engineering has made available.[30]

Others, however, welcomed the announcement by the archbishop of Canterbury that he intended to place spiritualism on the agenda of the 1920 Lambeth Conference.

Mail soon reached Lambeth Palace after Archbishop Davidson's announcement that the Lambeth Conference, scheduled to meet during the summer of 1920, would set up a committee to study the claims of spiritualism and its relationship to Christianity. Mr. W. Whately Smith, for example, wrote to Davidson and volunteered his services: "I should esteem it a privilege if your Grace would permit me to place at the disposal of the Committee such knowledge of the subject as I possess."[31] He then went on to explain his intentions. "The precise extent to which my experience might prove of value," Whately Smith continued, "would necessarily depend on whether the attention of the Committee would be primarily directed . . . towards the conflict . . . of Spiritualistic doctrines with those of the Church of England or to the scientific status of the phenomenal basis for those doctrines." He told the archbishop that he could offer assistance in the case of the latter, but also pointed out that it might prove difficult or impossible to separate these two subjects of doctrine and science. The proposed committee, no matter what line of investigation it decided to follow, would face problems.

> I feel that one of the main difficulties that will confront the Committee will be that of obtaining unbiased expressions of opinion on the many technical complexities involved . . . a danger lest their view of this aspect of the subject be wholly or mainly determined by the allegations of those enthusiasts whose zeal for their creed has inhibited their critical faculties . . . [these] are most likely to be regarded as representative leaders of Spiritualistic thought.

The archbishop of Canterbury must fully appreciate and understand the hurdles and obstacles which the committee of the Lambeth Conference must overcome. "An imperfect appreciation of these difficulties might lead," Mr. Whately Smith continued to stress, "to such erroneous results as the condemnation as religiously heretical of views which should more properly be characterised as scientifically unsubstantiated." Moreover, experts must be included in the membership of the committee as witnesses. Whately Smith told the archbishop that he would freely volunteer his time and expertise, which he described as "purely scientific." He closed his letter to the Archbishop Davidson by suggesting that the archbishop should approach the Society for Psychical Research for references about his credentials. Lambeth Palace responded and thanked Mr. Whately Smith for his interest. "The Committee to which the archbishop referred . . . in Leicester is a Committee of Bishops appointed in connection with the Lambeth Conference . . . [and] it will not be actually set up till the Lambeth Conference assembles."[32] This letter from the archbishop's secretary also asked Whately Smith for additional information on the subject of spiritualism, especially any material concerning "the scientific status of the phenomenal basis for those doctrines."

Whately Smith thanked the archbishop for his interest, and sent him "twelve copies of the paper which I have written for submission to the Committee on Spiritualism."[33] Archbishop Randall Davidson responded to Mr. Whately Smith and thanked the author for his essay, and he especially drew attention to the "clearness of statement, and a lucidity of arrangement which makes your paper one of the most valuable that I have seen on these matters."[34] Moreover, Davidson pointed out that "the conclusions you reach seem to me to be almost precisely those to which . . . I am myself led." The archbishop did, however, express some reservations about the publication of the paper on spiritualism: "I should prefer it should not be published (at all events before this Lambeth Conference) with any reference to the Conference as having been the purpose of its compilation." This, he concluded, "might be misleading to some people." With this exception, Archbishop Davidson saw no reason why the author should not publish his findings.

Archbishop Davidson earnestly sought to enlist expert opinions on the topic of spiritualism and its relationship to Christianity, and Whately Smith's paper, *A Critique of the Phenomenal Basis of Spiritualism*, was made available to the other members of the Lambeth Conference committee. His findings would not challenge the beliefs of any traditionally minded Anglican bishop. "The object of this paper," Whately Smith began, "is to summarise and critically to discuss the facts, and the alleged facts, on which the doctrines of Spiritualism are founded, the difficulties connected with their interpretation and such conclusions as appear to be logical and influences therefrom."[35] He pointed out that he personally did not hold a belief in spiritualism, and "his conclusions are not affected by any prepossessions beyond the belief that careful and scientific investigations of these phenomena is both legitimate and necessary." The conclusions, consequently, reflected this sense of objectivity. In the first place, "there is nothing in the strictly scientific interpretation of the facts to conflict with orthodox Christian doctrine—if only because of the meagreness of scientifically legitimate inferences." Moreover, the objectionable aspects of spiritualism derived from "ignorant interpretation rather than to intrinsic anomalies." The investigation of spiritualistic phenomena by "unqualified persons" should be discouraged "on the grounds of the scientific immaturity of the subject." But on the other hand, he concluded, "it should be recognized that there is a considerable chance that Survival may come to be regarded as experimentally confirmed."

Stanley de Brath, past temporary editor of *Light* and an advocate for a better understanding between Christianity and spiritualism, also took the occasion of the announcement that the Lambeth Conference would discuss spiritualism to write to Archbishop Davidson. And he approached the archbishop of Canterbury with a suggestion. "It is not without apprehension that many spiritualists view the discussion foreshadowed to take place at the next congress," he began, and "we [spiritualists] think we ought to be represented on the committee."[36] This would ensure objectivity and guard against those churchmen who might come to the meetings "with an antagonistic bias." He told Davidson that "I have solid grounds for thinking that the large majority of the clergy who do not know the real facts are disposed to take the line that whether the supernormal phenomena are true or not, they are unorthodox and pernicious *and ought to be suppressed*." The members of the committee, moreover, must not dismiss the claims of spiritualism with a smile of disbelief. Stanley de Brath concluded by drawing the archbishop's attention to the manner in which Anglicanism had treated spiritualism in the recent past. "It is on grounds of fact alone that we desire to see a more serious treatment of problems fraught with vast consequences, than the offensive . . . and ignorant jests of one or two speakers at the last congress."

Davidson's counterpart at York, Archbishop Cosmo Gordon Lang, also received letters dealing with the upcoming discussions on spiritualism scheduled for the summer's Lambeth Conference. One individual, for example, told Archbishop Lang that "it is most important that first-hand evidence be submitted."[37] Mr. W. T. Gates then informed Lang that his "Medium is a lady who has never accepted a fee or sat with other than personal friends . . . [and] Communion has been established with hundreds of . . . spirit people." And he identified some of these "spirit people": Charles H. Spurgeon, Henry Ward Beecher, Fr. Ignatius of Llanthony, and Richard Durnford, the past bishop of Chichester who died in 1895. Like similar letters dealing with the decision to include spiritualism on the agenda of the Lambeth Conference, this writer also volunteered his services as a witness. "Each one of these and a score of others, has given me most interesting descriptions of life on the 'other side,'" he pointed out, "and it seems to me that the Conference ought to be made acquainted with the evidence I have obtained before passing judgment." Gates offered to submit transcripts of his notes and also agreed to appear before the committee of the Lambeth Conference as a witness. Archbishop Lang forwarded this letter to Archbishop Davidson, who in turn invited Mr. Gates to send his material on "spirit communications" to Lambeth Palace.[38]

A member of the episcopal bench also had an interest in spiritualism, and he openly expressed his feelings on spiritualism as the opening of the Lambeth Conference rapidly approached. The new bishop of Lincoln, William Shuckburgh Swayne, preached a sermon in the London suburb of Stamford in April 1920 which addressed the issue of spiritualism. The bishop of Lincoln told his audience "that death had been so near to the people during the past few years that it was not surprising their thoughts turned in an unusual degree to the question of life beyond the grave."[39] The bishop admitted that the subject of spiritualism had fascinated him for approximately thirty years, and he believed that its claims and beliefs should not be dismissed flippantly or without careful study. He was "entirely unconvinced that the ordinary Spiritualist's interpretation of those phenomena as the means by which contact was established between the living and those who had passed to the next world was a true one." But traditional religion, he argued, still held the true answers. The Christian faith "could tell them more about the life beyond than the Spiritualist séance or phenomena could reveal." Many bishops at the Lambeth Conference would adopt this approach.

The English press also anticipated the opening of the 1920 Lambeth Conference, and a number of articles focused on the topic of spiritualism. In April, for example, one London religious newspaper printed a lengthy editorial which began by arguing that "we are now living in one of those periodical cycles when the teaching and practice of spiritualism dominate the human mind."[40] The author emphasized the horrible consequences of the Great War. "The appalling loss of life in the war is in a great measure responsible for the present revival in psychical questions," he pointed out. "Apart from the desire to communicate, if possible, with those who have passed away, there is a natural longing in the human heart to solve the mystery of the beyond." What then, the article queried, should be the position of the Anglican Church? Anglicanism should not condone spiritualism, but on the other hand the church should not remain silent. The Lambeth Conference, therefore, had the opportunity to give some authoritative guidance on the subject, and the newspaper offered a suggestion which the bishops might consider: "We should like to see established a permanent committee of competent Churchmen whose business it would be to cooperate with the Society for Psychical Research so that the Church might be kept officially informed of events in psychic circles."

Not surprisingly, numerous letters to the editor of the paper praised the merits and pointed out the shortcomings of spiritualism. No stranger to the columns of the English press, Sir Arthur Conan Doyle told the readers of the *Church Family Newspaper* that the Lambeth Conference had an obligation to study spiritualism from the viewpoint of objective and scientific observers and churchmen, and not through the prejudicial eyes of critics such as the Rev. J. A. V. Magee. If the bishops failed to adopt an unbiased approach, the result "must be a fiasco."[41] Another correspondent, on the other hand, captured the feelings of many and described spiritualism as essentially anti-Christian in character. He proceeded to list a number of spiritualist beliefs, for example, the denial of the divinity of Christ, and claimed that the followers of spiritualism wanted to establish a new religion on English soil. Other hostile critics maintained that spirit communications emanated from evil spirits, and one pointed out that St. Paul's condemnation of witchcraft also extended to spiritualism.[42] Before the summer of 1920 arrived, the meeting of the bishops at Lambeth Palace in London had attracted the attention of many people who wanted a clarification of the relationship, if any, between Christianity and spiritualism.

Initiated in 1865 at the insistence of the Anglican Church in Canada to address the concerns and apparent dangers of liberalism associated with the publication of *Essays and Reviews* and the actions of Bishop John William Colenso of Natal, bishops of the worldwide Anglican Communion met approximately every ten years at Lambeth Palace in London.[43] The archbishop of Canterbury functioned as the president of the assembly, and the resolutions passed by the bishops were merely directives and were not binding on the members of the Anglican Communion. The subjects discussed at the conferences extended beyond the boundaries of theology and matters religious, but rather concerned issues which affected Anglicanism in general. The 1897 Lambeth Conference, for example, discussed topics such as religious communities within the Church of England, foreign missions, Christian unity, industrial problems, and international arbitration, and later in 1908 episcopal committees addressed numerous subjects including foreign missions, problems associated with the married state, religious education, reunion and intercommunion, and the ministries of healing.

The bishops had touched upon the question of spiritualism, although briefly, before the 1920 Lambeth Conference. At the 1908 meeting, a committee had studied and reported upon the ministries of healing, the unction of the sick, faith healing, and Christian Science. The issue of spiritualism arose during the deliberations dealing with spiritual healing. The bishop of Winchester, Herbert Edward Ryle, chaired the committee. He cautioned his fellow bishops against "the temptation that these persons," who might have the gift of spiritual healing "owing to the mysterious influence which they feel they wield, may be led, into the very dangerous ground of occultism and spiritualism."[44] The report of the committee repeated its warning against the temptation of people involved in spiritual healing who might unknowingly wander "into the dangerous ground of occultism and spiritualism."[45] The question of spiritualism, therefore, did not appear out of place on the agenda of the 1920 Lambeth Conference.

"I think we can say, without fear of contradiction," according to a historian of the Lambeth Conferences, "that the Lambeth Conference of 1920 has been the most famous and best-known of all the Conferences."[46] Stephenson points to the names of some of the participants, such as, Randall Davidson, Herbert Hensley Henson, Frank Weston, and G. K. A. Bell, to substantiate his contention. *The Times* also recognized the significance of the gathering, and noted that several "of the subjects to be discussed are distinctly controversial."[47] The program of this meeting of bishops covered a wide area of topics, for example, relationship and reunion with other churches, missionary problems, issues dealing with marriage and sexual morality, the role and position of women in the church, Christianity and international relations, and questions raised by industrial and social problems. One committee would also study Christianity and its relationship to spiritualism, Christian Science, and theosophy. A change in procedure took place at this conference. "For the first time the Archbishop of Canterbury has had a number of papers prepared, not exclusively by Churchmen, on some of the subjects for discussion, and these will be at the disposal of the committee in preparing their reports."[48] The committee studying spiritualism, consequently, would make valuable use of the expertise of individuals who were not clerics. The memory of the recent war, however, permeated the workings of all the committees. According to the encyclical issued by the bishops,

> Men never prized the universal fellowship of mankind as they did when the Great War had for the time destroyed it . . . Nations became associated in alliances, which they cemented with their blood . . . Thousands gained quite a new impression of what human nature might be, when they experienced the fellowship of man with man in danger and death. Comradeship ennobled war. To-day, men are asking, Can it not ennoble peace.[49]

The 1920 Lambeth Conference first considered the subject of spiritualism and its relationship to Christianity at its afternoon session on 5 July 1920. The president, the archbishop of Canterbury, Randall Davidson, first proposed a list of names for membership on the committee, and announced that the group would meet under the chairmanship of Bishop H. M. Burge of Oxford.[50] Archbishop Davidson next introduced the subject for discussion, and suggested that the bishops consider the three topics of spiritualism, Christian Science, and theosophy separately. The chairman of the committee, Bishop Burge, then addressed the assembly, and he attempted to put spiritualism within a historical framework. Acknowledging the difficulty of tracing its growth and development, the bishop believed that spiritualism must be studied within the context of materialism and modernity. "We have been living in an age of immense material expansion and development of the material facilities of life," the bishop of Oxford pointed out, "and as the result of that you have, of course, the growth of great towns with large crowded populations, with all the restlessness and the rush of many converging streams of life."[51] Consequently, the worth of the "individual seems to count for very little and the purpose of his life seems to be limited to just the things of the day."

But what role or function should Christianity play in this new world? Did traditional Christian beliefs and practices adequately address the challenges of this modern age? According to the bishop, Christianity had failed to emphasize the spiritual dimensions or aspirations of its members. The Christian churches did not successfully stress the "increasing conviction of the reality and the supremacy of man's spiritual being and of the deep need of nourishing and strengthening that spiritual being by those means which have been revealed to us and bestowed upon us by Our Lord Jesus Christ." Consequently, he continued, an unhealthy skepticism and indifference to the claims of the spiritual dimension had become acceptable by an increasing number of Christians who now tended to explain and interpret the mysteries of life by simple physical phenomena. Bishop Burge also reminded the bishops of the old conflicts within the church's history between science and theology and between the realm of materialism and things spiritual. He noted that this antagonism, for the most part, had ceased. A so-called reconciliation marked out the appropriate areas of intellectual endeavors, and "all kinds of human speculation . . . have been turned more and more into a theological direction and have tended to concentrate upon the things which lie at the basis of religion."

The bishop of Oxford then brought the discussion back to the problems that the Anglican Church currently faced and urged his fellow bishops not to retreat from their "appointed task." Other periods of crisis and times of troubles had existed earlier in Christianity's long history, especially during the second century, and dedicated churchmen answered these challenges by emphasizing and reenforcing the "fundamental truths . . . which determine the meaning and order of the world." But before any discussion of spiritualism could continue, Bishop Burge sounded a word of caution to the assembly. "I want to say first of all that we have a duty, a very distinct duty, to restless dissatisfied souls that have never accepted the Christian revelation . . . [and] have never appropriated it and have never relied upon those means which our Church offers" to understand the truths of Christian Revelation. These people have already begun the journey from indifference "to a deep desire to feel after and to find the reality of the things unseen." These were the individuals, he believed, who were attracted or captured by the promises of spiritualism: "Such people think that they find in spiritualistic teaching the assurance of that unseen world which they desire."

The Anglican Church had a sacred and important obligation to instruct these searching souls, and all churchmen, moreover, also had a special duty to point out the weaknesses and shortcomings of spiritualism. But spiritualism also appealed to faithful and loyal Anglicans, and they likewise required attention from the church.

> On the other hand, we have a duty to members of our own Church who are led to believe that spiritualistic teaching and investigation give them assurance of the life of the unseen world and of man's power of moving in contact with it, which the traditional, and what they call the stereotyped, teaching of the Church does not present to them.

The bishop of Oxford believed that Anglicanism must necessarily consider two points of view when confronting this serious situation. Have scientific investigations produced any new revelations about the nature of human consciousness? "How far do those results confirm or modify or enlarge the teaching which the Church has given and gives about the meaning of man's life here in the world and the relation of that life to a world which transcends and lies beyond the limits of the material world in which he lives?"

He then proceeded to address these queries. Bishop Burge noted that the church welcomed scientific investigation and the results arrived at through a strict scientific method, even those dealing with "God's purpose and order in human life in this world." However, one must not forget two considerations. In the first place, he argued, there were difficulties when the mind investigates itself; this was especially true with psychical research. Another problem area which made scientific enquiries problematic concerned the presence in the mind of memories and the subconsciousness. In other words, the bishop told the assembly that the mind could influence the mind. And moreover, the scientific community had not reached any decisive conclusion about those areas which spiritualism and psychical studies held to be true, for example, "communication by physical means and psychical agencies with discarnate beings." He continued to dwell on the topic of spirit communications. Even if science eventually confirmed their validity, "we should have to be very much more certain than we are at present about the nature of the communications that we receive," especially in the area of interpretation. "How much of the incarnate mind is put into the communications of discarnate minds or discarnate beings?" Even members of the Society for Psychical Research and other scientists correctly recognize this danger. The bishop then made the connection to religion: "There is no scientific warrant so far for Spiritualism as it expresses itself in what are called spirit teachings and new revelations."

The bishop of Oxford then moved to the second question or consideration dealing with scientific investigations, namely, "How much do the results so far obtained . . . confirm or enlarge or modify the teaching which the Church gives and has given." In any discussion of this nature, the church must always reaffirm the traditional Christian view of life after death, and he gave a word of caution to those clerics who launched attacks on the followers of spiritualism from their pulpits with the claim that "spiritualistic phenomena are the work of evil spirits which man may invoke." Consequently, the bishop maintained, these well-meant critiques or criticisms might even "revive and encourage the doctrines and the practices of demonology, witchcraft, and the black arts which made European civilization for generations." Instead of adopting a negative approach, Bishop Burge urged his fellow bishops to emphasize the constructive aspects of traditional Christian revelation and its interpretations of the order and purpose of the world.

After this lengthy and general introduction to the subject of spiritualism, the role of scientific investigation, and some inherent shortcomings associated with this approach to the study of human affairs, Bishop Burge continued to stress a more positive approach to the issues. He tried to refocus the discussion:

> First of all, then we should begin, I think, by welcoming whatever inferences lay greater stress upon the reality and the conviction of the reality of some-

thing within and something essentially part of the human being which transcends the material circumstances of his life and enables him to hold fellowship with what lies behind and beyond him, which abides amidst all the changes and chances of this mortal life.

A Christian interpretation and view of reality necessarily required a conviction that a moral and spiritual order took precedence over "the life and order of this world." Consequently, "the one condition of communication and fellowship with any life or any beings that lie beyond this world . . . is the discipline of our spiritual faculties in nature and in life." The basis for a belief in the afterlife and personal immortality did not derive from logical or intellectual processes, the bishop of Oxford stressed, "but the belief itself in immortality is the spirit of man realising itself here and now through goodness, through the love of truth and the beauty of holiness, and becoming persuaded that neither life nor death can ever separate us from the love of God, which is in Christ Jesus Our Lord." He ended his opening address with a plea. A Christocentric view of the universe must be the starting point for any discussion of spiritualism and its relationship to Anglicanism; the historical creeds of the church supplied the necessary guideposts.

After Bishop Burge finished addressing the assembly, the bishop of Goulburn, L. B. Radford, rose and spoke to the bishops. The Australian bishop urged the Lambeth Conference to face and to explore new fields of thought fearlessly under the guidance of Christ. His address would emphasize specifically the topic of spiritualism, but Radford quickly pointed out all three topics—spiritualism, Christian Science, and theosophy—were interrelated since they dealt with the spiritual aspects of people. "They are three branches of one problem."[52] These three so-called philosophies enjoyed a common history, and moreover, they developed a creed of belief and then grew into cults. All three had always been conscious of Christian traditions and teachings and made "desperate efforts to find a footing in the title deeds of Christian faith in scripture and in creed," which they have distorted. Still they remained dangerous: "they have anxiously made the effort, not merely to commend this as an alternative form of Christianity, but I believe to vindicate the essential Christian character of the thing that they believe and feel to be real and true at the heart of their system, however grotesquely it has been wrapped in a science which is not scientific, and a philosophy which will not bear ten minutes thinking criticism."

The bishop continued in his harsh and rough criticism of these alternatives to traditional Christianity. They have abandoned the essential tenets and beliefs of Christianity; spiritualism, unfortunately, emerged as an alternative religious system. Moreover, faithful members of the Anglican Church have been touched and influenced. And Anglicanism should not avoid its responsibility in this situation. "There is an anxiety on the part of some people lest the Church should be blind to elements of truth that have gained a new distinctiveness or emphasis outside the door of the Church and its teachings." He also pointed out another area of concern to some Anglicans who appeared to be attracted to these so-called "psychicalisms." What if spiritualism did prove to be true? How would the Anglican Church react to this development? Bishop Radford ended his introductory remarks to the conference by strongly suggesting that the committee should study spiritualism, Christian Science, and theosophy as elements or parts of a single question.

The bishop of Goulburn then began to address his remarks to the question of the relationship of the Christian faith to spiritualism. The role of science could not be avoided, and the bishop made some observations about psychical studies and research: "We very gravely doubt the capacity of psychical investigation to carry us the whole way" in the search for truth. Psychical studies, for example, relied upon a high degree of probability in respect to communications with spirits. The task facing the Lambeth Conference, however, should be confined to the area of strictly religious or theological speculation. "We are trustees and interpreters of religious truth, and that is our sole function, and our sole duty in speaking on this matter." Spiritualism as a religion or creed deserved more attention. The bishop believed that it would be unfair to judge spiritualism in terms of some of its alleged dogmas or "some of the weird communications which are supposed to be received from the yon side." Nonetheless, he even saw those more sober aspects of spiritualism as "pitifully poor and meager." Proofs offered by psychical studies offered no substantial confirmation of the Christian faith. The bishop's real critique, however, rested on the observation that spiritualism stressed the "psycho-centric and not Christo-centric." "To depart is to be with Christ," Bishop Radford forcefully pointed out, "and he will surely reveal any communications from those who are a stage nearer where it is far better to be." The so-called new revelation had thus far failed to throw any additional light on the conditions of life after death.

Spiritualism might parade itself and market itself as a religion, but it also had developed into a cult. Not willing to address the purported psychological damages which might be associated with the séance or other psychical activities, the bishop nonetheless recognized two serious consequences: "it shifts the centre of interest from the normal current channels of truth and grace . . . and the second is, that it alienates minds from patient submission to the discipline of faith." Bishop Radford also noted that he found it exceedingly difficult to believe that any new spiritual or religious truth could come from a source other than the traditional Christian faith. Again he sounded a familiar refrain: what position or response should the Anglican Church adopt? He dismissed a policy of nonapproval, and he also repudiated those who argued for a suspension of judgment.

Nay, more, it seems to me that we have not merely to sum up the present situation, but we have to indicate tendencies; we have fearlessly to contemplate the directions in which new knowledge may come from psychical research, and, as far as we can, tentatively to indicate the directions in which that new knowledge will throw light . . . on the working of the old argument, as to what revelation we have of the mind of man in relation to itself and the mind of God.

Consequently, the bishop of Goulburn made two proposals: the Anglican Church should give more emphasis to the idea of the eternal and second, the church should articulate and teach more clearly the doctrine of the communion of saints. Both would counter the claims of spiritualism by offering instead the church's traditional and positive teachings on immortality.

The doctrine of the communion of saints, which had received serious attention by Anglican theologians such as William Temple earlier in the century, should stress the fact that mediation or communion between the living and the dead took place through Jesus Christ, "in whom the spirits are one." He urged his fellow bishops to "insist that the communion of Christian spirit with Christian spirit must be found through Christ." He has remained not only the "one mediator, but . . . the only medium." In spite of this insistence and contrary to his criticisms of psychical studies earlier in his presentation, the bishop then acknowledged that he saw some usefulness in psychical studies, namely, this type of research might give churchmen "a new insight into the working of the mind of man under the teaching of the mind of man, or the mind of God." Bishop Radford concluded his presentation by stressing that a true Christian spiritualism, therefore, might illuminate the dark caverns of faith.

The bishop of Grahamstown, F. R. Phelps, gave the last presentation of the afternoon. And he went straight to the heart of the problem facing the Anglican Communion: "there has been a remarkable recrudescence of spiritualism during the past few years."[53] "Everywhere men are accepting as facts a vast number of phenomena which they cannot explain, but upon which they proceed to rear imposing edifices." Whether one considered spiritualism as a cult or religion did not pose the important question. The bishop believed that the real danger existed in the fact that "spiritualism tends to weaken the sense of responsibility for present action as the basis of future condition by substituting the satisfaction of immediate longings natural in themselves, or by ministering to the popular desire for the abnormal and the uncanny." Spiritualism, he pointed out, claimed that a continuity of life exists before and after death, and spiritualists believed that they had effectively demonstrated this fact. According to the bishop, the chief difficulty with this proposition could be found in one essential point: it was almost impossible to analyze and examine the evidence competently. Bishop Phelps then thanked Archbishop Davidson for the work of Dr. W. Whately Smith, which had been placed at the disposal of the conference, and he voiced his support for a proper study of spiritualism for two reasons: the pursuit of knowledge remained a noble goal and the church was "bound to warn the faithful of the dangers which beset their spiritual and moral lives if they carelessly, or ignorantly, or willfully, embark on perilous courses, or walk in unauthorised roads."

The bishop expanded upon these concerns. Acknowledging the difficult problems of investigating topics such as mediumship and automatism, he nonetheless argued that

> psychical states and phenomena need investigation as offering a wide and promising field for the increase of knowledge concerning telepathy, the survival of sublunary consciousness, latent memory, crowd psychology, multiple personality, and other kindred topics, and, if such investigations by adequate and careful critics lead to a strong presumption or even proof of continuity, such as cases like the case of the Ear of Dionysius seem to indicate, then the resultant will simply be the addition of scientific corroboration to what the Church has already taught.

Moreover, the ultimate test of truth, even in regard to the possibility of communication with the dead, "is the revelation of the faith which is in Christ Jesus." The Anglican Church should welcome an investigation of any aspects of spiritualism by trained minds, especially in the field of psychology.

Unlike the previous two speakers, Bishop Phelps of Grahamstown vividly described the dangers associated with dabbling in spiritualism. And the church, consequently, must warn the faithful, especially the bereaved, of the serious risks involved. "It seems positively indecent and unspeakably rash," the bishop argued, "for ordinary unskilled persons, often enduring a soul-shocking grief, or bereavement, to rush lightly into the perils of the seance, or to practice automatic writing, or the like." One's nervous system, for example, might suffer incalculable harm, and the psychological harm appeared obvious to him. Sacred Scripture also contained numerous examples of personal risks such as false prophecy, demonic possession, the existence of malevolent spirits, and necromancy. Moreover, "the possession of abnormal psychic gifts is not in itself a protection" against these real dangers. The surrender or loss of one's free will might also result from experimentation with spiritualism. No automation, therefore "is permissible, for it is never God's plan to rule our actions without our consent."

In line with the suggestions of the previous speaker, Bishop Phelps called for a reaffirmation of traditional Christian beliefs, especially the communion of saints and the mediatorship of Christ, as a powerful antidote to the allurements and attractions of spiritualism.

> Therefore it follows that . . . holy souls who depend for their union with God upon the one mediator are *ipso facto* united one to another, and, inasmuch as the love of Christ has set no limit to the nearness of our approach to him it is

possible even in this life to be allowed to see and hear, not only our Lord himself, but all those others of the Communion of Saints who have their life by union with Him.

The Anglican Church, therefore, should not allow the idea of communion with the departed to be forgotten or disallowed. Spiritualism tended, on the other hand, to minimize this sacred practice. The bishop ended his presentation by urging the conference to take a hard and critical look at the issues raised by spiritualism, and he reminded the assembly of a serious episcopal obligation, namely, "to defend ignorant and unskilled persons from a peril which it seems clear meets them when they embark on spiritualistic practice."

Following Bishop Phelps's presentation, Archbishop Randall Davidson, as president of the Lambeth Conference, asked the assembly for a vote to establish a committee which would consider the issue of spiritualism. After other bishops had the opportunity to speak on Christian Science and theosophy, another vote would be taken to place these topics on the agenda. The wording of Davidson's proposal, however, caused some confusion, The archbishop of York, Cosmo Gordon Lang, proposed that one committee should be constituted to consider and report on the three subjects individually, rather than three separate and independent committees dealing with three different issues. Davidson responded to this suggestion and agreed with Archbishop Lang's idea, but he did not believe that the resolution which he had voiced ran contrary to Lang's proposal. "The resolution is 'that a Committee be appointed to consider (a), [spiritualism],' and then to consider (b) [Christian Science] and (c) [theosophy]," the archbishop of Canterbury pointed out. "We do not say three Committees, but when the Committee is appointed it will, of course, be for the Committee to decide how it will break itself up."[54] With no additional discussion from the floor and after the confusion had been cleared up, the assembly agreed to Archbishop Davidson's motion to establish a committee which would consider spiritualism first, and then Christian Science and theosophy.

On 5 August 1920, the Lambeth Conference again took up the question of spiritualism. Since the last meeting in July, the committee had drawn up several resolutions and had written a report. The chairman of the committee, Bishop Burge of Oxford, began the morning session and apologized for the late circulation of the revised set of resolutions from the committee, noting that the original but unrevised set had been distributed earlier. He also made some general comments about the scope of the work undertaken by the committee, especially the complexity of the three subjects, which extended "into the domains of Theology and Philosophy moral and metaphysical."[55] The type of methodology employed and the use and definition of important terms such as "personality," "soul," and "spirit," also made the task more difficult, and moreover the committee had to write resolutions "which will be understood by the plain man or the man in the street." The terms of reference, however, proved easier, namely, the relationship of Christian faith to the three topics, spiritualism, Christian Science, and theosophy. Consequently, the committee applied "the decisive test of the cardinal truths that lay at the basis of the Christian Faith to anything" associated with these three movements. And the incarnation of Jesus Christ formed the essence or keystone of Christian belief.

With this litmus test established, the bishop of Oxford introduced the first of four resolutions of the committee (appendix 1), and this dealt with the three movements in general.

> We reaffirm our conviction that the revelation of God in Christ Jesus is the supreme and sufficient message given to all mankind whereby we may attain to eternal life. We recognise that modern movements of thought connected with Spiritualism, Christian Science, and Theosophy join with the Christian Church in protesting against a materialistic view of the universe and at some points emphasize partially neglected aspects of the truth. At the same time, we feel bound to call attention to the fact that, in cults and practices which have arisen out of these movements, the teaching given or implied either ignores or explains away or contradicts the unique and central fact of human history, namely, the Incarnation of our Lord and Saviour Jesus Christ.

Archbishop Davidson interrupted the bishop's presentation and asked whether the final report of the committee should be discussed and received before the consideration of the resolutions. Bishop Burge replied that the report, previously circulated to the assembly of bishops, had already been amended and changed by the committee. The bishop of Oxford responded to a question from the floor, and noted the alterations in the report were minor. He also announced that he planned to introduce the report of the committee for discussion after the deliberations on the resolutions concluded.

Following this interruption, the bishop then moved the first resolution of the committee, and made comments about important sections, especially the wording, "partially neglected aspects of the truth."[56] Drawing the assembly's attention specifically to spiritualism, the bishop of Oxford noted that "we would admit that Spiritualism has drawn our attention to the fact that many people do not realise that we teach very definitely and very clearly the activity and the present consciousness of the departed and the reality of fellowship and communion between the living and the departed." Spiritualism, and the other two related movements of Christian Science and theosophy, did not supplement or add to beliefs already expounded upon by the church; however, he admitted, certain perspectives might have been "partially neglected" by the Anglican Church. Other queries came from the floor concerning the first resolution. The bishop in Tinnevelly and Madura, E. H. M. Waller, asked for a clarification about the cults and other practices which had evolved from these movements. Bishop Waller, moreover, wanted to include the word *philosophy* so that the resolution would be more inclusive. His amended statement would read: "both in the underlying philosophy and in cults and practices which have arisen the teaching given or implied."[57] Bishop Burge replied that the committee worded the resolutions in an attempt to warn all people about cults and practices associated with the three movements, and he accepted the amendment. This first resolution then received the approval of the assembly.

The bishop of Oxford then introduced the second resolution:

> We recognize that the new phenomena of consciousness have been presented to us, which claim, and at the hands of competent psychologists have received, careful investigation, and, as far as possible the application of scientific method. But such scientific researches have confessedly not reached an advanced stage, and we are supported by the best psychologists in warning our people against accepting as final theories which further knowledge may disprove, and still more against the indiscriminate and undisciplined exercise of psychic powers, and the habit of recourse to seances and seers.

Comments from the bishop followed. He told the assembly that it was important for the Lambeth Conference "to recognize how very carefully and scrupulously . . . some people have been investigating phenomena of consciousness." Bishop Burge singled out, for example, members of the Society for Psychical Research as both conservative and reputable in their investigations of psychical phenomena. The bishop maintained "that they themselves would welcome as much as anyone in the world a serious warning by us against people resorting at once to seances and seers before anything like certainty has been reached in these matters."

Questions from the assembly centered around the use of terminology in the resolution. In response to a query from the bishop of Edinburgh, G. H. S. Walpole, about the use of *seer* instead of *medium*, Bishop Burge replied that the former was more general and inclusive. Another bishop argued for the use of the words *Crystal Gazers*, as an appropriate description. Archbishop Randall Davidson spoke and made a suggestion that both *seers* and *medium* should be included in the resolution, and the bishop of Oxford accepted this wording. One concerned bishop wanted to delete the word *habit* from the resolution, but Bishop Burge refused to consider this amendment. One might attend a séance out of curiosity; to frequent one on a regular basis, however, might prove harmful. After this short exchange of views, the resolution, as amended, carried. The conference then adjourned, and the discussion would continue again in the afternoon.

The bishop of Oxford opened the afternoon session, which would consider resolutions dealing exclusively with spiritualism, and he introduced the first of the two.[58]

This Conference, while prepared to expect and welcome new light from psychical research upon the powers and processes of the spirit of man, urges strongly that a larger place should be given to the teaching of the Church to the explanation of the true grounds of Christian belief in immortality, and the true content of belief in the communion of saints as centreing in Christ.

Acknowledging the valuable work done by the Society for Psychical Research, Bishop Burge admitted that some members of the church turned to the SPR searching for something the Anglican Church has failed to provide. The concern over the alleged shortcomings of Anglicanism had already been voiced in public. "Conan Doyle attributes limitations to the teaching of the Church of Christ which do not in the least exist," he pointed out, "and the limitations which he attributes to our teaching have come as a very great surprise to some of us."

One bishop wanted to offer an amendment to this resolution which would draw attention to the "great danger to the mental balance of people who practice spiritualistic seances," but the bishop of Oxford replied and pointed out that this concern could best be dealt with in the last resolution which addressed the dangers of spiritualism as a cult. The American bishop of South Carolina, W. A. Guerry, then suggested that the wording should include some reference to the idea of eternal life. "The question of immortality and eternal life are quite distinct," he pointed out. And Bishop Guerry suggested the following addition to the resolution: "and the true content of belief in eternal life and in the communion of saints." The bishop of Oxford, however, urged caution. He had no objection "to accepting the words suggested if you think that the Resolution will then suggest that the whole idea of immortality is connected both with eternal life and the communion of saints." The exchange between the bishops continued, and they discussed the choice of words, the position of words, and the emphasis of the resolution. After a warning from the archbishop of Canterbury that the bishops must not be "too meticulous" about the order of words, a compromise was eventually reached which addressed the concerns of the bishop of South Carolina. (The amended section read: "the explanation of the true grounds of Christian belief in eternal life, and in immortality, and of the true content of belief in the communion of saints as involving real fellowship with the departed.")

G. H. S. Walpole, the bishop of Edinburgh, however, expressed some concern about the phrase "belief in the communion of saints as centreing in Christ." The ordinary man and woman, he believed, might be confused by these words. The bishop, consequently, suggested the following as an alternative: "belief in the communion of saints as involving real fellowship with the departed through the love of God in Christ Jesus." After the assembly accepted this amendment, the bishop of Burnley, H. Henn, offered another alteration, and this drew the ire of E. S. Talbot, the bishop of Winchester. Talbot acknowledged his fellow bishop's sincerity, but stated that he felt "a little inclined to protest against amendments so minute in a Conference so big as this." "We have sometimes lost time over them and I am sure that the bishop of Burnley will forgive me if I make his amendment the peg on which to hang a little word of caution or protest." Bishop Henn's amendment was defeated, and the Lambeth Conference voted to accept the amended resolution.

Following this, Bishop Burge of Oxford introduced the next resolution dealing with spiritualism and its relationship to Christianity.

> This Conference, while recognizing that the results of investigation have encouraged many people to find spiritual meaning and purpose in human life and led them to believe in survival after death, sees grave dangers in the tendency to make a religion of spiritualism. The practice of spiritualism as a cult involves the subordination of the intelligence and the will to unknown forces or personalities and, to that extent, an abdication of that self-control to which God has called us; it tends to divert attention from the approach to God through the one Mediator, Jesus Christ, under the guidance of the Holy Spirit; to ignore the discipline of faith as the path of spiritual training; and to deprecate the divinely ordained channels of grace and truth revealed and given through Jesus Christ our Lord.

Recognizing that this particular resolution represented an important statement by the committee, the bishop of Oxford proceeded to give a lengthy explanation of its meaning and purpose. He admitted that in the minds of some individuals spiritualism could bridge the painful void and help those people who had experienced a sense of grief because of the loss of a loved one. "They have never really felt the want of something to fill up their lives until the tremendous ordeal of bereavement came," the bishop reported, "and in their agony and bewilderment they have turned to . . . the offers of spiritualism." When everything else seemed to fail, spiritualism offered a means of personal satisfaction and comfort to these individuals.

What should the Anglican Church say about those individuals who looked to spiritualism in times of personal distress or sorrow? People who embraced spiritualism for this reason, the bishop maintained, were "doomed to bitter disappointment." Danger also threatened those misguided individuals who based their religious or spiritual life on the claims of spiritualism. He paraphrased the resolution to emphasize the risks involved in the "subordination of the intelligence and the will to unknown forces or personalities." Spiritualism could thus easily evolve into a religion, and this also posed many threats to the well-being of the Christian searching for comfort or meaning in life: the absence of a moral teaching could divert people from "the need of any other communion or fellowship," and beliefs and modes of worship antithetical to Anglicanism in particular and Christianity in general might develop. The bishop of Oxford ended his discourse and asked for suggestions on how to improve this important resolution.

The bishop of Kampala, H. Gresford Jones, immediately offered an amendment. The bishop wanted to strengthen the wording, and consequently suggested adding after *spiritualism* in the fourth line the following, "sees grave danger of the tendency to make a religion of spiritualism, and feels bound to give a serious warning against its general effect both upon mind and faith." The Anglican Church, he believed, needed to stress that the one medium was Jesus Christ. The primus of the Scottish Church, Bishop W. J. F. Robberds of Brechin, agreed with the emphasis of Bishop Jones's amendment. He noted, for example, the popularity of spiritualism in the large industrial centers among the working class, and he believed that the resolution should stress the adverse effects on one's psyche which would definitely result from dabbling in spiritualism. To illustrate his point, the Scottish bishop used the examples of a "medical officer in one of the great asylums near Edinburgh" and a West End doctor. Both had treated numerous people who had experimented with spiritualism. Consequently, he supported the bishop of Kampala's suggestion and urged that some reference be made to the serious psychological dangers.

The discussion continued, and it centered around the question of the adverse or unhealthy consequences which might be associated with spiritualism. Bishop G. L. King suggested the insertion of the phrase, "it is dangerous to the mental balance of many who practice it," into the resolution. According to his testimony, "Those who have worked on the Tyne side and who had to do with spiritualism amongst . . . the people who practice spiritualism there is a very great danger of their being what you would describe as not normal mentally." Bishop G. R. Eden of Wakefield, however, thought Bishop King's viewpoint represented a narrow interpretation. Any "concentrated form of religion acting upon certain minds," he argued, might harm one's mental health, and he used the example of the great Welsh revival when many people believed that the "extravagant and emotional forms which the revival took ended in a considerable number of cases of more or less permanent insanity." But on the other hand, he preferred Bishop King's phraseology in place of the sweeping and general terms of the bishop of Kampala.

Bishop E. A. Copleston of Colombo jumped into the discussion and argued that the resolution would lose its clout and force if references "to other kinds of dangers than those which tend to separate the soul from Christ" were introduced. At this point Archbishop Davidson, probably reflecting the feelings of other bishops, expressed some confusion and asked that the amendments be read again to the assembly.[59] After the bishop of Peterborough, F. T. Woods, read them to the assembly, Bishop H. L. Wild of Newcastle-on-Tyne spoke against King's amendment on the one hand, and he also wanted to modify the bishop of Kampala's statement to include "and faith" in addition to the possible dangers to one's mental balance. (It would read: "against the danger to the mental balance and faith of those who practice it.") The chairman of the committee, the bishop of Oxford had no objection to Wild's addition but opposed any statement which concluded "that it [spiritualism] is dangerous to mental balance." Consequently, the bishop of Kampala's rather strong amendment "was lost."

The discussion of the bishops then moved to a consideration of spiritualism as a cult. The bishop of Oxford told his fellow bishops that "the words 'The practice of spiritualism as a cult' were put in deliberately." According to the bishop, "We are very anxious to make it plain that we are not saying anything to condemn or depreciate what is being done by members of the Society of Psychical Research [i.e., the Society for Psychical Research]." Other more serious problems threatened the Anglican Church. "It is the practice of spiritualism as a cult or religion and as a substitute for the practice of the Christian religion is what we have in mind," he pointed out. At this point, Bishop King's earlier amendment, namely, the addition of "and it is dangerous to the mental balance of many of those who practice it," came up for consideration but failed to win approval. The deliberations of the Lambeth Conference then revolved around the choice of the appropriate words which would strengthen the force of the resolution in question.[60]

The bishop of Oxford resisted this approach. "We have to be very careful about the criticisms that we pass upon spiritualism," he argued, "and must not attribute to spiritualists things that they can very easily deny." Burge forcefully attacked the efforts to alter the sentence in question which, in its amended state, would read that spiritualists "deny the approach to God through the one Mediator, Jesus Christ." He received some support from the bishop of Exeter, Lord William Cecil, who believed that there was a "great danger . . . in correcting words which have been carefully chosen." Pointing out the problems and negative associations of the word *deny*, the bishop of Exeter stated that "we want to assert that which we can easily defend." The amendment to insert *deny* failed, and the bishops finally approved this amended resolution concerning the relationship of the Christian faith to spiritualism.

The deliberations and debates of the 1920 Lambeth Conference of Bishops, although confusing at times and carried out in the nuances of theology, represented the first formal and official attempt by the Anglican Church to understand spiritualism and its connection with traditional Christianity. Despite some prolonged and tedious wranglings over the choice of words, Bishop Burge successfully avoided attempts to turn the resolutions into harsh and strong critiques of spiritualism and its practices, although the resolutions did identify several dangers which might harm fragile Christians. On the other hand, the resolutions adopted by the Lambeth Conference never compromised essential Christian teachings, especially the incarnation and the mediatorship of Jesus. The public was not privy to the deliberations of the bishops. But in addition to the resolutions, the Lambeth Conference did publish an encyclical letter and the report of the committee which investigated the relationship of Christianity and spiritualism. These documents attempted to convey the position of the bishops to members of the Anglican Communion and to other interested parties, especially those Christians who saw positive aspects of spiritualism. The committee received valuable help in the preparation of these publications.

In line with the new procedure for the Lambeth Conference, which acknowledged the importance of outside experts, several individuals volunteered during the spring and summer of 1920 to appear as witness or offered to write position papers on spiritualism for the benefit of the committee. Archbishop Davidson had also collected a list of important books for the committee from acknowledged authorities dealing with spiritualism, and Sir Oliver Lodge even sent the archbishop a bibliography of books and articles dealing with psychical subjects.[61] The names of those people who eventually spoke to the committee has not survived, but it seems that the members of the committee certainly had access to the correspondence of interested people and had the opportunity to study any papers or essays they had submitted.[62] One individual, who described himself as a churchman for nearly sixty years and also a clairvoyant, offered his services to the committee, and he pointed out that "love is the 'wireless to and from the Spiritual world.'"[63] It does not appear that the committee encouraged any further contributions from this person. The Rev. Charles Tweedale also did not appear as an expert witness. He had to be content with the fact that Archbishop Davidson agreed to distribute his pamphlet, *Present Day Spirit Phenomena and the Churches*, to the entire membership of the Lambeth Conference. Tweedale suggested to Davidson's secretary that they should be distributed "*before* the discussion on Spiritualism takes place, in order that all may have a clear conception of the issues before the conference on this important issue."[64] Others did appear before the committee. For example, David Gow, from the *Light* newspaper, accepted the invitation to speak before the committee, and he told them that it was correct to study spiritualism.[65] Mr. F. Bligh Bond, the author, spoke from personal experiences, and argued before the committee that the spiritualist gifts of the early church were similar to contemporary psychical phenomena.[66] At times, the evidence was contradictory. An essay written by Miss L. Dougell offered a logical or rational explanation for psychical phenomena. The correspondence from Stanley de Brath, on the other hand, argued that spiritualism was a growing and popular movement and urged the Anglican Church to study the claims of spiritualism carefully and seriously.

Miss Dougall's paper, *The Natural Explanation of Spiritualist Phenomena*, appealed to the cynics and critics of spiritualism. In a synopsis of her arguments, Dougall maintained that "Spiritualism is to be treated as a pious superstition."[67] Moreover, "all superstitions are harmful to the individual and the church . . . [and] the argument against Spiritualism should proceed by discovery of the natural causes of its phenomena." Some alleged psychic happenings could be attributed to "deliberate or unconscious fraud," but, she then pointed out, there "remain a number of remarkable happenings which occur in the presence of honest 'mediums' or private people of unimpeachable honour which are inexplicable to the average mind in the present state of our knowledge." When rational answers could not be found for mysterious events or happenings throughout human history, people naturally attributed them to "the agency of discarnate spirits." Contemporary men and women have continued in this tradition and "should do the same thing until a natural explanation is produced." Automatic writing, for example, could be interpreted as the outpouring of one's subconscious memory.

Stanley de Brath had written to Archbishop Davidson in February 1920 and congratulated him on the decision to explore spiritualism at the summer Lambeth Conference. In July, de Brath sent the secretary of the Lambeth Conference, the bishop of Barrow-in-Furness, his views on the manner in which the Anglican Church should approach this difficult subject. He told Bishop Campbell West-Watson about his recent experiences at the 4 July conference of the Spiritualists' National Union held at Reading. According to his impressions, northern working-class people believed that spiritualism did constitute a religion. "But they are not affected towards the Church, mainly because of the antagonism which has been shown to spiritualism as they know it."[68] "There can be no doubt in the mind of anyone conversant with the facts," de Brath argued, "that the movement is alive and will grow." Would the church dismiss spiritualism or "countenance it and direct it?" Anglicanism should adopt the latter approach: "much influence could be regained by the admission of fundamental psychic facts without touching any theological questions at all."

The committee, therefore, had at its disposal the testimonies of experts in the area of psychical research in the preparation of written statements dealing with spiritualism and its relationship to Christianity. The encyclical letter, which gave a brief synopsis of the proceedings of the 1920 Lambeth Conference, began with a remembrance of the devastation and destruction caused by the Great War. Under the section entitled "Some Movements outside the Church," the letter then discussed the actions of the conference concerning spiritualism, Christian Science, and theosophy. It recommended the formal report of the committee to all people interested in these movements and pointed out that "the teachings which are connected with them are tested in the light of the Christian truth."[69] "Tried by the doctrines of the Incarnation and the Cross," it noted, "they are clearly shewn to involve serious error." People who adhered to these movements might experience harm to their spiritual life and their loyalty to the Anglican Communion might also be severely tested. Recognizing that these three movements grew out of a reaction against the growth of materialism in the nineteenth and twentieth centuries, the bishops' letter pointed out that the church must offer a sympathetic hand to those who seek a refuge from the wiles and temptations of the material world. Moreover, the Anglican Church had an obligation to provide a safe haven for these souls.

Speaking specifically about spiritualism and accentuating the church's belief in the communion of saints, the encyclical letter stated that "we who belong to the Church's lesser fellowship in this world are not separated from, but are one with, those who belong to the Church's higher fellowship in the other world." The thoughts of the bishops turned to the immense sorrow and bereavement caused by the last war: "the nearness of the other world has been deepened by the war." Moreover, the Lambeth Conference correctly recognized the popularity and magnetic power of spiritualism. "It is in this endeavour that many distracted souls turn to spiritualism for help, not realizing that the Church has abundant treasures of comfort, and assurance of the world beyond this, with which to bring to the sorrowing the solace which is the right and the heritage of Christians." A proper understanding of the communion of the saints would certainly give ample comfort and succor to grieving Christians. The Anglican Church, therefore, had a sacred obligation to present and preach the communion of the saints in a manner satisfying for one seeking consolation and answers about life after death.

In addition to this encyclical letter, the formal report of the committee which had investigated the connection between Christianity and spiritualism, Christian Science, and theosophy, which had been accepted by the bishops of the Lambeth Conference, went into greater detail about the relationship of Christianity to spiritualism.[70] This report, moreover, represented a public and comprehensive statement by the Anglican Communion on the questions and issues posed by spiritualism, and it began by telling its readers that the committee faced a twofold task: to study the relation of the Christian faith to spiritualism, Christian Science, and theosophy; and, second, to consider the duty and response of the Anglican Church to these movements. The committee members, it continued, had read the vast array of literature associated with the subjects, and in some instances interviewed experts.

Before talking specifically about spiritualism, the report described the common characteristics of all three movements. In the first place, "they protest against materialism and a materialistic basis of human life."[71] The Great War, not surprisingly, also played an important part in the recent popularity of these movements: "Upon all this has come the catastrophe and shock of the War and the desolating, bewildering questions which such an experience raises."[72] "It is easy to understand," the report continued, "the appeal which in times like our own the Spiritualist, the Christian Scientist and the Theosophist make, especially to those who may have been indifferent to the spiritual claim of religion and religious motives or absorbed in material interests." Second, all three had attracted followers because of the new appreciation of psychical powers in human nature. Third, "each of the three movements claims to supply something which the teaching and practice of the Church fail to give." People who felt unsatisfied, unfulfilled, or unconsoled by the teachings of Christianity gravitated naturally toward these alternatives. In the fourth place, nothing new or novel had appeared in their teachings and beliefs; the Gnostics and Neo-Platonists had addressed these issues and concerns earlier. Finally, "none of these movements finds its centre in the central revelation of the Christian Faith, namely the Incarnation of our Lord as the unique fact of human history." The report concluded that the Anglican Church must make the fundamentals of Christianity relevant to the faithful in the decades following the Great War. Anglicanism must not discard new scientific findings, but the church must always remain loyal to the basic tenets of Christianity: "Above all it is only by keeping firm hold of the cardinal truths upon which Christian faith and practice are established that new knowledge can be given its right setting."[73]

The committee's report then spoke specifically about spiritualism. Two questions had immediately confronted the committee, and these demanded clarification. How should the Anglican Church deal with the modern investigations of phenomena associated with human consciousness, especially the work of the Society for Psychical Research? Second, what position should the church adopt to those groups or cults founded on the premises of spiritualism? In respect to the first, the committee welcomed the contributions of scientific research and recognized the worthwhile work of the SPR, especially its efforts to expose fraud and deception. Consequently, the report listed the findings or conclusions reached by scientific investigations in the area of psychic phenomena: the reality or existence of telepathy; "the reality of a subconsciousness which may operate without the control of the normal consciousness and will"; the suggestion of communication with "beings no longer limited by the conditions of bodily existence as we know it here"; and the difficulties associated with the workings of the subconscious of both the medium and the person seeking a communication.[74] The report, however, drew two conclusions from the area of science. In the first place, a warning should be sounded against "unregulated and undue exercise of an element of human consciousness which acts independently of the reason and the will, and against allowing reason and will to abdicate in its favour."[75] Second, materialism per se could not offer an acceptable account of phenomena; a belief in spiritual explanations of phenomena must be advanced and encouraged. Nonetheless, the report concluded: "We welcome inquiry conducted in this reverent and scrupulous spirit."

The second question, namely, the consideration of "the religious cult and practice of what is called spiritualism," admittedly received more attention from the committee. In fact, the report referred to this subject as "our main and proper function," and it drew the attention of the reader immediately to the Great War and its influence on the growth and popularity of spiritualism. The committee found that spiritualism appealed to the occasional Christian who was unfamiliar with the basic teachings of Christianity. However, "we have evidence that, especially under the stress of the horrors and anxieties of the war, particularly in our crowded areas, spiritualism has affected in some instances even regular Church-goers, withdrawing them from the Church." The Anglican Church might have to accept some blame for this sad situation. "Many have felt and expressed dissatisfaction with the consolations offered by the Church," the report pointed out, and "have misrepresented . . . what the Church holds and teaches, and have imagined that Spiritualist doctrine supplies something which the Church lacks and which the spirit of man needs to strengthen and uplift it." Anglicanism, therefore, should admit its part in the inability or failure to convey basic Christian truths, especially those doctrines concerning the afterlife, to the faithful.

The Anglican Church, consequently, must present its message in a clear and forceful manner. The chief emphasis of any Christian teaching and education must find its center in God and the affirmation that Jesus Christ, through the incarnation and redemption, remained the sole mediator with God. Spiritualism came up short in this respect. "Spiritualistic religion and practice," according to the report, "throw a wholly different emphasis upon the motive power of man's life: immortality is there concerned with the survival of human persons more that with God; the life beyond is represented largely as an extension of what is experienced here and now; and the fact is overlooked that survival is not necessarily immortality, still less eternal life." The belief in the communion of saints, on the other hand, rightly declared "that we can and do have communion with the departed through the Love of God which is in Jesus Christ."[76]

But some spiritualists, the members of the committee noted, might agree wholeheartedly with these statements of the church. No chasm or divide existed between them and the traditional beliefs of Anglicanism. But the teachings of the Anglican Church, according to the report, did stand in direct opposition to a belief in "definite communication."

> To this we should answer that the constant search for definite communication as practised by Spiritualistic teachers does, in fact, arrest the development of faith, diverting us from the need and also from the means of our spiritual education to an interest in experiments to determine whether communication is possible or real and to the desire to escape from the discipline of faith.

The report listed other dangers: loss of the control over one's will, the real possibility of illusion and deception, and the harm to one's personality due to an habitual addiction to subconscious activity. Drawing attention to the fact that sacred Scripture made reference to "the existence of unseen beings who influence men for good or evil," the report also noted that "we cannot, therefore, dismiss the possibility of communications from such beings of either nature." However, no spiritual benefit results from "recourse to *séances* and 'seers.'" The report, not wishing to limit or confine the manner in which God reveals himself to men and women, did, however, end the section on spiritualism with a strong caveat. "But there is nothing in the cult erected on this science which enhances," it explained, but "there is, indeed, much which obscures, the meaning of the other world and our relation to it as unfolded in the Gospel of Christ and the teaching of the Church, and which depreciates the means given to us of attaining and abiding in fellowship with that world."

The report also included some harsh words about the other two "movements outside the church," namely, Christian Science and theosophy, which it investigated. Founded by the American Mary Baker Eddy (1821-1910), Christian Science claimed to heal or cure disease by spiritual means and not by accepted medical or scientific means. Because it questioned basic biblical doctrines on creation, the fall, and redemption and portrayed Christ as a spiritual healer, Christian Science did present dangers to Christians. The report of the committee addressed some of these concerns. "It appears to the Committee that too much emphasis has been laid in many quarters upon the distinction between what are called spiritual means of healing, and what are called physical means of healing."[77] This erroneous division was fatal to the search for truth; the Spirit of Christ guided people to truth. Consequently, the report pointed out that "we are justified in claiming as due to the operation of the Divine Spirit all progress in knowledge of the physical world, particularly such knowledge as is being constantly brought into the service of love through the relief of human suffering." Scientific research and advances in medical care were due "to the Spirit of the Incarnate Christ." Moreover, the Anglican Church must remind both the patient and the doctors and nurses "of the spiritual nature of their undertaking and to affirm our faith that in the lively sense of this lies the best hope of success."

Anglicanism, the report admitted, had failed in its mission to emphasize the healing aspects of God's love for all people and the joy and inner peace of the Gospel message. Christians could not ignore suffering but should "transfigure" it through the teaching and life of Jesus Christ. This neglect, consequently, has led to a reaction in the form of Christian Science, which "has undoubtedly helped to call attention to the importance of spiritual forces in the work of healing and in the promotion of happiness and general well-being."[78] In addition to the harmful disparagement of "all physical methods of healing and God's gift of scientific research and knowledge," this "pseudo-spirituality" disagreed with traditional Christianity in other areas: by stressing "the Oneness of God and of the Universe" it preached pantheism; it revived the old dualism of matter and spirit which stressed the evil of the former; its Christology made a distinction "between Christ the Ideal Truth and Jesus the human prophet of Galilee" and, by denying the reality of sin, questioned the Christian doctrine of atonement. The report, therefore, recommended that the Anglican Church should emphasize traditional beliefs about authentic spirituality and prayer and offer better instruction to its clergy in matters dealing with sickness, psychology, and the role of pain and suffering in the world.

The report also identified serious problems for the Christian in theosophy, and began by stating that the "Theosophical Society represents a vigorous revival of earlier mystical and occult philosophies."[79] In the broad sense, theosophy contained a number of beliefs and groups of people which drew their teachings from pantheism and mysticism, but in a more narrow sense it was associated with H. P. Blavatsky and H. S. Olcott, who jointly founded the Theosophical Society in 1875 in America. After Blavatsky died in 1891, Mrs. Annie Besant (1847-1933), an English woman who was attracted to Indian religions, became the accepted leader of the movement. Based on sacred Indian texts, theosophy denied many traditional Christian beliefs such as the existence of a personal God and immortality. According to the committee's report, the three main objects of the Theosophical Society, namely, the creation of a universal brotherhood of all humanity, the comparative study of religion, philosophy, and science, and the exploration of the unexplained laws of nature and powers within people, presented no real difficulty. Consequently, "there is nothing in the Christian faith which precludes sympathy with the three stated objects of the Theosophical Society."[80] The methods and the results of theosophical study and research, however, did raise serious questions.

> Theosophical leaders and teachers claim to impart knowledge derived from occult sources. They claim to be in communion with a brotherhood of pioneers of the human race who have reached the goal of their own evolution and now control and guide the evolution of their race by operations in the unseen world or by reincarnation on earth. They claim also that they have themselves by a process of mystical self-discipline the developed latent powers of consciousness which enable them to read occult traces left in the etheric records of the universe by past events and experiences.

The Anglican Church, the report continued, welcomed sound psychical research but could not "resist the impression that the methods of theosophical occultism are not free from psychical conditions of a morbid and demoralizing tendency." The secrecy involved in its methods, moreover, tended to create an unhealthy atmosphere in the search for divine truth.

Theosophy also seriously deviated from Christianity in its conception of God. "It is in the twin doctrines of reincarnation and karma that theosophy begins to come into more or less direct conflict with the Christian faith." Reincarnation represented a philosophically and scientifically unsound doctrine, and karma, "or the law of consequence, namely, the quantitative karma or result of man's conduct must be worked off gradually in this or some future existence, evacuates forgiveness of all spiritual reality."[81] The conflict or chasm between Christianity and theosophy became irreconcilable especially in reference to the latter's Christology, which denied the uniqueness of Jesus Christ. The report, however, stressed "the universality of His mission and message." Theosophy taught that beneath the exoteric form of all religions there lay and still lies the same esoteric body of essential truths—that the Christianity of the Churches is only the exoteric form of the Christian religion—and that the mission of Theosophy is to reveal and restore the lost esoteric truths of this and every religion.

But the report stressed that what people need "now is the fuller life and truth which can only come from conscious knowledge of the Word made flesh, the historical Christ who was and is the Son of God."[82]

The report ended its discussion by pointing out that "there is nothing in the avowed objects of the Theosophical Society which is in itself incompatible with loyal membership in the Church" but warned the faithful about the dangers in pursuing the study of theosophy. People must to be vigilant, for example, because theosophists employed the same language and terms as Christianity, and some might fail to recognize the real differences between the two systems of thought. Moreover, Christians must examine the credentials and the character of the leading teachers of theosophy and should avoid subscribing to their doctrines uncritically. The report on theosophy, however, ended on a positive note. Like Christianity, it presented life and faith in terms of a personal searching. "Christian faith is indeed a quest for truth yet to be revealed no less that a grasp of truth already revealed." Nonetheless, the report concluded, one must still exercise a certain amount of caution when dealing with theosophy.

> The Committee, while pleading for a larger place to be given in the teaching of the Church to the mystical elements of faith and life, desire earnestly to advise all thinking people to safeguard their Christian position by making the fullest study and use of the treasures of knowledge and thought to be found in Bible, Creed and Sacrament as they have been interpreted by sound Christian scholarship and philosophy.[83]

The Lambeth Conference of 1920 expended much time and effort exploring the relationship of the Christian faith to spiritualism. This assembly also published an encyclical letter, a series of resolutions, and a lengthy report which explained the church's position on spiritualism to those troubled souls who were attracted to its practices and claims. Few expected any significant shift or change in the position of the Anglican Church in regard to spiritualism, but the fact that the Lambeth Conference had discussed the subject of spiritualism did mark an important change in church attitudes. The Rev. Charles Tweedale, who had written and spoken in favor of a closer relationship between Christianity and spiritualism for years, remarked on the importance of the Lambeth Conference. Writing in the October 1920 edition of *Light*, Tweedale commented on the Anglican position before the conference.

> While the world at large has been filled with an eager awakening interest, the Church which claims to be the custodian of religious and spiritual truth, has,

strange to say, until quite recently, turned a deaf ear to all modern evidences bearing upon the reality of that spiritual world to which it is the main object of her existence to testify, and even now is only just showing faint signs that she realises how important the matter is becoming for her.[84]

But times had changed. He mentioned approvingly the discussion of "psychic phenomena at the Lambeth Conference, and the placing by the secretary of my brochure, 'Present Day Spirit Phenomena and the Churches' in the hands of all the bishops present, with the archbishops' consent."

But the Anglicans did not monopolize the investigation of spiritualism in the British Isles. North of the border, the General Assembly of the Church of Scotland also appointed a committee, which met between 1921-22, to study "supernormal psychic phenomena." In May 1922, the committee published its findings.[85] The history behind this report began on 25 May 1920, when the General Assembly of the Church of Scotland received a petition from the Rev. William A. Reid asking that a committee be appointed "to inquire into the alleged supernormal psychic phenomena so much in evidence at present." He listed some phenomena, which were mentioned in the Bible, such as clairvoyance, clairaudience, healing, and speaking in tongues, and Reid believed that they deserved careful investigation before being condemned by the church. The most important reason behind the petition, however, was the fact that a number of Christians did believe in the possibility of communicating with their departed loved ones and consequently "have lost interest in the Church and ceased to attend its services, so that spiritualistic meetings are on the increase, and Church services are correspondingly depleted." Reid pointed out that "Spiritualism is a method, not a religion," but nonetheless the church should not flippantly dismiss its appeal and beliefs. The final reason behind the petition concerned the relationship between modern psychic phenomena and biblical psychical phenomena. In the words of the Rev. William Reid, "it is believed by a large and increasing number that if modern psychic phenomena could be proved true the Bible would become to them virtually a new book, the experiences of the early N. T. Church might be revived, and the kingdom of God advanced."

After its establishment, the committee began its task by looking at the evidence of psychic phenomena in sacred Scripture. It appeared to the membership that the "Old Testament represents a triumph of rationalism over grotesque, absurd, and morbid theories of life." Sorcery, divination, necromancy, and traffic in the occult received stern condemnation, and the pages of the Old Testament explicitly forbade "many forms of experiment with psychic phenomena." The New Testament taught that the divine spirit could influence the human spirit. St. Paul, for example, noted instances of healings and glossolalia, and he gave "a reluctant toleration to the ecstatic behaviour of some Corinthians." But nonetheless he spoke against "undisciplined spiritualism." Consequently, the committee did not believe that the list of "spiritual gifts" mentioned in the petition formed an "indispensable part of her [the church's] equipment and service." Modern research, especially investigations carried out by the Society for Psychical Research, was inconclusive. The members of the committee, however, wanted to observe psychic phenomena for themselves.

Hoping to demonstrate that its members exercised a strong sense of independent judgment, the committee's report then gave examples of the manner in which they reached their conclusions: several members visited an individual's house to observe firsthand examples of psychical phenomena, and several members even attended séances, but these meetings did not confirm for them the existence of such phenomena.[86] The conclusions proved to be unsatisfactory and difficult to substantiate; some members of the committee believed that "conscious fraud was practised," and no convincing evidence proved the existence of psychical phenomena. "These experiences," the report stated, "produced no conviction favourable to spiritism in the minds of those of us who had not been previously convinced."[87]

The report to the General Assembly of the Church of Scotland eventually came to several conclusions based on these investigations and experiences. "Strange things do happen," it admitted, but cases of genuine phenomena appeared to be very few. "Investigation is lawful." New discoveries, however, would not alter the basic beliefs of the church; "faith, hope, and charity will not be superseded by successful psychical research." It became apparent that fraud tended to be rampant, and moreover, dishonest or unscrupulous actions of this nature could damage one's mental health. Like its counterpart published by the Lambeth Conference, the Scottish report also acknowledged the influence of the Great War on the popular appeal of spiritualism. "During and since the recent war there has been a natural anxiety to know whether there may be any possibility of communication with finite human personalities beyond the grave." The Church of Scotland, it remarked, believed in the existence of the blessed dead, "yet in its practice it has been severely reticent in regard to the future life," for example, the absence of religious commendations at the graveside. The church should provide some assistance to the bereaved and work to cultivate "a wholesome sense of fellowship with those who are gone forward before us."

The report ended on a pragmatic note and suggested four recommendations for dealing with psychical phenomena. In the first place, the church could not simply ignore or scoff at such phenomena; ministers must deal seriously with occurrences as they arise. Second, the "attendance of Christian people at spiritualistic séances is open to serious dangers." Spiritualistic meetings or assemblies could never take the place of traditional Christian worship, but church officials should not adopt a policy of discrimination or segregation: "there is room in the larger life of the Church for Christian spiritualists whose special experiences have been sufficient to convince them." Moreover, "such Christians should be encouraged to share in the life of the Church rather than to withdraw themselves from its communion." Third, more devotional meditations and prayers should be encouraged which might help those mourning the loss of a loved one. Finally, ministers should "give due recognition in public worship to the provision made in the ordinances of the Church for the reverent and affectionate commemoration of the faithful departed."

The 1920 Lambeth Conference, along with the Church of Scotland two years later, finally addressed the growth and popularity of spiritualism in Great Britain. The Lambeth Conference acknowledged the spread of spiritualism and also recognized the threat it posed to Anglicanism. A reaction against the materialistic philosophy, which had been developing for some time, appeared to be the underlying cause or stimulus, but the magnitude of deaths resulting from the Great War had forced some Anglicans who had suffered a personal loss to find comfort and support outside of their church. For many, traditional Anglicanism offered little solace. Spiritualism welcomed the bereaved with open arms. The bishops at the Lambeth Conference admitted their pastoral shortcomings, but they also called attention to the mystery of the incarnation, the role of Jesus Christ as the sole mediator, and the doctrine of the communion of saints. However, the deliberations and publications of the Lambeth Conference did not calm the waters. Many people wanted the Anglican Church to explore further the relationship of Christianity to spiritualism. And some even dared to ask an unsettling question. Might not the practices and beliefs of spiritualism augment, strengthen, or even contribute to the vitality and mission of contemporary Anglicanism?

Notes

1. R. Davidson, introduction to *The National Mission of Repentance and Hope: Reports of the Archbishops' Committees of Inquiry* (London: SPCK, 1919), iii.
2. *The Worship of the Church: Being the Report of the Archbishops' Second Committee of Inquiry*, in *The National Mission of Repentance and Hope*, 22.
3. Ibid., 38.
4. Ibid., 26.
5. Dawbarn to Davidson, 8 August 1919, Lambeth Conference Papers 1920, LC 135, Lambeth Palace Library, Lambeth Palace, London.
6. *The Times*, 28 July 1919.
7. Dawbarn to Davidson, 9 August 1919, Lambeth Conference Papers 1920, LC 135, Lambeth Palace Library.
8. Sheppard (Archbishop Davidson's private secretary) to Dawbarn, 11 August 1919, Lambeth Conference Papers 1920, LC 135, Lambeth Palace Library.
9. *Daily Chronicle* (London), 13 August 1919.

10. Dawbarn to Davidson, 14 August 1919, Lambeth Conference Papers 1920, LC 135, Lambeth Palace Library.
11. Davidson to Dawbarn 18 August 1919, Lambeth Conference Papers 1920, LC 135, Lambeth Palace Library.
12. Church Congresses were unofficial gatherings of Anglican clergymen beginning in 1861. They discussed numerous topic and questions which the challenged the Anglican Church. The last meeting of this gathering took place in 1938.
13. *The Official Report of the Church Congress Held at Leicester on October 12th, 13th, 14th, 15th, 16th and 17th 1919* (London: Nisbet, 1919), 41.
14. Ibid., 42.
15. Ibid., 91.
16. Ibid., 96.
17. Ibid., 97.
18. Ibid., 99.
19. Ibid., 100.
20. Ibid., 106.
21. Ibid., 111.
22. Ibid., 113.
23. Ibid., 114.
24. Ibid., 115.
25. Ibid., 115-16.
26. Ibid., 116.
27. O. Lodge, "The Attitude of the Church to the Phenomena Known as Spiritualistic," *Hibbert Journal* 18 (1920):259.
28. Ibid., 260.
29. Ibid., 263.
30. Ibid., 274.
31. Whately Smith to Davidson, 2 November 1919, Lambeth Conference Papers 1920, LC 135, Lambeth Palace Library.
32. Sheppard to Whately Smith, 18 December 1919, Lambeth Conference Papers 1920, LC 135, Lambeth Palace Library.
33. Whately Smith to Davidson, 27 February 1920, Lambeth Conference Papers 1920, LC 135, Lambeth Palace Library.
34. Davidson to Whately Smith, 1 March 1920, Lambeth Conference Papers 1920, LC 135, Lambeth Palace Library.
35. W. Whately Smith, *A Critique of the Phenomenal Basis of Spiritualism*, Lambeth Conference Papers 120, LC 135, Lambeth Palace Library.
36. De Brath to Davidson, 29 February 1920, Lambeth Conference Papers 1920, LC 135, Lambeth Palace Library.
37. Gates to Lang, 29 June 1920, Lambeth Conference Papers 1920, LC 135, Lambeth Palace Library.
38. W. T. Gates sent his notes on "spirit communication" to Archbishop Davidson, but asked the archbishop to protect the identity of those individuals to whom he made reference in the transcripts. Gates to Davidson, 12 July 1920, Lambeth Conference Papers 1920, LC 135, Lambeth Palace Library; Gates to Davidson, 14 July 1920, Lambeth Conference Papers 1920, LC 135, Lambeth Palace Library.
39. *The Church Family Newspaper* (London), 30 April 1920.

40. Ibid., 23 April 1920.
41. Ibid., 30 April 1920.
42. Ibid., 7 May 1920.
43. For a general history of the Lambeth Conferences, see Alan M. G. Stephenson, *Anglicanism and the Lambeth Conferences* (London: SPCK, 1978).
44. Proceedings of the Conference, 1 August 1908, LC 69, Lambeth Palace Library.
45. *Report of the Committee Appointed to Consider and Report upon the Subject of Ministries of Healing: (a) The Unction of the Sick; (b) Faith Healing and "Christian Science,"* Lambeth Conference Papers, 1908, LC 78, Lambeth Palace Library.
46. Alan M. G. Stephenson, *Anglicanism and the Lambeth Conferences*, 128.
47. *The Times*, 25 June 1920. *The Times* printed the agenda of the 1920 Lambeth Conference and explained the inner workings of the meetings at Lambeth Palace. The bishops would discuss the agenda items at a business session, the readers of the newspaper learned, after which a committee would be formed "to go more thoroughly into its ramifications." A second round of business sessions would then "consider the reports and take final decisions."
48. Ibid.
49. Quoted in Alan M. G. Stephenson, *Anglicanism and the Lambeth Conferences*, 128.
50. The membership of the Committee Appointed to Consider and Report upon the Christian Faith in Relation to (a) Spiritualism; (b) Christian Science; and (c) Theosophy included the archbishops of Armagh and Nova Scotia, the bishops of Asheville, Assam, Barrow-in-Furness (secretary), Barbados, Derby, Exeter, George, Glasgow, Goulburn, Grafton, Grahamstown, Jarrow, Kensington, Knaresborough, Kootenay, Lincoln, Llandaff, Madras, Newcastle, Ossory, Ottawa, Quincy, Oxford (chairman), Sierra Leone, Southwark, Stafford, Tuam, Victoria (Hong Kong), Virginia, Wakefield, Western New York, West Virginia, Wyoming, and the Coadjutor bishops of Capetown and Newark.
51. Bishop of Oxford, *Proceedings of the Conference*, 5-7 July 1920, LC 105, 5 July, 52-61, Lambeth Palace Library.
52. Bishop of Goulburn, *Proceedings of the Lambeth Conference*, 5-7 July 1920, LC 105, 5 July, 61-68.
53. Bishop of Grahamstown, *Proceedings of the Lambeth Conference*, 5-7 July 1920, LC 105, 5 July, 69-74.
54. Archbishop of Canterbury, *Proceedings of the Lambeth Conference*, 5-7 July 1920, LC 105, 5 July, 75.
55. Bishop of Oxford, *Proceedings of the Lambeth Conference*, 5 August 1920, LC 5/36, 30-34.
56. For the wording of the amended resolutions which were accepted by the conference, see appendix 1.
57. Discussion, *Proceedings of the Lambeth Conference*, 5 August 1920, LC 5/36, 34-38.
58. "The Christian Faith in Relation to Spiritualism, Christian Science, and Theosophy," *Proceedings of the Lambeth Conference*, 5 August 1920, LC 5/36, 38-58.
59. The bishop of Peterborough, F. T. Woods, read the proposed amendments. "The Bishop of Kampala's amendment is: after the word 'spiritualism,' line 3, page 2, read 'and feels bound to give a serious warning against its general effect both upon

mind and faith.' If that is rejected there is a further amendment from Dr. King, after the words 'called us' in the sixth line on page 2 add 'it is dangerous to the mental balance of many of those who practice it.'"

60. The debate raged over the choice of words *deny* or *to negate*. The suggested new wording would read: "it tends to divert attention from and even to negate [or *to deny*]."

61. Lodge to Davidson, 3 July 1920, Lambeth Conference Papers 1920, LC 135, Lambeth Palace Library.

62. David Gow from *Light* and F. Blight Bond, the author of *Gate of Remembrance* and *Hill of Vision*, did appear before the committee to give evidence. The identity of the others is not known. The committee probably relied a great deal on the papers which several people submitted.

63. S. Smith Yelland to West-Watson (Campbell West-Watson was the bishop of Barrow-in-Furness and the secretary of the committee) 24 May 1920, Lambeth Conference Papers 1920, LC 135, Lambeth Palace Library.

64. Tweedale to Davidson, 29 June 1920, Lambeth Conference Papers 1920, LC 135, Lambeth Palace Library.

65. Gow to West-Watson, 20 July 1920, Lambeth Conference Papers 1920, LC 135, Lambeth Palace Library.

66. F. Bligh Bond to West-Watson, 24 June 1920, Lambeth Conference Papers 1920, LC 135, Lambeth Palace Library.

67. L. Dougall, "The Natural Explanation of Spiritualist Phenomena," Lambeth Conference Papers 1920, LC 135, Lambeth Palace Library.

68. De Brath to West-Watson, 22 July 1920, Lambeth Conference Papers 1920, LC 135, Lambeth Palace Library.

69. Encyclical letter "To the Faithful in Christ Jesus," 1920 Lambeth Conference, printed in *The Lambeth Conferences (1867-1930)* (London: SPCK, 1948), 28.

70. *Report of the Committee Appointed to Consider and Report upon the Christian Faith in Relation to (a) Spiritualism; (b) Christian Science; and (c) Theosophy*, printed in *The Lambeth Conferences (1867-1930)*.

71. Ibid., 106.
72. Ibid., 107.
73. Ibid., 108.
74. Ibid.
75. Ibid., 109.
76. Ibid., 110.
77. Ibid., 111.
78. Ibid., 112.
79. Ibid., 113.
80. Ibid., 114.
81. Ibid., 115.
82. Ibid., 116.
83. Ibid., 117.
84. Quoted in Arthur Conan Doyle, *The History of Spiritualism*, 2:266.
85. *Report of the Committee on "Supernormal Psychic Phenomena" to the General Assembly of the Church of Scotland*, 26 May 1922, Lambeth Palace Library.

86. At these séances, members of the committee experienced "the direct voice," "trance utterance," "table-tilting," and "thought reading." Moreover, the "communications received were vague, ambiguous, and often commonplace." "If a sitter were eagerly expectant and sympathetically uncritical, conviction might be produced."

87. *Report of the Committee on "Supernormal Psychic Phenomena" to the General Assembly of the Church of Scotland.*

Chapter Three

Psychical Studies, the Crisis of Faith, and the Anglican Church: Spiritualism and Religion during the 1930s

The resolutions of the 1920 Lambeth Conference left many questions unanswered concerning the relationship between spiritualism and orthodox Anglicanism. The printed material which came from this 1920 conference and other church meetings during the decade might have satisfied the theological and philosophical minds of the Anglican bishops and scholars, but it still did not address the personal and emotional needs of a great number of the faithful. The growth of the interest in spiritualism and the question of its relationship to traditional Christianity before the 1939-1945 war testified, in the opinion of some, to the inability of Anglicanism to meet the pastoral needs of its members. During this period, consequently, numerous people began to demand that the Anglican Church seriously investigate spiritualism from a Christian perspective, and they continued to ask the same questions others had asked earlier. Did spiritualism have something positive to offer traditional Anglican theology? Why should the two, which both preached about the other world, be at odds with each other? Could the tenets of spiritualism shore up the Anglican view of life after death, and thus give comfort to the bereaved?

The interest in spiritualism continued to grow in England between the two wars. Because of the policy adopted in 1920 the numbers of the Society for Psychical Research declined.[1] The membership of Spiritualists' National Union, on the other hand, increased. The societies affiliated to the SNU grew from 309 at the end of the Great War to 530 in 1938.[2] "In fact, by the mid-1930s, there were reported to be over 2,000 properly-constituted local spiritualist societies, and it was estimated that the total number of committed members might be in excess of a quarter of a million." Spiritualism touched all segments of the population, and "Jews, agnostics and Anglicans founded their own societies, for grief-stricken widows and mothers who sought 'the touch of a vanished hand and the sound of a voice that is still.'" A number of factors contributed to the strength of spiritualism during the 1930s, "the high water mark of the Spiritualist Movement."[3]

One reason for its popularity was the support and backing spiritualism received from influential people. Arthur Conan Doyle, "probably the greatest propagandist the Spiritualist movement ever had and a truely charismatic figure,"[4] worked to spread the gospel of spiritualism. Not only did Conan Doyle write *The History of Spiritualism* in 1926, but he also traveled throughout the world speaking on the subject. Robert Blatchford, the socialist writer, and Hannen Swaffer, the editor of *The People*, both converted to spiritualism. The English press was not as critical as it had been in the past and began to publish reports and stories favorable to spiritualism.[5] Spiritualism also caught the public attention by promoting measures designed to benefit society in general. Before the outbreak of war in 1914, a commitment to social reform could be seen in its association with socialism, the temperance movement, and animal welfare. Pacifism had always been strong in spiritualist circles. Spiritualists opposed violence and war, and this position presented a problem during the Great War. Most, however, backed the war effort. After 1918, spiritualists continued to encourage pacifism, which had also become popular throughout the country. "During the inter-war years the majority of Spiritualists seem to have supported every effort to preserve the peace, and the literature of the spiritualist movement frequently mentioned the activities of such bodies as the National Peace Council."[6] Geoffrey Nelson lists other organizations or activities which indicate the manner in which spiritualism had grown between the two world wars, such as spiritualist and psychic research societies and book clubs which provided literature on spiritualism at inexpensive prices.[7] He also notes that spiritualist leaders frequently condemned fraudulent individuals and practices which would hurt the reputation of spiritualism. During this period, moreover, spiritualism also became more identified as a religion, and some groups began to establish churches to preach its beliefs.

Most Christian churches in England were naturally critical of spiritualism. These churches dismissed the beliefs and claims of spiritualism as nonsense. The pressure which the followers of the prophetess Joanna Southcott (1750-1814) exerted on the archbishop of Canterbury during and after the Great War illustrates the manner in which Anglicanism tended to react to unorthodox movements which existed outside the boundries of traditional Christianity. Before her death, Southcott, who enjoyed some popularity during the upheavals of Napoleonic Europe, placed a number of her prophecies in a box, the so-called Great Box of Sealed Writings, and left instructions that the contents should be made public during a national emergency in the presence of twenty-four Anglican bishops, who symbolized the number of elders in the book of Revelation.

The disclosure of Southcott's writings would herald an era of peace. Beginning in November 1915 and continuing until the end of the war, several people wrote to the archbishop of Canterbury, Randall Davidson, and begged him to preside at the ceremonial opening of the sealed box, which was located in Devon.[8] The words of Southcott, these people believed, might stop the bloodshed in Europe. Davidson did not want to appear hostile to these concerns, but successfully distanced the Anglican Church from the pressures to open the sealed box. With the end of the war in 1918, the campaign on the part of Southcott's followers subsided, but the interest in her prophecies did not disappear.

The Panacea Society, a group interested in the study of modern prophecy, approached Archbishop Davidson and urged him to arrange for the opening of the sealed box in the presence of the required number of bishops.[9] Moreover, zealous individuals wrote to individual Anglican bishops, printed pamphlets which attempted to force the Anglican Church to take action, and also took their campaign to the archbishop of Canterbury. The secrets of the Southcott box might help England in the perilous times which followed the end of the war. Davidson, however, again refused to become involved and would not allow his archiepiscopal office to be associated with Southcott's prophecies. The pressure picked up in 1925, and those who wanted the archbishop to authorize the opening of the box took their crusade to the British press. The Panacea Society also tried to influence individual bishops but failed. Harry Price, the honorary director of the National Laboratory of Psychical Research, an organization founded by Price as a rival to the Society for Psychical Research, offered to officiate at the opening of the Southcott box, and he invited Davidson to attend. Not surprisingly, Archbishop Davidson refused to be present or to sanction this event. On 11 July 1927, the box was eventually opened at Church House, Westminster, in the presence of Price and the bishop of Grantham, John Edward Hine. Instead of the precious prophecies, the box contained a woman's nightcap, a book, a pistol, an eighteenth-century lottery ticket, a calendar, a medal, and a few coins. Members of the Panacea Society, however, quickly challenged the authenticity of this box, and claimed they possessed the real Southcott box. When Cosmo Gordon Lang became archbishop of Canterbury in 1928, the Panacea Society hoped that he would participate in the opening of its box. But Lang, like his predecessor, refused to become involved with the Southcott prophecies. This movement to associate the Anglican Church with the Southcott prophecies did alienate churchmen and never gained much popular support. The more sober methods and beliefs of spiritualism, however, did have a more positive impact on the Anglican Church. Moreover, its attempts to establish a church did enjoy some success.

Some Christian spiritualists worked for a reconciliation between the traditional churches and their own. During the nineteenth century, some spiritualists believed that their beliefs would revive Christianity by giving support to its supernatural teaching, but on the other hand some individuals wanted to establish spiritualism as a new and independent religion which would challenge traditional Christianity.[10] "The conflict between Christian and non-Christian spiritualists did not come to a head until the years between the two world wars when the movement as a whole was blooming."[11] Some wanted to develop a unified Christian spiritualist movement. After an unsuccessful attempt to persuade the Spiritualists' National Union to accept Christianity "as a principle of their beliefs," the first successful organization of Christian spiritualists, the Greater World Spiritualist League, was established.[12] Another group which existed during the 1930s, the Christian Spiritualist Church Union, "was eventually absorbed by the Christian Psychic Society in 1938 . . . [and] this Society was reported to have fifty-nine affiliated or near affiliated churches" in the following year.[13] Geoffrey Nelson estimates that during the 1930s approximately 30,000 spiritualist churches existed and could boast a membership of a quarter of a million people.[14] The Anglican Church could no longer avoid the popularity of spiritualism, and by the end of the 1930s it would begin to study the claims of spiritualism in a serious and responsible manner. Anglicanism also began to look at its responsibilities to comfort its bereaved members.

The Anglican Church did not run away from its pastoral responsibilities, and the history of the unsuccessful efforts to revise the *Book of Common Prayer* during the early twentieth century reveal that the church did address areas of concern. The proposed new *Book of Common Prayer*, which could be used in addition to the 1662 *Book of Common Prayer*, was presented to convocation after two decades of preparation and included two practices—reservation of the sacrament and the concept of prayers for the dead—which might help those Anglicans experiencing sorrow or bereavement. "The mounting casualty lists of the First World War widened the demand for reservation beyond the ranks of extreme Anglo-Catholics, but in 1918 the bishops declared that the rubric was not intended to cover perpetual reservation."[15] The introduction of explicit prayers for the dead, some believed, also signaled a change in doctrine away from Protestant traditions. "The new eucharistic rite, the provisions for reservation, the prayers for the departed—here were elements in the new Book which for the Evangelicals indicated a move in the direction of Rome."[16] Convocation and the church assembly gave their approval to the new book. Some Anglican bishops, such as E. A. Knox of Manchester, and other evangelicals in the Anglican Church, vigorously resisted its approval because of alleged Roman Catholic practices, especially reservation of the sacrament.[17] The Commons eventually rejected the new prayer book in 1927 and then again in 1928.

Doctrine in the Church of England, published in 1938, was the report of a commission established in 1922 "to consider the nature and grounds of Christian doctrine with a view to demonstrating the extent of existing agreement within the Church of England and with a view to investigating how far it is possible to remove or diminish existing differences."[18] Their findings and conclusions spoke to some of the pastoral and theological difficulties which the Great War had brought into relief. It did not represent the official statement of Anglican faith, but the commission did suggest some modifications in existing doctrines which some saw as a move away from a strict Protestant interpretation. After reaffirming the doctrine of the communion of saints, a belief in "a doctrine of life hereafter which (whether or not the *word* Purgatory be used or the element of purification emphasised) is at least conceived in terms of development and growth,"[19] the commission concluded that "there is no theological objection in principle to Prayer for the Departed."[20] The report of the commission received a cool, and in some cases, a hostile reception from churchmen. A spiritualist newspaper, *Psychic News*, believed that the report "sounds the death-knell of Orthodoxy" and criticized it for some antispiritualist sentiments: "Just as, according to the Bible story, [Jesus] was rejected by the orthodox of his day, so the same truth, accompanied by the same phenomena, is despised by the Church today."[21] A modern commentator described its failure to contribute to the life of Anglicanism by remarking, "It was a pondered, rather dull document, as was inevitable given the drawn out circumstances and varied views of its producers."[22] During the 1930s some Anglicans still needed advice and counsel from their church, and a number turned to the archbishop of Canterbury.

In early 1934, a Yorkshire widower wrote to the archbishop of Canterbury, Cosmo Gordon Lang, describing his personal grief and sorrow which stemmed from the death of his wife. He had sincerely tried to cope with the loss of his spouse. Mr. E. Adamson admitted to the archbishop that he was lonely, and consequently he had "tried to get into communication with her."[23] "I succeeded in doing immediately, *absolutely immediately*," Adamson told Archbishop Lang, and "she wanted to tell me of her happiness and freedom from pain . . . and of my coming happiness." The communications continued. "Since then I have been in *constant* communion with her." The writer of this letter noted that previously he had always viewed spiritualism as an academic subject, "for *exactly* the same reason as I reject the office of pope," and he never used the services of a medium. Adamson ended his letter to Archbishop Lang with words which would become familiar to the archbishop during the next several years: his communication was with the "highest Christian or *Christ* plane."

The archbishop of Canterbury's private secretary, the Rev. Alan Don, answered Mr. Adamson and told him that the archbishop had indeed read his letter with great interest. "His Grace can only say," the reply from Lambeth Palace stated, "that he is sure you are right in acting quietly and confidently on the belief that a communion of spirit continues between those who have loved each other here."[24] Moreover, the letter continued, Lang believed that "this communion of spirit must be of a more intensely spiritual character and not depend on such doubtful methods." But Archbishop Lang did express some caution: "you are equally right in refusing to complicate this simple belief by any traffic with mediums and the like." Moreover, automatic writing should also be treated as suspect. This letter of comfort from the archbishop of Canterbury did not reject or ridicule the writer's experience. According to Lang's opinion, "the communion of saints must be of a more intensive character and not depend on such doubtful methods" such as séances.

Cosmo Gordon Lang (1864-1945)[25] appeared to be the ideal person to entertain questions concerning the relationship between spiritualism and Christianity. Born into a Presbyterian family living in Aberdeenshire, Lang entered Balliol College, Oxford, in 1882 after schooling in Glasgow. After a period studying for the bar, he shocked his family and friends by announcing his intention to seek Holy Orders in the Anglican Church. After ordination to the priesthood in 1891, Lang gained a reputation for his work and preaching in London's East End. He declined the nomination to become the bishop of Montreal, but shortly afterwards agreed to become the archbishop of York, and he was enthroned in January 1909. Like many other men and women, the Great War also brought Archbishop Lang a personal loss. The death of his chaplain in action touched him deeply. After nearly two decades of service in York, the prime minister, Stanley Baldwin, nominated Lang in 1928 to succeed Randall Davidson as archbishop of Canterbury, and he was enthroned in Canterbury in December of that year. Among other ecclesiastical and civil matters, Archbishop Lang had to deal with the increasing popularity of spiritualism within certain Anglican circles.

Not all the concerns and queries about the relationship of spiritualism and Christianity came from the letters written by the laity. In November 1935, John Victor Macmillan, the bishop of Guildford, approached Archbishop Lang about the activities of the Rev. G. Maurice Elliott, vicar of St. Peter's, Cricklewood, "who seems to be going into the diocese around London speaking about Spiritualism."[26] Macmillan reminded Lang that the bishop of London, Arthur Foley Winnington-Ingram, had spoken about Elliott's questionable activities at a recent Bishops' Meeting. The cleric's apparent disregard of ecclesiastical protocol had irked Bishop Macmillan. According to the bishop of Guildford, Elliott had scheduled a meeting at a parish within the boundaries of his diocese, and only then informed the bishop of the arrangement. Macmillan replied to Elliott and reminded him that an invitation from the local parish to a visiting priest was necessary, and this had not been extended to him. The Rev. Maurice Elliott, however, disregarded the bishop's words and attended the meeting.

The purpose and message of these meetings associated with the Rev. G. Maurice Elliott also troubled Bishop Macmillan. "The matter has now gone further," the bishop informed Archbishop Lang, "in that Mr. Elliott together with a certain Mrs. St. Clair Stobart have advertised a Meeting to be held at Camberley [Surrey], described as being 'In conjunction with the Confraternity between Clergy and Spiritualists.'" Elliott, according to the bishop, had also suggested that the parishioners should urge their local clergy to attend. Moreover, among "the papers circulated is one of the long interview which Mr. Sharp [an Anglican cleric] purports to have had with the late Archbishop Davidson in the other world!" Was the Diocese of Guildford the only one experiencing attempts to mix or to confuse Christianity and spiritualism? Some of the spiritualist literature, described as "being done with a certain amount of cleverness," which promoted this particular meeting, openly criticized the Anglican Church. The opulence of the bishops and "the practical difficulties, financial and other, of the clergy" received much attention. The bishop of Guildford ended his letter to Lambeth Palace and pointed out that meetings of this sort might find friendly ears among certain Anglicans. "A district like Camberley is rather good hunting ground for this type of propaganda, as there are a number of leisurely people who have not got regular occupation."

The reply from Archbishop Lang expressed surprise at the activities of the two clerics, Elliott and Sharp. The latter, "at the Bishop of London's instigation, [had] resigned his post of Rural Dean."[27] Moreover, according to the archbishop, the "Bishop of London, who has been considerably troubled by these people, has prohibited spiritualist meetings being held in any churches or church halls within his diocese." Consequently, interested people journeyed outside of the Diocese of London in search of gatherings of this nature. Lang told Bishop Macmillan that he had acted appropriately in warning the clergy and laity of the dangers associated with "spiritualistic seances and the like." Yet Archbishop Lang did not have a closed mind on the subject. "If Spiritualism has anything in it," he told Bishop Macmillan, "the matter ought to be investigated by skilled and trained scientific enquirers and certainly not by the ordinary clergy." The bishop of Guildford responded the following day and thanked the archbishop for his time and concern. He told Lang that he would address his diocesan conference on the dangers associated with spiritualism, and ended by adding that "I very much agree . . . about what the Archbishop says about the unhealthiness of the whole thing."[28]

Early in the new year, January 1936, another letter appeared on the archbishop's desk concerning the subject of spiritualism. And this time the writer, a prominent and respected churchman, proposed a plan to study the relationship between spiritualism and Christianity. The Rev. Francis Underhill, dean of Rochester, wrote to Archbishop Lang[29] and formally withdrew a resolution which he had made at a meeting of the church assembly during the previous summer which read: "That in view of the growth of Spiritualism among the clergy and communicant laity of the Church, this Assembly respectfully requests their Graces the Archbishops to consult with the Convocations as to the appointment of a Commission to investigate the matter and to report to the Assembly."[30] Underhill explained that the motion had asked for the appointment of a commission of enquiry to study spiritualism. A commission appointed by the archbishops, he believed, seemed more appropriate. The dean also sent to Archbishop Lang a list of suitable people drawn from the ecclesiastical, academic, and professional worlds who might be invited to serve as members of the commission.[31]

Archbishop Lang replied within a week to Dean Underhill's proposal. The archbishop expressed some confusion with the wording of Underhill's letter. "What His Grace had in mind when he spoke of the subject," Lang's secretary began, "was not anything in the nature of a formal Commission but rather a committee of enquiry somewhat on the lines of the Archbishop's Advisory Council on Spiritual Healing of which . . . you have been a member."[32] Archbishop Lang wanted to know if the dean had any objection to the establishment of an informal committee or commission which would study spiritualism. Underhill's reply left the question of the nature of the group up to the decision of Archbishop Lang, but again he offered suggestions on the composition of the committee. According to his thinking, should "there not be on this council those who are avowed Spiritualists being also members of the Church . . . some who are regular communicants?"[33] He also believed that expert witnesses should be called upon to give evidence. Without waiting for an answer from Lang, Dean Underhill hurried off another letter to Lambeth Palace. He enclosed additional names and a book, *A Christian Searchlight on Spiritualism*, by the Rev. D. H. D. Wilkinson,[34] "which gives . . . the point of those Churchmen and women who have become Spiritualists."[35]

Two letters came quickly from Lambeth Palace. The first told Dean Underhill that Archbishop Lang intended to approach the archbishop of York, William Temple, about "the proposed Committee on the subject of Spiritualism."[36] The second, written two days latter, thanked Underhill for the copy of Wilkinson's book and commented on the potential list of members. Archbishop Lang, this letter ended, "will give consideration to the names which you mention when the time comes for him to talk over with the Archbishop of York the question of the appointment of a Committee."[37] Again Dean Underhill did not wait for a report of the discussion between the two archbishops. In early March, he sent Lang a lengthy typescript, *Psychic Phenomena with Reference to the Christian Tradition*, which dealt with the relationship of spiritualism to Christianity. The author wanted to remain anonymous, but Underhill vouched for his character and credentials. "It seems to me," the dean told Archbishop Lang, "that it is the kind of document with which the Advisory Committee might well begin its work."[38]

The typescript began with a succinct statement of purpose: it was an "attempt to summarise the more usual psychic phenomena with special reference to the Christian tradition, and the present situation."[39] The author noted that such phenomena have been essential in the history of Christian and non-Christian religious beliefs. "Psychic phenomena have been used as channels of what we call revelation." Moreover,

> It is a fact that instructed and open-minded Christians who have had the courage to make a first-hand study of psychic phenomena have found an altogether new light shed upon one thing after another both in Scripture and in the traditions of the Church that in recent times have become matters of grave difficulty in consequence of the attitude of modern science.[40]

In respect to cases of bereavement and despair, many believed that the church had not been equipped to offer any comfort or support. However, "it has been the experience of psychic phenomena that has in actual fact brought conviction, removing the fear of death itself, and thereby making for health and sanity of outlook."[41] Consequently two developments had emerged in recent memory: a hostility on the part of the Christian churches toward spiritualism and a schism or break within traditional Christianity on the part of those who have experienced "the new light."

The popularity of spiritualism, the anonymous author noted, had grown rapidly. Newspapers appeared and so-called spiritualist churches dotted the countryside. The clergy, unfortunately, have grown ignorant of these "churches" and the beliefs of their congregations.

> But could they [the Anglican clergy] establish some sympathetic contacts they would also find very real psychic phenomena mixed with questionable material, and numberless cases of conversion of atheists and agnostics and materialists into believers in God and in a future life, practising with conviction the Christian ethics of life here, though often combined with some very wrong ideal on certain religious questions.[42]

After laying down this challenge to the Anglican Church, the essay listed and explained numerous examples of psychic phenomena.[43] The author then described these phenomena in clinical and objective terms, and with the exception of "descriptions of the other world," references to the Judeo-Christian traditions and beliefs were rare.

Any discussion of this nature which addressed the existence of the other world naturally touched the theological and doctrinal nerve of the Anglican Church. The author maintained that "a vast amount of material has been communicated about the future life and there is much common ground in messages from widely different sources."[44] After explaining the classical belief in the different planes of existence, the paper remarked that the substance of these communications in the majority of instances dealt with Christian ethics and morals. Creeds and religious doctrines did not divide the spirits after death; the important matter was that these people, or spirits, still lived. Some spiritualists, consequently, questioned whether it was necessary to embrace or profess the Christian faith, and some even became exceedingly hostile to Christianity.

The author ended his essay by appealing to the Anglican Church to adopt an open mind to spiritualism. He also made several suggestions which might help those Christians being attracted by the mysteries and appeals of spiritualism. In general, the recommendations saw spiritualism in a positive light. The validity of psychic phenomena, in the first place, provided ample evidence of a future life and formed part of the natural order of life. Moreover, the "the affirmation of the occurrence of such phenomena . . . [was] the basis of religious experience including that of the Christian faith."[45] But the list also contained cautions against fraud, palmistry, the irresponsible use of psychical phenomena "for the consolation of the bereaved" and as a bulwark against the claims of materialism, and finally the "mischievous propaganda of the Anti-Christian Spiritualists." The Anglican Church, however, should not discount or ignore recent advances in education and scientific research. Dean Underhill's letter and the gift of this typescript did not go unacknowledged. A letter from Lambeth Palace thanked him, remarked that Archbishop Lang intended to read the document shortly, and told Underhill that the archbishop would discuss the appointment of a committee when he next met with the archbishop of York, William Temple.[46] This anonymous essay, moreover, would eventually be distributed to members of the committee on spiritualism and would serve as evidence to help them in their deliberations.

The archbishop of Canterbury met with Archbishop William Temple in London during late March 1936. At the meeting, the question of spiritualism surfaced, and Archbishop Lang gave Archbishop Temple a copy of *Psychical Phenomena with Reference to the Christian Tradition* to read. After Lang's return to Bishopsthorpe, Temple wrote a letter of appreciation to Lang and expressed his views on the subject of spiritualism. "It seems to me full of uncriticised matter which calls aloud for very careful testing," he told Archbishop Lang.[47] "The trouble with the whole question," Temple argued, "is that people either despise the subject and therefore cannot attend to the alleged evidence, or else become enthusiastic and lose their critical balance." The question of a committee and its membership also became a subject of this letter. Archbishop Temple pointed out that he was acquainted with individuals who possessed an objective and critical sense, such as members of the Society for Psychical Research. These, he believed, would make outstanding contributions to a committee investigating the issue of spiritualism. According to Temple, "It seems to me that what we want is a *group of scientists* who will really study the alleged physical facts and try to work out the uniformities governing these." To understand the underlying laws, he believed, was important; only then one could easily proceed to discover the causes of psychical phenomena.

Archbishop Lang replied the following day, and again asked the archbishop of York some questions about the composition of the committee, especially the number of representatives from the scientific community. "Is His Grace to understand that you consider that if any Committee is to be appointed it ought to be of a purely scientific nature?"[48] The difficulty, in the mind of the archbishop of Canterbury, would be identifying interested scientists who did not hold membership in the Society for Psychical Research. But the need to establish a committee under the aegis of the church to study the relationship seemed overwhelming and urgent. According to Archbishop Lang, "a good many Christian people, clergy and otherwise, are at present dabbling in Spiritualism." He mentioned, for example, the master of the temple, Harold Anson, who frequently attended séances. Lang ended his letter and again asked Archbishop Temple for his thoughts on the appointment of a committee. Should it follow lines similar to what the dean of Rochester wanted, namely, "going carefully into the whole matter and reporting upon its bearing upon the Christian faith and religion"?

Archbishop Temple's response to Lang tried to clear up any ambiguities in his thoughts on the matter of a committee. Concerning the membership, Temple told Archbishop Lang that he hoped "that any group whom we appoint would urge the necessity of investigation with real thoroughness."[49] Men and women of science, consequently, should not be avoided or neglected. They would add respectability and expertise to a group dominated, naturally, by representatives from the church. Temple emphasized that the committee could not possibly avoid investigating the scientific basis of psychic phenomena. His private thoughts on spiritualism also surfaced. "Personally I am sure that much of it is foolishness, all of it is dangerous, but some of it may be well founded, and if only we could track the foundations, it might be possible to allay the danger." In short, Archbishop William Temple gave his support and backing to the establishment of a committee or commission which would study spiritualism.

In spite of this encouragement, Archbishop Lang still continued to adopt a rather cautious approach to the appointment of a church body to investigate spiritualism. He feared what ramifications or consequences it might have on Christian practices and beliefs, and from March to June 1936 the archbishop continued to weigh all possibilities. A note, simply entitled "Spiritualism," recorded his thoughts on the matter. In it, Lang recalled his meeting with Dean Francis Underhill at Lambeth Palace on 2 April when he told the dean that he had some reservations about appointing "some sort of Commission" to consider the question of spiritualism.[50] During the discussion between the two churchmen, Underhill expressed some opposition to the archbishop's timidity. According to Lang's notes, Underhill "felt rather strongly that a mere private request to some individuals to undertake some examination of the problem would not suffice because it would be difficult . . . [for] the right sort of people to give up so much time and thought in a merely private enquiry." Archbishop Lang's recollections reveal that he did see some merit in Underhill's arguments, but the archbishop also pointed out to the dean that before he would appoint a formal commission or committee he would first place the matter on the agenda of the next Bishops' Meeting and ask them for their advice.

Before the Bishops' Meeting, which had been scheduled for the first week of July 1936, Dean Underhill again approached Archbishop Lang. After apologizing for another letter on the subject, which he had marked "confidential," Underhill told the archbishop that he had recently devoted much time and effort to reading and researching the topic of spiritualism. The dean even admitted that he had attended a number of "'sittings' with several mediums."[51] Underhill reminded Lang of the archbishop's confessed skepticism about communications with departed spirits and admitted that he had recently arrived at the same conclusion. The sittings had brought him to this position. "I am supposed to have been in touch with many persons 'on the other side,' including Archbishop Davidson and my own father and mother," Underhill revealed. "In these and other instances, while there have been trifling matters which might be called evidential, the general impression I gained is that, if these are the persons they purport to be, they have deteriorated mentally and spiritually since death."

Dean Underhill also confessed that after talking to several of his friends, "convinced Spiritualists," he could not find anything worthwhile that came from their spiritualistic experiences. Underhill did not like the manner in which "great names are being used for trivial purposes," and he also expressed his opinion that "real dangers" were involved in spiritualism. He had initially urged the archbishop to bring the matter of spiritualism to the floor of the Bishops' Meeting for consideration, but he now admitted that this approach might not be the appropriate course of action. " I am inclined to believe," he told Lang, "that if you could, quite privately, set a few of us to work with your authority, good would come of it." Consequently, he urged Archbishop Lang to proceed with the appointment of a committee along these lines. The archbishop responded immediately and told the dean of Rochester that he took great interest in his thoughts on the matter of the committee. Nonetheless, Lang told him that "I propose to speak of the matter quite generally at a meeting of the Bishops here on Wednesday."[52] The archbishop of Canterbury still hedged on the appointment of a formal commission or committee, but he confessed that after a consultation with the bishops on the matter he might consider appointing "a small body to carry on quiet investigations with you and coming to such conclusions as they are able to reach."

The Bishops' Meeting did discuss the question of spiritualism and the possibility of setting up a committee to study its relationship with Christianity. Archbishop Lang informed the meeting that he had recently been in constant contact with Dean Underhill of Rochester. The archbishop continued and argued that the "subject was undoubtedly daunting, in that it pointed to the existence of undiscovered and unrelated capacities of the human mind."[53] Moreover, he revealed, Underhill had expressed a keen interest that a small group of responsible people be set up under the aegis of the archbishop of Canterbury "to conduct a quiet and private investigation into the subject." A frequent and open critic of spiritualism, Arthur Foley Winnington-Ingram, the bishop of London, responded and spoke in favor of a committee such as Archbishop

Lang had described. "The cult of Spiritualism was apt to become an absorbing obsession," Winnington-Ingram told the assembly, and he mentioned a Member of Parliament "who was in the habit of conversing through a tube with his Great-Grandfather." Walter Godfrey Whittingham, the bishop of St. Edmundsbury and Ipswich, argued that spiritualism should not be dismissed or disregarded as "mere foolishness," and he likewise called for an investigation "undertaken by people of scientific temperament capable of sifting evidence." Bishop Bertram Pollock of Norwich agreed. He believed that the committee ought to include people who had an attraction to spiritualism and suggested that the committee move toward positive and constructive conclusions. Likewise, the bishop of Carlisle, Henry Herbert Williams, did not want the deliberations of a committee to become a venue for "mere criticism of Spiritualism."

Other bishops gave their opinions. One maintained that the Anglican Church ought to make plain and clear the implications of the doctrine of the communion of saints, and another prelate, beginning his remarks with a critique of "the deplorable theology of many popular hymns," also believed that the church had an obligation to teach the true Christian doctrines about life after death. However, the bishop of Birmingham, Ernest William Barnes, saw matters in a different light; he doubted if any additional studies or investigations were really necessary. In his opinion, "The Society for Psychical Research had gone very thoroughly into the matter." "Spiritualism," he argued, "was on the decline whereas Christian Science was increasing in popularity." Moreover, mediums and other advocates of spiritualism would use a report, whether positive or negative, and exploit it for purposes of advertisement and recruitment. After this statement by the bishop of Birmingham, Archbishop Lang ended the discussion of spiritualism with a brief summary of the bishops' thoughts. In the first place, he "would deprecate the appointment of any formal commission upon which eminent scientists would hesitate to serve." He would, however, encourage Dean Underhill to undertake a "private" investigation assisted by a group of interested friends. The bishops agreed with Archbishop Lang's suggestion.

Archbishop Lang, consequently, wrote to Dean Underhill and informed him that the consensus of the Bishops' Meeting favored "the appointment of a private and informal committee to co-operate with you in the investigation of the subject" of spiritualism.[54] Before pursuing the matter any further, especially the invitation to suitable individuals asking them to participate in the study of spiritualism, Lang thought it would be appropriate and necessary to confer personally with Underhill first. And they eventually agreed on 4 August 1936 as a suitable date for a meeting at Lambeth Palace. According to Archbishop Lang's notes, both concluded that a commission should be private in nature, the participants should be invited personally by the archbishop, and the size should be limited to eight or nine with Dean Underhill as the chairman. A preliminary list of possible members also emerged from this luncheon meeting:

the dean of St. Paul's, the master of the temple, Professor C. Raven, Professor L. W. Grensted, Mr. Cyril Baily, Dr. William Brown, Evelyn Underhill (Mrs. Stuart Moore), Mrs. A. E. J. Rawlinson, and Mr. Walter Wigglesworth.[55] The latter might be approached to serve as the secretary of the group, and the Rev. J. K. Mozley might be an alternate. Lang's notes reveal that Underhill planned to be away on holiday in Scotland until the end of September, and thus the archbishop decided to wait until October to send the archiepiscopal invitations to the prospective members of the committee.

Dean Underhill, however, did not wait until the autumn. He began immediately after the 4 August meeting to approach possible members of the committee. Underhill informed Lambeth Palace that Cyril Baily had declined ("but would I think, yield to a letter . . . from the Archbishop"), and that his cousin, the religious writer, Evelyn Underhill, "to my great surprise and satisfaction yielded at once"[56] to the invitation. "I'm afraid I don't know much about the subject," her reply read, "but if the Archbishop wishes it . . . I am prepared to do the best."[57] Dean Underhill was overjoyed with the successes of the initial responses to the first round of invitations, but advice from Lambeth Palace urged caution and tried to cool the dean's growing enthusiasm for the project. A letter told him that the archbishop's secretary would be away during the month of August and that Archbishop Lang had already decided to wait until early October before sending out the actual invitations.[58]

On the second day of October, Archbishop Lang wrote to Dean Francis Underhill. He wanted to have another talk with the dean to confirm the list of names which had been discussed at the August meeting. Dean Underhill responded and agreed to come to London on the date proposed by the archbishop of Canterbury, 16 October, but he continued to push Lang into action, suggesting two additional names as possible members.[59] Dean Underhill met with Archbishop Lang nearly a fortnight later at Lambeth Palace. Lang's notes reveal that both clerics went over the preliminary list agreed upon in August, with the addition of Mr. Paul Sandlands, K.C., recommended by the master of the temple, Canon Harold Anson, who was also a potential member. Both agreed that the Rev. J. K. Mozley, canon and chancellor of St. Paul's Cathedral, and Lady Gwendolen Stephenson would be considered as possible alternate or substitute members. Dean Underhill would act as the chairman and convener of the committee, and Mr. W. S. Wigglesworth, barrister and later vicar-general of the province of York, would serve as the secretary. The archbishop and the dean also set the main guideline for the discussions: "To investigate the subject of communications with discarnate spirits and the claims of Spiritualism in relation to the Christian Faith."[60] Archbishop Lang told Dean Underhill that he planned to send out the invitations immediately.

By the end of October, however, Archbishop Lang had still not mailed out the invitations. He wrote to Dean Underhill and apologized for the delay. The archbishop explained that he thought it best to consult the dean on the wording of the invitation and thus sent him a copy of "the proposed draft of such a letter" for any possible suggestions or amendments.[61] Underhill thanked the archbishop for his thoughtfulness, told him that the invitation seemed fine, and wished him good luck on the responses.[62] This lengthy letter of invitation from the archbishop of Canterbury outlined the reason and purpose behind the establishment of the committee. "I have for some time past been aware of the influence of the phenomena with which Spiritualism is concerned upon members of the Church and indeed upon Christian people generally," Archbishop Lang began the letter.[63] "In the case of some these phenomena are causing much perplexity and even disturbances of mind, and in the case of others they seem to afford some assurance of the Christian belief of the survival of life after death."

Lang then pointed out that he believed that the time was propitious for an investigation of spiritualism and psychic phenomena in a quiet manner by a small committee composed of members of the Anglican Church. The invitation noted that the Society for Psychical Research had been conducting investigations of this nature for some time, and the committee should avoid duplicating the valuable work of the SPR. Lang suggested that the committee "should undertake some independent investigation quietly and without undue publicity especially as to the bearing of these phenomena on the Faith of Christian people." Archbishop Lang also formally appointed Dean Francis Underhill as the chairman and convener of the committee. The archbishop expressed his heartfelt hope that the reader would accept his invitation to participate, and he stated that if any questions or queries exist, Dean Underhill should be consulted. "I cannot doubt that if you are willing to accede to may request," the archbishop of Canterbury ended the letter, "you will be rendering a very real and valuable service to the church."

Within days, responses to Archbishop Lang's invitation began arriving at Lambeth Palace. Professor L. W. Grensted, Nolloth Professor of the Philosophy of Christian Religion, wrote from Oxford University and accepted the invitation, pointing out, however, that he had duties at the university and was already scheduled to undergo an operation. The Regius Professor of Divinity in Cambridge University, the Rev. Charles Raven, expressed an interest but would not commit himself until he knew more about the work of the committee from Dean Underhill. (Raven eventually declined, telling Lang that after hearing from Underhill he came to the conclusion that this "seems to me a task for which I am in no way especially suited.")[64] Mr. P. E. Sandlands, although professing his lack of knowledge on the subject, Mrs. A. E. J. Rawlinson, expressing some critical words about spiritualism, Walter Wigglesworth, and Dr. William Brown, psychiatrist and Wilde Reader in Mental Philosophy in Oxford University, all accepted the archbishop's invitation. Evelyn Underhill, the dean's cousin, also agreed to serve. Openly admitting her prejudice, she told Archbishop Lang that she was "very strongly opposed to spiritualism . . . especially to any tendency on the part of the Church to recognize or encourage it."[65] Mr. C. Bailey, Fellow and Classical Tutor of Balliol College, flatly refused the invitation to participate.

In early December, Lang's secretary wrote to Dean Francis Underhill and informed him of the results of the responses to the archbishop's invitation. He also solicited Underhill's opinion on the names of two people to fill the vacancies created by the refusals of Raven and Baily. The dean promptly suggested the Rev. Henry de Candole of Chichester, the Rev. Guy Mayfield, assistant editor of the *Guardian*, and Mr. Kenneth Ingram of London. But Lang's response to these suggestions revealed some confusion or misunderstanding concerning the process of choosing potential members. The archbishop, after studying the correspondence with Dean Underhill and his notes on the subject, found what appeared "to be contradictory recommendations as to whom should be invited to serve on the Committee."[66] Because of an error or oversight, the names of the dean of St. Paul's, W. R. Matthews, and the master of the temple, the Rev. Canon Harold Anson, had been left off the list, although both had been mentioned previously as valuable participants and contributors. Should they be invited to join? The letter also acknowledged Underhill's suggested replacements but wondered about possibility of the Rev. J. K. Mozley and Lady Stephenson being included.

Dean Underhill wrote back and agreed that the dean of St. Paul's and the master of the temple should most certainly be asked to participate. He withdrew his previous support for Dr. Mozley ("he is too antagonistic") but agreed that the name of Lady Stephenson should be added to the list of potential members. Consequently, the archbishop sent out a second round of invitations, but he did not accept all of Underhill's recommendations. Archbishop Lang contacted Lady Stephenson, Harold Anson, and W. R. Matthews, and they all agreed to serve. Canon Anson responded enthusiastically. "I have been interested in the phenomena of Spiritualism for many years," he told the archbishop, "and before speaking on the subject at a Church Congress some years ago [I] made a special study of it and published a paper on it."[67] The letter of appreciation from Lambeth Palace to Lady Stephenson indicated the direction the committee would take: "I am sure it is the sort of enquiry that ought to be made though it will be difficult for the Committee to carry on much independent investigation . . . [and] I suppose its main work will be to consider the relation between these investigations and the Christian Faith and Church."[68] After much thought, however, Henry de Candole asked to be excused. Because of Dean Underhill's earlier recommendation, an additional invitation was sent to the Rev. Guy Mayfield of the *Guardian*. Underhill wanted to move quickly, and he planned to schedule a preliminary meeting early in February 1937.

The committee on spiritualism soon suffered another casualty. After only two meetings, Evelyn Underhill, an acknowledged expert on mysticism, wrote a letter of resignation to Dean Francis Underhill. She explained that regular attendance at meetings had become impossible, but more fundamental reasons also contributed to her resignation. She again confessed to a prejudice against spiritualism. After reading the literature circulated to the committee members, Underhill admitted that she was "struck once more with the utterly sub-Christian, anthropocentric, hopelessly unsupernatural character of the Spiritualist outlook."[69] "It is all about man," she continued, "his survival, prospects, etc., hardly at all about God, and really represents *au fond* the nineteenth-century naturalistic attitude with a little superstition stirred in." Utilitarian and pragmatic in nature, spiritualism did not emphasize the "glory of God but our own consolation, future well-being, etc., is in the foreground." Her hostile position toward spiritualism would harm the objective nature of the committee. She also addressed some of her comments to the leaders of the Anglican Church and warned that "it will be a very ill day for the Church of England when she allows it to be assumed that she can come to terms with the 'Spiritualist outlook' and abandons the theocentric point of view." The church, she believed, "is already too much concerned with sub-religious interests and this one cuts at the very root of the spiritual life." Miss Underhill drew attention to the scientific character of the archbishop's committee, and she pointed out that an organization such as the Society for Psychical Research should undertake an investigation into spiritualism. Consequently, the "Church should stick to her supernatural job as the Body of Christ."

The appointment of an ecclesiastical committee to study spiritualism became public knowledge. By October 1936, the spiritualist press began to inform its readers that it had become necessary to appoint such a commission to investigate the subject. The news of the committee had, not surprisingly, spread to the northern province, and in February 1937 Archbishop William Temple of York asked Lang about the status and goals of the committee on spiritualism. Confusion also accompanied the reports about the committee northward. Archbishop William Temple told the archbishop of Canterbury's secretary that he had received several letters which mentioned that he had appointed the committee! The archbishop of York, therefore, wanted some information. "Is it actually a Commission set up by the Archbishop of Canterbury, or at his invitation," Temple queried, "or is it at the invitation of the two archbishops?"[70] Archbishop Temple expressed his support and backing for the establishment of a committee to study spiritualism, and pointed out that he did not question the fact that the invitations came from Lambeth Palace. He also informed Lang that the existence of the committee "has become more public . . . and of course one cannot deny that it exists."

A reply from Archbishop Lang arrived quickly at Bishopsthorpe. This letter reminded Archbishop Temple that the question concerning the appointment of the committee had been discussed at the Bishops' Meeting in July 1936, and at that time the "Archbishop of Canterbury made it clear that he would deprecate the appointment of any formal Commission."[71] Moreover, Lang continued, "all he suggested was that the Dean of Rochester should, with his encouragement, undertake a private enquiry with assistance of a group of friends." The archbishop of Canterbury, therefore, had invited several people to take part in the discussions, and he had informed the Bishops' Meeting of the names of those individuals whom he had asked to serve on the committee. Archbishop Temple, therefore, had no official ecclesiastical involvement in the formation of the committee apart from the fact that he knew about it in his role as a member of the Bishops' Meeting.

And the committee did take its job seriously. Dean Francis Underhill faithfully fulfilled his position as chairman and convener of the committee. During the spring and summer of 1937, Underhill and the committee met several times, and numerous witnesses gave evidence, later included as part of the committee's formal report, but only sketchy records of these deliberations have survived.[72] In the autumn of that year, an event changed Francis Underhill's life and his position in the Anglican Church, but did not drastically affect the workings of his group. On 6 October 1937, Underhill was nominated as bishop of Bath and Wells, and was later consecrated on 30 November as bishop of that western diocese. In the midst of his move from Rochester to the episcopal residence in Wells, Archbishop Lang sent him a confidential letter asking about the progress of the committee dealing with spiritualism. Had a report been concluded yet? "The reason I ask," Archbishop Lang continued, "is that I have just had a long and very interesting talk with the retiring Swedish Minister (Baron E. K. Palmstierna) who has gone very deeply into these matters not in the least after the manner of the ordinary spiritualist but in a more philosophical way."[73] According to the archbishop, the baron "has tried to find a basis in philosophy and religion for what seems to be credible and worthy in communications which he and some of his friends believe they have received."

It appeared, moreover, that this meeting with Baron Palmstierna gave Archbishop Lang a bit more enthusiasm for pursuing the question of the relationship of Christianity to spiritualism. Lang told the bishop-elect of Bath and Wells that the baron had never personally attended a séance; "he is quite outside that department." The archbishop then got to the point of the letter: "It occurs to me that if you have not finished your evidence he might be an exceedingly useful and constructive witness, or if you have not yet completed your Report it might help your Commission to look at the problem in a larger way if you could have some talk with him." The baron knew about the existence of the commission, Lang reported, and he had already volunteered to appear as a witness. Archbishop Lang ended the letter by referring Underhill to some of the baron's writings and remarked that it might be "profitable to consider the matter with him."

Francis Underhill replied to Archbishop Lang's letter, telling him that Palmstierna had been in contact with him and that the baron had already sent him a copy of *Horizons of Immortality*.[74] Archbishop Lang acknowledged this letter and told Underhill that it remained up to the committee, scheduled to meet again in early December 1937, to come to a decision whether or not to interview the baron. It appeared that Archbishop Lang eagerly wanted Palmstierna to appear before Underhill's committee, and the baron also anxiously desired to give testimony. Writing in late November, Baron Palmstierna thanked Archbishop Lang for thinking about him in respect to the committee's work. "I feel greatly indebted to you for the kind interest taken in our experiences . . . with the beyond," he wrote to Lang, "and your wise judgement on these matters was a great encouragement.[75] He also promised to send the archbishop a copy of his recent paper on the subject, "Horizons of Immortality and the Subconscious Mind," which refuted the contention that the subconscious mind had an influence on psychic findings. According to the paper,

> The Subconscious mind as created by some modern psychologists may in certain respects have been useful as a working hypothesis but its evidence in reality seems very doubtful, to say the least, and my experience tells that it is nothing else than a functioning of the ever living . . . human soul itself under the conditions offered by a life on earth.[76]

Palmstierna pointed to the facts surrounding the recent discovery of a lost Schumann concerto and argued forcefully that the subconscious mind could not possibly have contributed to its recovery.

The work of the bishop Underhill's committee continued throughout the autumn, and by December 1937 it had sketched out a rough outline of a report. The committee sent a copy to Archbishop Lang for review, but the archbishop declined to comment on the preliminary draft. He expressed a keen interest in the work, but he wrote in reply to the Rev. Professor L. W. Grensted, who sent Lang the report in the name of the committee, that "it would he wholly improper for me, to whom the Report is to be submitted, to make any comment upon its proceedings or to give any indications about what might or might not desire its report to be."[77] The archbishop ended by thanking Grensted for his time and effort and told the secretary that he would await the finished report with much interest.

In spite of most of the work being completed and a preliminary draft of a report already written, Bishop Underhill listened to Archbishop Lang's suggestion about the valuable assistance Baron Palmstierna might give the committee. Underhill, consequently, invited the baron to attend a séance with other members of the committee. This resolution and dedication to reach an objective understanding of spiritualism also demonstrated the seriousness of the committee in discharging its task. In addition to listening to witnesses, some members personally experienced examples of psychical phenomena such as the séance in question. In addition to Baron Palmstierna, W. R. Matthews (the dean of St. Paul's), Harold Anson (master of the temple), Mr. Sandlands, and Mr. Wiggleworth (secretary of the committee) represented the committee. Mr. and

Mrs. Fachiri and Miss d'Aranyi were in charge of the session. Once the initial communication (message) had been established, the master of the temple asked for information about his mother, and the reply told him that "questions of a personal nature we do not answer. It is not our work."[78] Responses to other questions proved more fruitful.

During the séance, the Very Rev. W. R. Matthews, the dean of St. Paul's, asked the communication what advice it could give to the committee on spiritualism. And Matthews received an answer to this query: "First of all we wish to make it clear to you that unless one is a believer in the love and the light of the Great One one cannot come into contact with us, not because we are exclusive, but because the wave-quality is out of harmony." What the committee was doing had value, Matthews was told, but the doubt or skepticism of some people tended to throw up walls between the "world of the spirits and earth." The message then moved to the area of theology and announced that "none of you is quite convinced about the purity of God," and because of this "weakness" He sent Jesus Christ to earth. Jesus "will bring you near the light of God." The communication also expressed an anxious desire "to associate with the clergy but they must be pure in every respect so as to be worthy of repeating the words of Jesus." When asked who was speaking, the communication refused to reveal an identity. Again, it cautioned those present about asking personal questions, changed the topic briefly to the resurrection of Jesus, and then continued to describe the requirements necessary to communicate successfully with the spirit world. "For you to recive [sic] coherent messages from a departed takes three earthly years . . . [and] Beware of those near earth who make fun of sacred things . . . That is the danger of spirit messages." Finally, one must have pure and honorable intentions.

Some other questions from the group followed. One person focused on the resurrection of Jesus and asked: "If Christ was raised on the third day was it His earthly material body or not?" The communication answered in the negative. A second question wondered whether "Christ . . . [was] supernaturally born or was He born of two parents like other people." According to the words of the message, which probably shocked some ears,

> He came down with the knowledge of what was expecting Him but this had to happen through earthly intercourse of two very pure loving souls. That the birth of Jesus was predicted to Mary in a dream is equally true. But the immaculate conception is all a legend. Beloved friends, we entreat you to meet as often as you can. We long for the church to join us. The time has come to reveal to mankind all that Jesus taught.

The notes of this meeting ended with the following observation. "Neither Miss d'A. nor Mr Fachiri or Baron Palmstierna touched the pointer during the meeting. Some of the present tried to receive messages without the aid of Mrs

Fachiri, but the pointer only made irregular movements in that case."[79] Another meeting of some members of the committee, which also included Baron Palmstierna, took place on 8 February 1938 again at the home of Mr. and Mrs. Fachiri. "The members present had had an opportunity of observing the method whereby Baron Palmstierna and Mrs. Fachiri had received communications by means of an inverted tumbler which spelt out messages by touching letters of the alphabet."[80]

As the work of the committee reached the end of its assigned task, many interested people became anxious about its findings and recommendations. Throughout the spring of 1938, several articles appeared in the press. Mr. E. W. Oaten, who had given evidence before the committee, asked W. R. Matthews, dean of St. Paul's, and Bishop Francis Underhill to write a letter for the press dealing with the committee's work on spiritualism. Bishop Underhill asked Archbishop Lang for advice, and Lang suggested that Bishop Underhill and the dean of St. Paul's compose an answer for Oaten, "pointing out that the Report of the Committee over which you [Bishop Underhill] preside has not yet been issued and advise people not to jump to conclusions beforehand, which may prove to be unwarranted."[81] A statement written by Bishop Underhill did appear in the 19 March edition of *Psychic News*, and began by noting that the committee "is investigating 'psychic phenomena'—not Spiritualism."[82] He denied press reports that "the Church is determined to fight Spiritualism." Hoping to dismiss cynics, Bishop Underhill stated that "the Commission consists of a number of men and women amply qualified to hear and weigh evidence," and "their sole aim is to arrive at the truth, and the work of the Commission proceeds without prejudice." The article ended by stating that no report "has yet been made to the Archbishop."

In spite of this statement, some believed that the report of the archbishop's committee would contain hostile remarks about spiritualism and warned of a possible witch hunt on the part of the ecclesiastical and civil authorities. "The Church plans war against Spiritualism, and clergymen who openly practise Spiritualism will be severely disciplined," one paper predicted.[83] "Legal proceedings will be instituted against certain mediums on the grounds of false presences. A nation-wide campaign will be undertaken to warn the public against the dangers of Spiritualism." The spiritualist paper which reprinted this particular story, *Prediction*, adopted a more objective approach to the work of the committee. It doubted whether "the Commission's views have been accurately presented" by some interested people.[84] The paper defended the hard work and the integrity of the archbishop's committee; however, the conclusions might still disappoint some Christian spiritualists. "Whether the Church will reject the 'philosophy' of Spiritualism is another matter entirely," the editorial stated, and "there are many who believe that the philosophy of Christianity contains all that is needful for the seeker after truth. The Commission may ignore the Spiritualists here." Regardless of the outcome, however, one must not forget "that the phenomena of Spiritualism when sifted of all that is fraudulent and deceptive, bear close resemblance to the 'miracles of Holy Writ.'"

By summer, it appeared that the committee had accomplished its task. The work of the committee was rapidly coming to an end. The last formal meeting of the archbishop's committee on spiritualism, as it was officially called, took place on 3 June 1938, with all members present except W. R. Matthews, Dr. William Brown, and Mrs. A. E. J. Rawlinson.[85] The committee approved the amended minutes of the last meeting, which took place on 21 January, accepted apologies from the absent members, and read two letters which offered additional information on the subject. The secretary also reported on Baron Palmstierna's notes of the meeting which had taken place at the Fachiri household on 8 February. And then the secretary, W. S. Wigglesworth, introduced the important point of business, the finished report. He told the members present that the drafting committee, which consisted of himself, the Rev. Guy Mayfield, and Professor Grensted, had met in early March. At that meeting, Grensted's preliminary report, which Archbishop Lang had earlier refused to comment upon, had been amended and shortened. Consequently, the members of the committee set out to consider the wording of this text.

The committee, however, failed to act in a unanimous fashion. The following members indicated their willingness to accept this draft as an acceptable text: Bishop Underhill, the dean of St. Paul's (Matthews), the master of the temple (Anson), Professor Grensted, Dr. Brown, Mr. Sandlands, and Lady Stephenson. The other members could not agree with some of the wording and conclusions, and consequently they proposed to draw up a minority report and forward it together with the report and conclusions of the majority to the archbishop of Canterbury. The entire committee, therefore, passed a resolution which stated:

> that these Reports be submitted to the Archbishop for his consideration and that he be asked to consider the advisability of bringing these Reports to the attention of the Bishop's [sic] at the next Bishops' Meeting, but that the submission of these Reports to the Archbishop should be postponed until after the receipt of any evidence submitted by Dr. Fodor [one of the individuals who offered to submit additional evidence for the consideration of the committee] in order that the Committee might have an opportunity of making any amendments which they thought necessary.

Finally, all members agreed that the question of publishing the report, which would eventually become an emotional and controversial issue, should be left to the discretion of the archbishop. After completing some other business, such as the costs of printing and publication, the archbishop's committee adjourned.

It was not until 1 November 1938, however, that the secretary of the committee, W. S. Wigglesworth, sent a summary of the final meeting to Lambeth

Palace. Wigglesworth went straight to the important point which had split the membership of the committee and created two opinions.

> The majority of the members (seven out of ten) were in favour of presenting a Report to the effect that, subject to certain safeguards, the Church should maintain some relations with Spiritualism, while the minority, consisting of the remaining three, recommended that the Church should not seek to establish any relations with Spiritualism.[86]

Wigglesworth then gave a brief outline of both the majority and minority reports. Revealing his own personal feelings, he described those who wrote the latter report as "malcontents." The secretary pointed out that the "reports are really in their final form but at our last meeting [3 June 1938] we received a letter from Dr. Nandor Fodor," research officer of the International Institute for Psychical Research, Ltd., who expressed a desire to appear before the committee.

The secretary devoted a large portion of this letter to Archbishop Lang about Fodor's evidence before the committee. Wigglesworth had asked Dr. Fodor to submit a short synopsis of the testimony he planned to give in person, and he would circulate this among the membership. The final report to Archbishop Lang, therefore, would not be sent until the committee had ample opportunity to consider this evidence. Unfortunately, and this appears to be the reason for the long time lapse between the last committee meeting and this letter, Dr. Fodor had failed to send any additional information immediately to the secretary. With the eventual addition of Fodor's evidence before the committee, this part of their work had come to an end. Wigglesworth, consequently, told Archbishop Lang that he "would like to bring the affairs of the Committee to a conclusion so far as possible." Speaking on behalf of the committee, the secretary recommended that the archbishop present both reports or conclusions to the bishops at the next Bishops' Meeting. He also wanted to know how many copies of the report should be made, and Lambeth Palace suggested that fifty-five copies should be printed before the end of the year. Archbishop Lang's secretary promised to circulate them "to the Bishops on the next occasion on which they will be meeting."[87]

If the members of the committee or the archbishop of Canterbury believed that the finished report would not become an emotional issue and would not contribute to additional controversies, the month of December 1938 quickly destroyed these illusions and also gave a preview of the furor which would eventually surround the question of its publication. In early December, an interested cleric, Canon L. W. Bird, wrote to Archbishop Lang and innocently asked, "What is holding up the publication of the Report on Spiritualism?"[88] The canon also hit on a point which would be repeated for the next several years by other interested parties. "Friend and foe seem agreed that the report is more favourable than the archbishop cares for," he suggested, "and being the shrewd man that he is, he is attempting to shelve it." This alleged ecclesiastical coverup quickly become a hot topic in both clerical and lay circles, and the official silence about the report and the delay in publication gave credence to this rumor. Bird explained that he would appreciate any advice or help the report might give, talked about his positive experiences with mediums, and confessed that he, like many others, needed assistance in the face of contradictory, heretical, or even laughable explanations of spiritualism.

The attitude of silence on the part of church officials did become an important issue. Archbishop Lang's secretary hurried off a letter to Mr. Wigglesworth, the secretary of the committee, and asked about a possible date of publication of the committee's report, telling the secretary that an individual had already written and suggesting "that the delay in issuing the Report is being interpreted in certain quarters as being due to objections raised by the Archbishop of Canterbury who is stated to be attempting to shelve it."[89] Wigglesworth replied to this letter and stated that the report would be ready for distribution by the end of December, and he also reminded Lang's secretary that he had already informed Lambeth Palace of this publication date in an earlier letter.[90] Mr. Wigglesworth also drew attention to the fact that Bishop Francis Underhill, the chairman of the committee, had been ordered to rest for three months by his doctor. After some final corrections, Wigglesworth promised that Archbishop Lang would receive his copy of the text as soon as possible. Armed with this information, Archbishop Lang's secretary wrote to Canon Bird and informed him that the report would "probably come out early in the year."[91] He also dismissed the rumors of an archiepiscopal conspiracy concerning the findings of the committee; Lang had no desire to "shelve it." In fact, the archbishop had not even read the report yet.

The timing of publication became an important and crucial issue for some interested individuals. The secretary, Wigglesworth, sensing that Lang wanted to see the finished product immediately, wrote again to Lambeth Palace. In this letter, he told the archbishop's secretary that with the exception of the bishop of Bath and Wells, Francis Underhill, all the members of the committee had the opportunity to study the proof of the report, and consequently the final and corrected draft of the report on spiritualism could be printed immediately. Wigglesworth explained that he did not want to trouble Bishop Underhill because of his illness, and had sounded out his chaplain about the Underhill's health. The chaplain's response cautioned Wigglesworth not to trouble Bishop Underhill at the present time but also noted that "the Bishop ought to see the Report before it is presented to the Archbishop."[92] This necessarily might mean another unavoidable and unwelcome delay. "Perhaps you will let me know," the secretary of the committee asked Lang's secretary, "whether the Archbishop thinks it more important for the Report to be presented now or for it to be seen again by the Chairman of the Committee [Bishop Underhill] before it is presented."

Archbishop Lang's response indicated that he saw no rush in having the report printed, and Lang also began to express some doubts about making its contents known to the general public. The archbishop told his secretary that Bishop Underhill should certainly see the report before the printer, and publication might have to wait until after the Bishops' Meeting in June 1939, nearly six months in the future. "Between ourselves," the archbishop wrote, "I think that it may be a matter for further consideration whether the Report even when it is printed ought to be published for the general public."[93] Publication would depend on the contents and conclusions of the report. The archbishop's secretary conveyed Lang's thoughts to Mr. Wigglesworth, especially the possibility of a delay in publication until the Bishops' Meeting in June, and asked that a copy of the report be sent to Archbishop Lang soon after Bishop Underhill had read and approved it. Underhill also agreed with this approach. He wrote to Archbishop Lang, told Lang that he was recuperating, and gave his approval to the delay. The bishops of the Anglican Church must have the opportunity to review and discuss the committee's findings. "The presentation of the report will be a difficult and intricate business," Bishop Underhill told the archbishop, "and I would very much rather its consideration was deferred until our meeting in June."[94] Both prelates, therefore, agreed to a delay and concurred that the report should be placed on the agenda of the June Bishops' Meeting. The archbishop did not have to wait long to examine the work of his committee. On 16 January 1939, Mr. W. S. Wigglesworth sent the finished printed copy of the report on spiritualism to Archbishop Lang.

Notes

1. See page 8-9.
2. D. Cannadine, "War and Death, Grief and Mourning in Modern Britain," 229.
3. G. Nelson, *Spiritualism and Society*, 161.
4. Ibid., 159.
5. Ibid., 159-60.
6. Ibid., 154.
7. Ibid., 161-62.
8. R. Kollar, "Prophecy, Anglicanism, and the Great War: The Archbishop of Canterbury and Joanna Southcott's Sealed Box," *Dutch Review of Church History* 78 (1998): 94-112.
9. R. Kollar, "The Church of England and Joanna Southcott: The Revelation of Her Secret Writings in 1927," *Journal of Religion and Psychical Studies* 22 (April 1999): 68-82.
10. G. Nelson, *Spiritualism and Society*, 147.

102   Chapter Three

11. Ibid., 148.
12. Ibid., 149-50.
13. Ibid., 161.
14. Ibid.
15. G. J. Cuming, *A History of Anglican Liturgy* (London: Macmillan, 1969), 233.
16. R. C. D. Jasper, *The Development of the Anglican Liturgy, 1662-1980* (London: SPCK, 1989), 130.
17. A. Hastings, *A History of English Christianity*, 204-8.
18. *Doctrine in the Church of England: The Report of the Commission on Christian Doctrine Appointed by the Archbishops of Canterbury and York*, 19. Bishop Burge of Oxford served as chairman of the commission until his death in 1925. He was succeeded as chairman by William Temple, bishop of Manchester.
19. Ibid., 213.
20. Ibid., 216.
21. *Psychic News*, 22 January 1938.
22. A. Hastings, *A History of English Christianity*, 261.
23. Adamson to Lang, 25 January 1934, Lang Papers, vol. 123, Lambeth Palace Library.
24. Don to Adamson, 2 February 1934, Lang Papers, vol. 123, Lambeth Palace Library.
25. For biographies of Archbishop Lang, see *The Dictionary of National Biography 1941-1950*; and J. G. Lockhart, *Cosmo Gordon Lang* (London: Hodder & Stoughton, 1949).
26. Macmillan to Lang, 27 November 1935, Lang Papers, vol. 133, Lambeth Palace Library. The Rev. G. Maurice Elliott continued to write in support of spiritualism. Pointing out the similarities between spiritualism and sacred Scripture, he argued that spiritualists were friends of the Anglican Church. "Should the Church Preach Spiritualism?" *Prediction*, September 1936, 341-42. His language became increasingly more hostile toward traditional Christianity. In 1937, for example, he maintained that if spiritualism was accepted by Anglicanism, "there would be a revolution in the Church's beliefs and teaching." In addition to some drastic changes in the doctrines of the church, the prestige of priests would also suffer. "If the Church Accepted Spiritualism," *Prediction*, September 1937, 357.
27. Don to Macmillan, 4 December 1935, Lang Papers, vol. 133, Lambeth Palace Library.
28. Macmillan to Don, 5 December 1935, Lang Papers, vol. 133, Lambeth Palace Library.
29. Underhill to Lang, 27 January 1936, Lang Papers, vol. 70, Lambeth Palace Library. The personal and official papers of Francis Underhill (1878-1949) could not be located. Educated at Shrewsbury School and Exeter College, Oxford, he served as dean of Rochester from 1932 to 1939, and following this he was bishop of Bath and Wells until his death.
30. Resolution of the Dean of Rochester on Spiritualism, 10 July 1935, Lang Papers, vol. 70, Lambeth Palace Library.
31. The Dean of Rochester suggested the following as possibilities: the bishops of Ely, Carlisle, Liverpool, Lincoln, Croydon, and Chichester; the deans of St. Paul's and Liverpool, the archdeacon of London, the master of the temple; and Professor Charles Raven, Professor L. W. Grensted, Dr. Perkin (sacristan of Westminster Abbey), Sir

Walter Moberly (University of Manchester), Dr. Pickard (Cambridge University), Dr. Cyril Bailey, Sir Raymond Beazley, Mr. A. Clifton Kelway, Lord Mamhead, Sir Michael Sadler, Mr. F. C. Eeles, William Brown, Lady Bridgeman, one of the Misses Gregory, Miss Evelyn Underhill, Miss C. M. Ady, Mrs. Rawlinson, Miss Sybil Thesiger, Mrs. Wordsworth, Mrs. Guy Rogers, Mrs. Smith-Marriott.

32. Don to Underhill, 3 February 1936, Lang Papers, vol. 70, Lambeth Palace Library.

33. Underhill to Lang, 4 February 1936, Lang Papers, vol. 70, Lambeth Palace Library.

34. Wilkinson wanted the Anglican Church to study spiritualism in an objective manner, and he argued that the church should at least know what spiritualism professed before it was dismissed. "So the purpose of this book," he argued, "is primarily to urge that it is a subject which should be investigated with an open mind, and should not be condemned without being understood, nor run away from because there are dangers in it." D. H. D. Wilkinson, *A Christian Searchlight on Spiritualism* (London: Hillside Press, 1935), 3. He also recognized the influence of the First World War on the growth and popularity of spiritualism: "The movement was on the increase before the Great War, but the appalling sorrows, the heartrending bereavements and the shattered hopes of those sad years, gave a further great impetus to it." Ibid., 17.

35. Underhill to Lang, 7 February 1936, Lang Papers, vol. 70, Lambeth Palace Library. In addition to the earlier list, Underhill also suggested Dr. William Brown, "one of the most important and learned psychologists," Doctors Dudley and L. Copper Johnson, "medical men who have had wide experience," Professor Fraser, a physiologist better known in Canada, and Miss Nea Walker, who was the secretary to Sir Oliver Lodge. Underhill also drew Archbishop Lang's attention to a Colonel Clarke, Mrs. Forman, and Miss Stevenson, and noted that "these had years of experience . . . but very cautious and know all the difficulties." The dean again mentioned Mrs. Smith-Marriott, whom he described as "a good Churchwomen, also clairvoyant and a trance medium but financially quite independent."

36. Don to Underhill, 11 February 1936, Lang Papers, vol. 70, Lambeth Palace Library.

37. Don to Underhill, 13 February 1936, Lang Papers, vol. 70, Lambeth Palace Library.

38. Underhill to Lang, 6 March 1936, Lang Papers, vol. 70, Lambeth Palace Library.

39. "Psychic Phenomena with Reference to the Christian Tradition," Lang Papers, vol. 70, 1.

40. Ibid., 2.

41. Ibid., 2-3.

42. Ibid., 4.

43. The author gave a brief description and explanation of the following: trance phenomena, direct voice, clairvoyance and clairaudience, exteriorisation, automatic writing, materialization, healing, photographic evidence, psychometry, telekinesis, hauntings, impersonations, the evil side, mysticism, evidential communications, and descriptions of the other world.

44. "Psychic Phenomena with Reference to the Christian Tradition," 20.

45. Ibid., 24.

46. Don to Underhill, 11 March 1936, Lang Papers, vol. 70, Lambeth Palace Library.
47. Temple to Lang, 23 March 1936, Lang Papers, vol. 70, Lambeth Palace Library.
48. Don to Temple, 24 March 1936, Lang Papers, vol. 70, Lambeth Palace Library.
49. Temple to Don, 25 March 1936, Lang Papers, vol. 70, Lambeth Palace Library.
50. "Spiritualism," Lang Papers, vol. 70, Lambeth Palace Library.
51. Underhill to Lang, 26 June 1936, Lang Papers, vol. 70, Lambeth Palace Library.
52. Lang to Underhill, 27 June 1936, Lang Papers, vol. 70, Lambeth Palace Library.
53. Bishops' Meetings, 1932-1938, BM 10, Lambeth Palace Library.
54. Don to Underhill, 31 July 1936, Lang Papers, vol. 70, Lambeth Palace Library.
55. "Spiritualism," August 1936, Lang Papers, vol. 70, Lambeth Palace Library.
56. Underhill to Lang, 11 August 1936, Lang Papers, vol. 70, Lambeth Palace Library.
57. E. Underhill to Underhill, 9 August 1936, Lang Papers, vol. 70, Lambeth Palace Library.
58. Don to Underhill, 13 August 1936, Lang Papers, vol. 70, Lambeth Palace Library.
59. Underhill to Don, 3 October 1936, Lang Papers, vol. 70, Lambeth Palace Library. The two additional people, suggested by the master of the temple, were the archdeacon of Kingston, the Venerable G. H. Marten, and Mrs. Sitwell of Barmoor Castle, Northumberland. Dean Francis Underhill admitted that he did not know either of these individuals.
60. "Proposed Committee on Spiritualism," 16 October 1936, Lang Papers, vol. 70, Lang Papers, Lambeth Palace Library.
61. Lang to Underhill, 31 October 1936, Lang Papers, vol. 70, Lambeth Place Library.
62. Underhill to Lang, 4 November 1936, Lang Papers, vol. 70, Lambeth Palace Library.
63. Invitation, 20 November 1936, Lang Papers, vol. 70, Lambeth Palace Library.
64. Raven to Lang, 25 November 1938, Lang Papers, vol. 70, Lambeth Palace Library.
65. E. Underhill to Lang, 24 November 1936, Lang Papers, vol. 70, Lambeth Palace Library.
66. Don to Underhill, 8 December 1936, Lang Papers, vol. 70, Lambeth Palace Library.
67. Anson to Lang, 12 December 1936, Lang Papers, vol. 70, Lambeth Palace Library.
68. Don to Stephenson, 14 December 1936, Lang Papers, vol. 70, Lambeth Palace Library.
69. *Archbishop's Committee on Spiritualism: Report of the Committee to the Archbishop of Canterbury* (1939), printed in *The Christian Parapsychologist* 3 (March 1979): 40-41.

Psychical Studies, the Crisis of Faith, and the Anglican Church 105

70. Temple to Don, 27 February 1937, Lang Papers, vol. 70, Lambeth Palace Library.
71. Don to Temple, 1 March 1937, Lang Papers, vol. 70, Lambeth Palace Library.
72. For the testimony of these witnesses, see the discussion of the completed report in chapter four. By June 1938, records indicate that twelve meetings of the committee had taken place.
73. Lang to Underhill, 23 November 1937, Lang Papers, vol. 70, Lambeth Palace Library.
74. E. K. Palmstierna, *Horizons of Immortality: A Quest for Reality* (London: Constable, 1937).
75. Palmstierna to Lang, 25 November 1937, Lang Papers, vol. 70, Lambeth Palace Library.
76. E. K. Palmstierna, *"Horizons of Immortality" and The Subconscious Mind*, Lang Papers, vol. 70, Lambeth Palace Library, 94-95.
77. Lang to Grensted, 11 December 1937, Lang Papers, vol. 70, Lambeth Palace Library. The typescript which Lang received was essentially the same as the final *Report of the Committee to the Archbishop of Canterbury* (1939).
78. Meeting, Netherton Grove, 14 January 1938, Lang Papers, vol. 70, Lambeth Palace Library.
79. Two days after the 14 January meeting, other messages arrived which made references to the earlier gathering. There is no indication that members of the committee on spiritualism were present to experience this communication. The message expressed an interest in having clergy present, and if they could not attend, the messages and information should be sent to them. This message contained some clarifications on the earlier interpretation of the resurrection. Once the "spirit left the body the body was not quite the same as before." Jesus "represented the absolute purity and finally He raised His body with Himself." It stated, "Of course He was divine but He was not God." Again, the message addressed the clergy: "We want the clergy to ask the clergy not to permit any films in the churches but to have personal discussions and then prayers together. If the clergy would harken to what we say their churches would not be empty. They must also refrain from keeping their churches closed at any hour whether day or night."
80. Minutes, Archbishop's Committee on Spiritualism, 3 June 1938, Lang Papers, vol. 70, Lambeth Palace Library.
81. Don to Underhill 26 February 1938, Lang Papers, vol. 70, Lambeth Palace Library.
82. *Psychic News*, 19 March 1938.
83. Quoted in *Prediction* (London), April 1938.
84. Ibid.
85. Minutes, Archbishop's Committee on Spiritualism, 3 June 1938, Lang Papers, vol. 70, Lambeth Palace Library.
86. Wigglesworth to Don, 1 November 1938, Lang Papers, vol. 70, Lambeth Palace Library.
87. Don to Wigglesworth, 9 November 1938, Lang Papers, vol. 70, Lambeth Palace Library.
88. Bird to Lang, 7 December 1938, Lang Papers, vol. 70, Lambeth Palace Library.

89. Don to Wigglesworth, 9 December 1938, Lang Papers, vol. 70, Lambeth Palace Library.

90. Wigglesworth to Don, 14 December 1938, Lang Papers, vol. 70, Lambeth Palace Library.

91. Don to Bird, 16 December 1938, Lang Papers, vol. 70, Lambeth Palace Library.

92. Wigglesworth to Don, December 1938, Lang Papers, vol. 70, Lambeth Palace Library.

93. Lang to Don, 21 December 1938, Lang Papers, vol. 70, Lambeth Palace Library.

94. Underhill to Lang, 30 December 1938, Lang Papers, vol. 70, Lambeth Palace Library.

Chapter Four

The Archbishop's Committee on Spiritualism: The 1939 Report of the Committee to the Archbishop of Canterbury

Appointed by the archbishop of Canterbury in January 1937, this committee under the chairmanship of Francis Underhill, the bishop of Bath and Wells since autumn 1938, finally produced a statement, consisting of a majority and minority report (appendix 2 and 3), which explored the relationship between Christianity and spiritualism. This report represented the first in-depth study of spiritualism through the eyes of the Anglican Church. Witnesses gave evidence, conclusions were reached, and recommendations were put forward. The report received its first crucial hearing at the June Bishops' Meeting, and following this reception an increasing number of interested persons attacked Archbishop Lang for adopting a policy of secrecy or silence about the material contained in the report. Through letters and articles in the press and direct appeals to the archbishop of Canterbury, these curious and concerned individuals campaigned, although unsuccessfully, for the immediate publication of the report. The reaction to Lang's decision to embargo the committee's conclusions also demonstrates the anxiety felt by some churchmen about its findings and the popularity of spiritualism in some religious circles. The decision not to publish, therefore, attracted as much attention as the contents of the report itself.

Lambeth Palace acknowledged the reception of the report on spiritualism from W. S. Wigglesworth, secretary of the committee, on 23 January 1939. Lang's secretary also requested an additional fifty-five copies of the report, which he would distribute to the bishops before their June meeting. By the end of the month, Archbishop Lang had read the report and then wrote a rather long letter to the chairman of the committee, Bishop Francis Underhill of Bath and Wells. Lang apologized for failing to read the report sooner, but assured Bishop Underhill that he had recently studied it with great interest and care. The archbishop then expressed his thanks and gratitude to the bishop and his committee for the time and energy they had devoted to spiritualism, "this difficult subject."[1] Archbishop Lang then began to give his personal impressions of the report. In the first place, "it seems to me to give a very useful and impartial account of Spiritualism as a movement and of the various phenomena with which Spiritualism deals." The archbishop did admit that he found it difficult at times to distinguish between the evidence per se, which the report contained, and the comments made about the evidence.

Archbishop Lang's emphasis, however, dealt with the findings of the report. "As to the conclusions of the majority, interesting and valuable as they are," he told Bishop Underhill, "you must forgive me if I am somewhat disappointed." And he proceeded to outline his major critiques and concerns. In the first place, the archbishop took exception to the style and the presentation of report's conclusions: "I wish they could have been expressed with greater clearness of language and in a more systematic way." The elusiveness and the difficulty of the subject, he admitted, probably contributed to his concerns. Two conclusions brought some disapproval from the archbishop's pen. Lang questioned the encouragement given to individuals "who resort to the methods of Spiritualism," especially when it was followed by the admission in the next conclusion "that there is every probability that this assurance of personal contact cannot involve assurance of the accuracy and the authority of the messages involved." The archbishop pointed out the apparent danger to Bishop Underhill. "I fear that many people would be more inclined to act upon the measure of encouragement which your Conclusions give them than to pay heed to the warnings which they contain."

Although Lang admittedly found some faults with the wording and the conclusions of the minority report, the archbishop more importantly could not forget or dismiss his questions about the conclusions of the majority. "But I confess I wish that the Report of the Majority had laid greater stress upon the dangers awaiting individuals who may be inclined to dabble in Spiritualist methods and who have not the necessary powers of discrimination or the weighing of evidence." The archbishop of Canterbury, however, clearly recognized the positive aspects of both reports, especially the stress both the majority and minority positions gave to the importance of the belief in the communion of saints. The question of making the report public also surfaced. Drawing attention again to his concerns about the report, Archbishop Lang pointed out that the issue of publication "raises many difficult issues about which I must consult the bishops when the Report is brought before them at their next meeting" in June.

Bishop Francis Underhill wrote and thanked Archbishop Lang for his comments and questions about the report on spiritualism. Underhill confessed that the committee did indeed face a difficult and burdensome task. The number of meetings, in the first place, had presented several problems, but Bishop Underhill also confessed that he "was constantly beset and much abused by many spiritualist cranks."[2] Underhill acknowledged Lang's criticisms and promised that he would reread the report in light of them. Publication of the report also occupied Bishop Underhill's thoughts. "I confess I should dread it from my own point of view," he told the archbishop, "for I can well imagine the spate of letters which will descend upon me." The bishop ended his letter to the archbishop with the hope that the Bishops' Meeting would offer some useful suggestions and modifications which would make the report more acceptable to them. Bishop Underhill also understood that as chairman of the committee he would present the report at the meeting of the bishops in June.

The report on spiritualism, which would receive its first public and formal scrutiny at the Bishops' Meeting, represented a comprehensive document on the relationship of Christianity and spiritualism. It contained an opening statement, introductory observations agreed upon by all members of the committee, the evidence of witnesses and experts, and finally the conclusions of the majority and the minority.[3] The preliminary remarks of the report immediately drew attention to the charge of the committee, namely, "to investigate the subject of communications with discarnate spirits and the claims of Spiritualism in relation to the Christian Faith."[4] These introductory statements also informed the reader of the origin of the committee, which had emerged out of a motion of the church assembly in 1936, noted that the committee had met twelve times, and that subgroups had also gathered to discuss particular points. The loss of Miss Evelyn Underhill, it acknowledged, was a serious blow to the work of the committee, and the report reprinted her reasons for resignation.

Part 2 of the report contained some general remarks agreed upon by all the members of the committee. The Anglican Church, it stated, could no longer avoid or dismiss spiritualism as a fluke. "In recent years," this section of the report began, "Spiritualism has aroused great interest in all sections of the community."[5] "In its more public manifestations it is a popular movement of wide extent." In addition to numerous publications dealing with psychic phenomena and the increasing information coming from spiritualist organizations, several so-called spiritualist churches have been constituted, and "Spiritualism as a whole claims to have a religious character, and must be held to be a religious force." People tended to gravitate toward spiritualism for three reasons: by establishing communication with discarnate spirits, the bereaved hoped to receive consolation; messages from the spirit world might provide guidance; and finally spiritualism offered more proof of the survival after death than traditional religions. Reports from the Anglican clergy, moreover, confirmed this steady drift of the faithful into the arms of spiritualism. "Some break away from the fellowship and worship of the Church altogether," these churchmen maintained, and "others, who remain loyal to their membership of the Church, supplement their religious experience through the practice of Spiritualism." The writers of the report disavowed any intention of pursuing a "full investigation of the character and claims of Spiritualism." This, they argued, would consume an enormous amount of time and effort, and the nature of the subject was too complex to be investigated by the members of the archbishop's committee. Even the use of scientific methods could not unravel the mysteries of the subject. Science, moreover, could not begin to study the relationship of spiritualism to Christian beliefs; it "is this special need that we [the committee] have had in mind in this Report."

The report next talked about an appropriate and acceptable definition of spiritualism. The members found fault with the wording contained in the *Shorter Oxford Dictionary*, which saw spiritualism exclusively as a belief. In the minds of most people, certain practices were also associated with doctrines and creeds. The proper relationship of these activities to traditional Christianity also proved to be problematic. With these difficulties in mind, the committee defined spiritualism in the following terms: "Spiritualism is a belief, with attendant practices, that the spirits of the dead can hold communication with the living, or make their presence known to them, through mediums and in other ways which are not a part of the accepted Christian tradition." Not all spiritualists, however, would accept this definition. One witness, Miss Mercy Phillimore, secretary of the London Spiritualist Alliance and the Quest Club, took exception. For her,

> Spiritualism means the demonstrated survival of human personality after bodily death. It includes the knowledge of the interaction of matter and spirit. Further, it implies a comprehension of the intelligent progressive spiritual principle which underlies the whole of creation, of mankind and nature in this present life, and of continuous individual progressive life in the hereafter.

The committee took exception with Miss Phillimore's description of spiritualism. Her definition stressed the survival of the human personality after death to such a point that it fell far short of the Christian understanding of immortality, "and must be clearly distinguished therefrom, as survival after bodily death is not necessarily identical with immortality." Another shortcoming, the members of the committee noticed, was the fact that this definition stressed knowledge rather than the realm of faith. Consequently, Phillimore's position shared more in common with Gnosticism and Christian Science than with the traditional Christian beliefs. "It would not necessarily mean that a Christian cannot be a Spiritualist . . . but if this definition is accepted, it does mean that Spiritualism cannot be regarded as a religion in the same sense as that in which Christianity is a religion." In addition to having serious religious or theological shortcomings, this alternative definition would have to accept certain standards of science, and this raises "serious difficulties of proof which many Spiritualists do not seem to face at all adequately."

The report, in addition to its accepted definition of spiritualism, also chose to view spiritualism is several ways. In the first place, it possessed the characteristics "of a system with numerous adherents with many of the elements of a cult, or even of a religion." Spiritualists, moreover, have constructed a philosophical system which deals with the universe and the future destiny of human beings. And finally, adherents to the beliefs and practices of spiritualism have succeeded in collecting and accepting facts "which fall outside the normal range of our experience." Tracing its development from the experience of the Fox sisters in 1848, the report pointed out that spiritualism enjoyed a relatively recent history, but its development has nonetheless been rapid. Public interest grew; mediums, both honest and fraudulent, multiplied; and the Society for Psychical Research tried to assess and judge the validity of psychical phenomena. The report again relied on the testimony of Miss Phillimore for an evaluation of spiritualism in England during the 1930s. According to her interpretation,

> Spiritualist societies and individual Spiritualists hold widely divergent views upon particular mediums, psychic phenomena, and on the presentation of Spiritualism and allied subjects. There is unanimity of opinion on one point only, and that is the critical point, namely the proof of the survival of human personality, and the accompanying knowledge as expressed in my definition of the word "Spiritualism."

Spiritualism and its followers, therefore, could not be stereotyped or conveniently fit into any mold or category. The relationship of spiritualism with Christianity also varied from person to person and from group to group. Some believed "that they possess the means of amplifying and confirming the Christian revelation." On the other hand, "Others are neutral, and regard the practice of Spiritualism as a religion in itself to which Christianity may or may not be relevant." And finally a minority of spiritualists have expressed an open hostility to the beliefs and practices of Christianity. One common thread between the spiritualists and the Christians, however, did exist: "there is a very widespread resentment at the refusal of the Church to accept the evidence offered and to endorse the general teaching of Spiritualism."

The report also attempted to estimate the size and the number of spiritualist societies and organizations throughout the country. The secretary of the Spiritualists' National Union supplied the statistics. According to his information, "the Union had affiliated to it some 520 societies distributed over the whole of Great Britain, in each of which a purely religious service was held at least once every Sunday, while in the majority two or sometimes three services were held." The secretary estimated that at least twice as many more meetings took place each Sunday under the auspices of organizations not associated with the Spiritualists' National Union. He estimated the attendance at Sunday "services" for those churches affiliated with the union at 90,000, and he set the figure of those attending the churches associated with the other groups at 160,000.[6] The common denominator of the various spiritualist organizations, the report noted, was the belief, which closely approximated some Christian tenets, in the "Seven Principles of Spiritualism": the fatherhood of God, the brotherhood of man, the communion of spirits and the ministry of the angels, the "continuous existence of the human soul, Personal Responsibility," the compensation "and retribution here or hereafter for all good and evil deeds done on earth," and the possibility of eternal progress for every soul. Some people, on the other hand, did not enjoy any formal connection with a spiritualist organization or church but nonetheless did believe that they had experienced some contact or communication with their departed loved ones. The report acknowledged that these types of personal experiences, although not as well publicized as some others, should not be dismissed as insignificant.

The topic of psychic phenomena, naturally, concerned the thinking of the committee, and the report addressed this area. According to the findings of the report, the "Spiritualist movement depends . . . upon the validity of the hypothesis that it offers definite proof of survival and the means of communication with the spirits of those who have passed through death to 'the other side.'" These messages or communications might come, for example, through the medium at the sitting by means of "table-turning," the planchette, or the Ouija board. The committee unanimously recognized that messages obtained in this fashion were usually incomplete or fragmentary. When a complete or understandable communication did appear, however, the problem became the interpretation, an issue which the committee did not address. Finally, the committee printed a general survey of the varieties of psychic phenomena from the pages of the manuscript, *Psychic Phenomena with Reference to the Christian Tradition*, which Bishop Underhill had given Archbishop Lang for consideration and which in turn had been distributed to the members of the committee.[7]

After these general comments and observations dealing with the question of psychic phenomena, the committee turned to the question of their validity. Were they authentic? The majority of spiritualists, the report noted, accepted the reality of communication with the departed "but are very critical of the evidence for the more bizarre forms of paranormal phenomena." A conservative interpretation, however, could be detected in several spiritualist circles. According to the report,

> the better spiritualist organizations are extremely cautious both in the acceptance of evidence and in the recommendation of mediums, and continually insist that it is only when mediums and sitters are of sincere purpose and high character that results of value can be gained.

Despite some problems such as the knowledge of the conditions of the sitting and the exact nature of the tests used, the committee also recognized that it "is of great importance in estimating the relation of Spiritualism to Christianity to note that the evidence upon which its claims rest lies very largely within the sphere of scientific observation and investigation."

Emphasizing the distinction between fact and hypothesis, the committee raised some questions about certain phenomena. Telekinesis, materializations, spirit photographs, clairvoyance and clairaudience, and telepathy represented "simply groups of facts, capable of attestation by witnesses, and of verification through the occurrence of other and similar facts." On the other hand, ectoplasm, the astral body, planes of existence, and the "'controls' and 'communicators,' which apparently make use of mediums, are rather hypotheses rather than facts." The trance state, closely related to hypnotism, belonged properly to the field of psychology. What, then, was the relation between fact and hypothesis and the Christian beliefs or teachings? The report conveyed the feeling of the members in straightforward and succinct language. "We regard it as of the first importance to note that neither scientific facts nor scientific hypotheses, as such, involve any questions for Christian doctrines," it pointed out, and it "is no business of Christians either to oppose them or to accept them lightly." The report urged serious and scientific study, arguing that "no sphere of truth lies outside the truth of God himself." One should adopt the same attitude to psychical phenomena as the individual who approached or studied any other type of scientific happenings.

But what about the question of Christian revelation? Did spiritualism participate in direct, divine, or spiritual revelation? On the one hand, some might argue that any "evidence of survival is truly a revelation." A medium might make an interpretation, and the evidence might fall outside the realm of the scientific. But, on the other hand, other individuals pointed out that psychic happenings did fall "strictly within the sphere of scientific hypothesis or fact." Certain teachings of spiritualism depended on mediums or "guides," and, consequently, certain schools of thought attached the notion of revelation to aspects of spiritualism. The report, therefore, had to address two questions and then formulate an answer: "what elements in Spiritualism are of this character, and what are the principles of spiritual verification which ought to be applied to them."

The committee's report conceded that the main beliefs of spiritualism "should be regarded as claiming this kind of authority": the survival of the human personality after death and its power to communicate with the living, the progressive movement or development through a hierarchy of planes after death, the law of love, "and the principle that the consequences of our conduct here and hereafter cannot be averted." Other tenets associated with spiritualism, since they cannot be proved or rejected by science, also "must have the character of revelation." The report then listed a series of so-called "useful and evidential communications from the spirit world," such as the "wickedness of suicide," directions or guidelines on cremation, the notion that "no one is alone at death but is then and immediately afterwards accompanied and assisted by others . . . [and] such help is made easier and more effective if there has been communication with friends and relations who have passed on," a guide or guardian angel watches over the living, and the "spirits of still-born children grow up in the next world."[8] This section of the report ended by reminding the reader that the "fundamental truth and principles of Christianity are our sufficient guide and strength," and not the above "useful and evidential communications from the spirit world." Moreover, it strongly stated, "We have already, in Jesus Christ and in His Church, all that we need to direct us 'in the way that leadeth to eternal life.'"

An important aspect of the deliberations of the archbishop's committee on spiritualism centered on listening to the testimony of witnesses and experts. Guarding the anonymity of the individuals who appeared before the committee, the report printed the extracts of the testimony of nine witnesses. (The report of the committee, however, identified the witnesses who gave evidence by letters of the alphabet.) Miss Mercy Phillimore, secretary of the London Spiritualist Alliance and the Quest Club, gave a definition of spiritualism, which the committee had printed in the text, and then she began to speak about "the bearing of Spiritualism on Christianity."[9] In the first place, "Spiritualism proves that man is a soul having a body, and not *vice versa* . . . [and] at death there is no sudden break or cessation of life, or memory, or affection." Moreover, mental and psychical phenomena demonstrated "the immanence of God." Spiritualism, she argued, also stressed another important Christian principle, namely, personal responsibility for one's earthly actions.

Phillimore then directed her attention to specific Christian beliefs. In respect to the resurrection, she pointed out that the "physical phenomena of Spiritualism show laws of nature rarely seen in operation." Consequently, she continued, these "offer a rational explanation of the Resurrection." Commenting on the existence of miracles, Miss Phillimore argued that psychical happenings associated with spiritualism again offered a logical parallel. Thus, biblical miracles could become more believable to doubters or cynics. Spiritualism, like Christianity, emphasized the value and worth of every human being, especially the soul. This line of argumentation pointed to a picture of a personal and loving God, which was no stranger to traditional Christian thought. Finally, she introduced the subject of inspiration and maintained that "Spiritualism proves that all human minds may be enlightened by the Divine Spirit." After making several other brief comments on psychical phenomena, the witness concluded by saying that individuals who experienced help and consolation in traditional religions would not be drawn to spiritualism. "People, however, who did not believe in any religion have found it a step towards a religious life, for Spiritualism is capable of demonstrating a rational and practical basis for the Christian faith." Phillimore believed that the Anglican Church would benefit greatly and be strengthened if its leaders could find a way of incorporating or adopting aspects of spiritualist teachings and practices.

Dame Edith Lyttelton, Witness B,[10] sent her written statement to the committee. It concluded that "psychical research supported and strengthened the religious sense and the Christian religion."[11] Moreover, Dame Edith believed that the spiritualist "claims to certain visions, communications and materialisations do not, if they are properly understood, weaken the evidence for direct revelations by saints and prophets." Likening her own experiences of psychic communication to forms of Christian meditation, she argued that messages ultimately came from the Holy Spirit. Finally, Dame Edith made a plea that the Anglican clergy should teach "people to use their 'curious mental powers.'" The next witness, Kenneth Richmond, a member of the Society for Psychical Research, spoke from the psychological point of view. If wisely developed and used, psychic faculties could have a positive influence on people's lives. But "Spiritualism cannot be joined to the Church in any way," he argued. However, church officials should "recognise Spiritualism and leave it to the clergy to condemn or bless as they think fit." Richmond recognized that communication with discarnate spirits presented proof for immortality, and could thus offer support and succor for the bereaved. Spiritualism might, therefore, strengthen a weak or doubting faith. "Evidence cannot supersede faith," he concluded, "but it is becoming a body of fact to which those who need it consider that they should have a right of access."

Witness D, described by the report as a typical Anglican, was the Hon. Mr. Justice Atkinson. A skeptic of spiritualism at first, he became attracted to its teachings and practices after the death of his daughter in 1930. During numerous sittings, Atkinson reported that he had received several communications from her. Commenting on the effect that spiritualism had on his life, "the witness said that until he studied Spiritualism he was beginning to lose interest in religion because he did not hear anything that he had not heard many times before." It had also given him a renewed interest in matters spiritual. The next testimony came from E. W. Oaten, the editor of *Two Worlds*, who told the committee that during the past five years, he had attended over 1,000 séances at which he had witnessed numerous examples of psychic phenomena. Oaten said that he had been a spiritualist for approximately forty years, and during that time "he had never known a single moment of doubt concerning the love and purpose of God or the actuality of a spiritual world; he had not felt the need of any other religion."

On the other hand, a longtime member of the Society for Psychical Research, Dr. William Brown, not to be confused with the member of the archbishop's committee with the same name, gave a negative view of spiritualism and any benefit it might have for Christianity. This witness critiqued certain physical phenomena such as telekinesis, ectoplasm, materialization, and spirit photography as fraudulent or based on faulty human observation. Brown admitted that other phenomena could not be easily dismissed, but the possibility of dishonesty still persisted; moreover, science could prove the reality of psychical research. In respect to the relation of spiritualism to religion, he argued that "Spiritualism had little or no value from the point of view of religion, or as a means of conversion to the Christian faith." Brown's final comment on the subject contained a harsh verdict: "Religion must avoid being compromised by Spiritualism which is beset with unsatisfactory elements."

The committee heard from three additional witnesses. Another critical view came from Dr. Oliver Gatty (Witness G), sometime Fellow and Natural Science Tutor of Balliol College, Oxford, and Bedford Lecturer in Physical Chemistry. According to the report, "he has no belief in Spiritualism." His numerous years of experiments have "nowhere demonstrated the existence of paranormal phenomena." Baron E. K. Palmstierna, Witness H, gave evidence based on his recent writings. The committee, however, decided not to print his testimony but referred interested parties to his books. Dr. Nandor Fodor, research officer of the International Institute for Psychical Research, Ltd., was the final witness. Pointing out that "Spiritualism is based on professional mediumship," Fodor argued that the "so-called phenomena of Spiritualism are at least in 99 per cent of cases due to conscious and unconscious fraud." "The majority of Spiritualists are unable to judge the value of evidence." Problems and difficulties did exist, but the witness maintained that "the Church would make an error in taking an attitude of condemnation." "Spiritualism does tend to make its believers Christians," he concluded, and the "Church should have deep concern in the means of its appeal." The section of the report dealing with the evidence ended by acknowledging that all members of the committee had attended at least one séance and had acquired additional knowledge of the subject either by years of experience or by reading and research.

At this stage, the report noted, the committee on spiritualism was in the position to present its findings and make recommendations, but it became apparent that two different positions or interpretations had been formed. A majority and minority list of conclusions, therefore, were both attached to the official report. The former, endorsed by Bishop Francis Underhill of Bath and Wells, W. R. Matthews, Harold Anson, L. W. Grensted, William Brown, P. E. Sandlands, and Lady Gwendolen Stephenson, began by speaking about the inherent difficulties associated with messages, communications, mediums, and the related problems of verification or interpretation.[12] This majority view then addressed the question of the relationship between spiritualism and Christianity. It did not accept fully the contention of some individuals that spiritualism "in many cases re-affirms the highest convictions of religious peoples, and that it has brought many to a new assurance of the truth of teaching which had ceased to have any meaning for them." Some spiritualists did openly profess anti-Christian positions. The majority of the committee members did not believe that spiritualism had added anything new or significant to religious truths, and moreover some alleged communications came across to them as juvenile. Even spiritualism's clear and strong emphasis on love seemed to "fall very far below the full teaching of the Christian Gospel, seeming to depend rather upon some power of working a miracle or materialisation." In spite of these reservations, the majority conclusion pointed out some positive aspects.

> Nevertheless, it is clearly true that the recognition of the nearness of our friends who have died, and of their progress in the spiritual life, and of their continuing concern for us, cannot do otherwise, for those who have experienced it, than add a new immediacy and richness to their belief in the Communion of Saints.

Consequently, no compelling reason existed "why the Church should regard this vital and personal enrichment of one of her chief doctrines with disfavour, so long as it does not distract Christians from their fundamental gladness," which comes from fellowship in Jesus Christ. The majority position continued to explore the relationship between spiritualism and Christianity, especially the arguments of many spiritualists that a close and intimate connection between the two existed. The similarities with the Bible could not be brushed aside so easily. Some spiritualists claimed that many of the supernatural events which the Gospels recorded represented nothing more than psychic phenomena, and moreover "the evidence for the paranormal occurrences . . . confirms the historicity of the Gospel records." The biblical miracles and the healings, for example, paralleled the activities of contemporary mediums. Finally, some spiritualists argued that if Christians rejected the existence or the reality of psychic phenomena, then certain parts of the Gospel message were also discredited.

The majority report of the committee attempted to answer these serious challenges. One could not deny the parallels and similarities between some spiritualist teachings and practices and those found in the Bible. The report also stated that scientific methods could not possibly verify the Gospel miracles and the resurrection. "We must therefore ask what the proper Christian grounds of belief in these central truths of Christianity are." Christianity rested on faith, and not "demonstrable scientific knowledge." According to the thinking of the majority, "Our grounds for this faith are to be found either in a direct mystical assurance that Jesus of Nazareth, as we have received Him, is indeed God's Word to us, or, more broadly, in the apprehension of ethical and spiritual values." One should not accept the Gospel message because of miracles or other wondrous activities, but because it appealed to one's deepest spiritual self. In spite of these words of caution, however, one should not dismiss spiritualism lightly. The majority of the members recognized that parts of spiritualism were "not properly capable of scientific verification or dispute, but, at the same time, as deserving the consideration of Christians upon grounds of another kind."

The committee could not honestly avoid the question of science, which since the nineteenth century had enjoyed a stormy or tense relationship with the teachings of traditional Christian beliefs. Science, and its attendant methodology, must not be seen as the panacea, especially in the discussion of the survival of the human personality after death. One could also not disregard the Christian insistence on faith. In respect to spiritualism, the majority conclusion stated, "It is thus a weakness, rather than a strength, in the spiritualist position that it has been represented as resting upon scientific verification. If rigid scientific methods are applied it is probable that verification will never be attained." The majority, consequently, drew several conclusions dealing with the importance or the role of science. In the first place, scientific evidence did not prove the existence or the reality of psychic phenomena. In fact the findings of the scientific community tended to be critical and disbelieving. "Thus the strictly *scientific* verdict on the matter of personal survival can only be one of *nonproven*." Considering, on the other hand, communications from the other world,

> When every possible explanation of these communications has been given, and all doubtful evidence set aside, it is very generally agreed that there remains some element as yet unexplained. We think that it is probable that the hypothesis that they proceed in some cases from discarnate spirits is the true one.

The conclusions of the majority report ended by drawing attention to the consequences which these members culled from their investigation and the testimony of the witnesses. The majority clearly recognized the possibility of fraud and deception associated with spiritualism, and warned against being drawn to psychical studies out of a sense of curiosity. Christians could rightly investigate spiritualism from a scientific point of view, but "it is not legitimate, and it is unquestionably dangerous, to allow an interest in Spiritualism . . . to replace that deeper religion which rests fundamentally upon the right relation of the soul to God Himself." If one eventually accepted the reality of communications or messages from the discarnate spirits, this did not abrogate or alter one's basic Christian obligations. However, "those who have the assurance that they have been in touch with their departed friends may rightly accept the sense of enlargement and of unbroken fellowship which it brings." One must always rely on human reason directed or inspired by the Holy Spirit, but "there is no reason why we should not accept gladly the assurance that we are still in the closest contact with those who have been dear to us in this life, and who are going forward, as we seek to do ourselves, in the understanding and fulfillment of the purpose of God."

The 1920 Lambeth Conference had criticized the claims of spiritualism because it de-emphasized a Christocentric universe. In the same manner, the majority report also found serious fault with spiritualism. Because of its stress on the human, spiritualism, in spite of numerous and persistent disclaimers, tended to emphasize aspects of the material world. According to the report, therefore, spiritualism had become "a substitute for religion, and is not, in itself, religious at all." One reason for the popularity of spiritualism and its magnetic power of attraction was due to the fact that "the Church has not proclaimed and practised its faith with sufficient conviction." The majority report again echoed the spirit of the 1920 Lambeth Conference in this regard. The reality and the importance of the doctrine of the communion of the saints, for example, "is often a dead letter." On the other hand, however, real fellowship among Christians had become all too obvious. But the fascination with spiritualism might also be attributed to the human propensity to be drawn to the bizarre; spiritualism might offer an opportunity to escape from the harsh realities of daily life.

The majority members also made brief mention of the alleged unhealthy aspects of spiritualism, such as the risks associated with any obsession or addiction and the dangers it might cause emotionally unbalanced personalities. And the report pointed out that "Spiritualism has every need of the high standards of Christianity and of its witness to a life which rests by faith upon God, and which is thereby freed from the conflicts of desire and of purpose to which all lives not so grounded are liable." Noting the possibility, which other critics of spiritualism had for a long time maintained, that some psychic phenomena might be the results of evil spirits, the majority of the committee, on the other hand, also accepted the possibility that some psychic phenomena might also proceed from contact with good spirits, such as the guardian angels in the Christian tradition.

The last three paragraphs of the majority conclusions contained some vague suggestions or recommendations for the Church of England to consider when discussing spiritualism and its relationship to Christianity. Some dealt specifically with the question of bereavement and the church's responsibility to minister to people in need of comfort or consolation. Historically, because of certain Roman Catholic practices, Anglicanism had avoided or distanced itself from strong pastoral references to the dead. "Anglican prayers for the departed do not satisfy people's needs, because the prayers are so careful in their language that it is not always evident that the departed are being prayed for, as contrasted with the living." The majority urged a stronger recognition on the part of the Anglican Church of that unity between the living and the dead. Second, the majority certainly did not recognize or accept spiritualism as a new religion, but if it did contain certain positive aspects, "it is important to see that truth not as a new religion but only as filling up certain gaps in our knowledge, so that where we already walk by faith, we may now have some measure of sight as well." The final recommendation of the majority suggested that "representatives of the Church should keep in touch with groups of intelligent persons who believe in Spiritualism."

The conclusions put forward by the majority of the committee's membership hardly represented a radical acceptance or validation of spiritualism and its practices, but three members, Guy Mayfield, Mildred Rawlinson, and W. S. Wigglesworth, felt compelled to voice their disagreement, and consequently they wrote a minority statement which became part of the official report.[13] With the important exception of the tenor of the conclusions reached by the majority of their colleagues, these three individuals had no problem accepting the findings of the report. Mayfield, Rawlinson, and Wigglesworth saw no close connection or common ground between spiritualism and Christianity, and therefore they could not comprehend how Christianity could benefit in any way from an association with the practices and teachings of spiritualism.

The first objection from the minority members concerned the verity and the reality of psychical phenomena. No evidence existed, the minority report stated, that "would convince a scientist or an open-minded layman that Spiritualists do communicate with discarnate spirits. The alleged communications may not only be valueless but may also be misleading and therefore dangerous." The contents and messages of these alleged communications also tended to be meaningless, and therefore added nothing to "our knowledge of the Christian revelation." Experimentation with spirit communications and psychical phenomena, moreover, could not be regarded as harmless or benign. "We have had evidence of the lack of balance which spiritualist practices encourage in certain types of people." The individual who dabbled with spirit communication and who believed in the worth of their messages unfortunately had forsaken ordinary human logic and common sense, and this person "becomes his own judge of right and wrong." Consequently, these three members argued, when "spirit guidance comes into conflict with the authority of the Church, the Spiritualist is likely to prefer the former and ignore the latter."

The minority also expressed serious reservations and misgivings about the contention that the knowledge of life after death obtained through spirit communication would benefit the "Christian religion and establish the faith of many now outside the Church." Since science could not possibly verify or establish the validity of these messages, the essentials of Christian belief and teachings must ultimately rest on faith, and not psychical phenomena. Faith, and not the teachings of spiritualism, must remain at the center of Christianity. But what about the revelations and the visions of the holy men and women which have become an accepted and important part of traditional religion? Were they not similar to the psychical phenomena identified with spiritualism? The minority members, unfortunately, chose not to address these queries or to suggest any answers. They simply advised people to distance themselves from any revelations or visions associated with spiritualism.

Consequently, the minority report believed that "these reasons persuade us that Spiritualism is not necessary to Christianity and has nothing to add to it." The Apostles' Creed and the Nicene Creed contained everything "that Spiritualism at its best seeks to preach." The minority then leveled its chief critique against spiritualism. "The Christian believes in immortality and in the Communion of Saints because he believes in God," their statement noted, and "our objection to Spiritualism apart from the reasons we have already given, is that it reverses this order." That is, the spiritualist believed in God because of those communications received from the departed spirits. For the disciple of spiritualism, direct prayer to God had taken a back seat to communication with discarnate spirits. Arguing that the spiritualist did not enjoy a "monopoly in believing in the continuance of our personalities after death," the minority members pointed out that there "is an irreconcilable difference between the Church's teaching on the future life and the spiritualist's account of an existence, very like our own, in which God is but dimly apprehended and where spirits yearn, not to see God, but to communicate with their relations and friends on earth." Both the sovereignty and redemptive power of Jesus, they argued, had been lessened and weakened.

Beginning first with a brief history of spiritualism, the minority report then turned its attention to the relationship that the Anglican Church should seek to maintain with spiritualism. Doubts concerning honesty and integrity had always plagued the development and growth of spiritualism as a movement, and thus "we think it undesirable in the extreme that the Church should give the least shadow of approval to a movement which is still being gravely abused by the unscrupulous." Although many serious, honest, and sincere people have become involved in spiritualism, on the other hand, fakes, charlatans, and hypocrites also occupied its ranks: "some are anti-Christian, some are religious but non-Christian, and others are queer mixtures of corruption and superstition." In the thinking of the minority, the curse of superstition had deeply permeated and colored spiritualism. It would be a grave mistake, even taking into account the number of honest and sincere spiritualists, for the Anglican Church to encourage a cautious or even a selective relationship with spiritualism in general or with individual, specific groups. Moreover, the question of alleged communications associated with psychical phenomena, which received much attention in the majority report, also came under scrutiny from the minority. "We are not satisfied that the communications received proceed from discarnate spirits," the minority members argued, and "considerable allowances must be made for coincidence, mal-observation, honest self-deception, auto-suggestion and credulity and in particular for fraud and collusion among mediums." In addition to these, the minority statement listed other numerous rational explanations for the existence of spirit messages.

The minority finally arrived at its recommendations. What position or policy should the Anglican Church adopt in relationship to spiritualism? In the first place, Anglicanism had the serious responsibility to emphasize traditional Christian practices and beliefs such as the value of prayers for the dead, the doctrine of the communion of the saints, the reasons for the belief in the afterlife from a

Christian perspective, the centrality of the eucharist "as the meeting place for souls present and departed," and the rich mystical tradition of Christianity. Finally, the church should accentuate the "truth that knowledge of and faith in God can be the only true consolation for mourners." Based on these observations and the recognition of some apparent shortcomings in the Anglican Church, the minority strongly suggested the following points for serious consideration. Most importantly, Anglicanism should avoid any relations or contacts with spiritualism; it represented a field to be explored and studied by science and not by churchmen. Prayers for the dead should be encouraged, the language of these prayers should clearly tell people that the dead were the object of the prayers, and the Anglican Church should adopt an Office for the Dead. Moreover, "well-informed literature about the possible dangers of Spiritualism is badly needed." Anglicanism needed to communicate to the faithful in a better manner the doctrine of the communion of the saints, the Christian beliefs about eternal life, "and the grounds in experience for the Christian hope."

According to Archbishop C. G. Lang's directive, the formal report of the committee would be given first to the Anglican bishops for their consideration. Released only in 1990, the minutes of the Bishops' Meeting in June 1939 describe the reception the diocesan bishops gave to the archbishop's report on spiritualism. The agenda for the Bishops' Meeting, scheduled for 28-29 June, contained a wide variety of items and topics which the forty-three bishops had to study and discuss.[14] This long and oppressive list and the fact that Archbishop Lang did not distribute the report on spiritualism to the bishops until less that a fortnight before the meeting proved an inconvenience and irritation to many of the prelates. An issue such as spiritualism, moreover, did not have the gravity and importance of other items which confronted the Anglican bishops. During the tense summer of 1939, discussions dealing with the role of the Anglican Church in wartime and other problems created by the European crisis, such as air attacks on the civilian population and women in the labor force, naturally seemed more urgent and timely. The report of Bishop Underhill's committee which dealt with spiritualism appeared rather esoteric and peripheral.

As the chairman of the archbishop's committee, the bishop of Bath and Wells, Francis Underhill, introduced the topic and remarked that "the Report which had been circulated to the bishops was intended to be an Interim document."[15] Underhill told the assembled bishops that the committee had met twelve times, and it soon became apparent that the group could not reach an unanimous opinion on some matters or agree to a common statement, hence the majority and minority reports. The bishop then told the assembled prelates that he would not recommend that the report should be published. As to any additional or future action or study in regard to spiritualism, Bishop Underhill believed that "continued research undertaken by men and women belonging to the Church" should be encouraged. He spoke against any future investigation into psychical phenomena being commissioned on strictly scientific lines or undertaken exclusively by men and women of science.

After Bishop Underhill took his seat, a number of other bishops expressed their opinions on the report, especially addressing the question of communication with discarnate spirits. Several, such as, E. W. Barnes of Birmingham, A. F. Winnington-Ingram of London, C. F. Garbett of Winchester, A. E. J. Rawlinson of Derby (whose wife was a member of the committee and a supporter of the minority point of view), and Archbishop William Temple of York "were agreed in holding that the evidence for such communications was at present so unconvincing as to be almost negligible." Moreover, the assembly of bishops did not want to give the impression that the Anglican Church recognized or gave any official approval or approbation to the teachings and practices of spiritualism. The bishop of Lincoln, F. C. N. Hicks, consequently, repeated a conclusion reached by both the 1920 Lambeth Conference and Bishop Underhill's committee, namely, "the growth of Spiritualism was partly due to a failure to emphasise sufficiently the orthodox teaching about the communion of saints." And Anglicanism must remedy this defect.

At the end of this rather short discussion, Bishop Underhill again addressed the bishops and tried to soften the harsh comments of some of his fellow bishops. Believing that "there was a residue of truth in Spiritualism which deserved further research," Underhill suggested that additional investigations into the subject should be undertaken on behalf of the church at some time in the future. The archbishop of Canterbury, C. G. Lang, then concluded the deliberation on spiritualism by thanking Bishop Underhill and the committee for their time-consuming efforts. Lang believed that the subject of spiritualism did deserve further attention, but "men of science . . . ought to undertake further enquiry into the subject of spiritualistic phenomena." Men and women associated with or acting on behalf of the Anglican Church, he added, did not possess the necessary skills and training required for such a task. Finally, the other bishops also expressed their appreciation to Bishop Underhill and his committee, and also made it clear that they did not want to publish the report.

Archbishop Lang most likely realized Bishop Underhill's disappointment at the outcome of the Bishops' Meeting. The brief amount of time devoted to the report on spiritualism and some of the critical remarks made against spiritualism by some of the bishops probably fell short of Underhill's expectations. In late July, therefore, Lang wrote a letter to Bishop Underhill. The archbishop began by again expressing his gratitude for the time and energy "which were given to the most obscure and difficult subject."[16] He also revealed his own feelings on the decision to withhold the report from the general public. "As you know," the archbishop told Bishop Underhill, "the Diocesan Bishops of England and Wales whom I consulted advised that your Report should not be published." Lang then offered an explanation for this decision.

The Bishops I think felt that having regard to the dangers which might arise if people were encouraged by the Majority Report to put trust in the admittedly doubtful character of alleged communications from discarnate spirits and to the strong opinion of the Minority Report, publication would not be desirable.

Archbishop Lang tried to make Bishop Underhill feel better by telling him that the report, even though unpublished, would immensely help other bishops when asked to give advise or guidance to the laity on the subject of spiritualism. He also reminded Underhill that the consensus of the Bishops' Meeting also recognized the need for additional studies on spiritualism "of a more full and scientific character than was possible for your committee. But inasmuch as your Committee has already given so much time and thought to the subject I do not propose that it should continue." Lang ended by again thanking Bishop Underhill and his committee for their valuable work, and he assured Underhill that their labors were not undertaken in vain.

Archbishop Lang's conciliatory letter to Bishop Underhill did not produce the desired results. Underhill's bruised feelings surfaced in his reply to Lambeth Palace. He pointed out that the three members in the minority argued that the report should not be published, and "they will no doubt be relieved by the decision of the Bishops in that sense."[17] The bishop expressed his disappointment over the small and insignificant amount of time given to the report at the Bishops' Meeting. "No doubt we were all tired by the long and difficult discussion which preceded my presentation of the report," Bishop Underhill wrote, "but in view of the great importance of the subject, I had hoped that there would have been a fuller discussion." Underhill ended his letter to Archbishop Lang by asking the archbishop's permission to send a copy of this letter to the other members of the committee.

The archbishop of Canterbury responded within the week. Lang shared Bishop Underhill's regret that the Bishops' Meeting did not discuss the report more fully. And he did offer an explanation of the bishops' actions:

> Some of them may have been too busy to read it right through but the probability is that in the majority of cases they felt convinced that it was undesirable that the Report should be made public, and when they ascertained that that appeared to be the general opinion they did not feel disposed to go into the matter in any detail.[18]

Archbishop Lang, however, did not want Bishop Underhill to distribute his earlier letter among the membership of the committee. Lang explained that "it is not customary to make any allusion to what takes place at the Bishops' Meetings." The archbishop probably hoped that the committee's work and the deliberations of the Bishops' Meetings would not generate much interest. But some curious individuals soon approached Archbishop Lang for information on the report.

Baron Palmstierna, one of the experts who gave testimony before Bishop Underhill's committee, wrote to Archbishop Lang in October 1939 and told him that Harold Anson, master of the temple and a member of the committee, recently informed him that the group had made its report and sent it to the archbishop.[19] The baron asked Lang for permission to read the copy in Anson's possession. Harold Anson had already agreed to this arrangement if Lang approved, and Palmstierna had promised to keep the contents confidential. Archbishop Lang contacted Bishop Underhill immediately and told the bishop that he did not want to give permission without the approval from the chairman of the committee. The archbishop, however, did express some reservations. "However strongly the word 'confidential' may be stressed it is always difficult for people like him to refrain from alluding to a report though it has never been published."[20]

Bishop Underhill gave his consent in a telegraph, and Archbishop Lang sent Baron Palmstierna the good news immediately. "Although it was not considered desirable that at least at the present the Report of the Committee . . . should be published," the archbishop informed the baron, "I am quite willing that you should read the copy which is in the possession of the Master of the Temple [Harold Anson], provided of course that you recognize in the fullest possible manner that the contents are entirely confidential and that therefore you must not quote them or any of the conclusions to other persons."[21] In reply, Baron Palmstierna assured Archbishop Lang that he would adhere faithfully to the condition of confidentiality.[22] Lang also sent a copy of this letter to Bishop Underhill with the additional notation, "I hope he will observe these conditions."[23] The bishop fully endorsed Lang's decision to allow Palmstierna access to the report. According to Underhill's estimation of the baron, "I find him singularly credulous about the phenomena of spiritualism, but no doubt he is enough of a diplomat to keep secrets."[24]

Other interested or curious parties also wanted to see the contents of the report. In early December 1939, the editor of *Psychic News* wrote to Bishop Underhill and asked for a copy of the report so that his newspaper could publish it. Underhill wrote to Lambeth Palace and asked for advice. Archbishop Lang's secretary replied and told the bishop of Bath and Wells that the "Bishops decided that the Report on Spiritualism should not be published."[25] He even suggested the appropriate wording for the reply back to the editor: "The Report itself disclosed much difference of opinion and it was consequently felt that there was need of further careful investigation into the subject . . . [and] it was decided that the Report should not be made public."

But requests to examine the report continued to arrive in the archbishop's post. A joint letter signed by Mrs. M. A. St. Clair Stobart (chairman and founder of the Spiritualist Community and of the Confraternity of Clergy, Ministers, Laymen, and Spiritualists), George Lethem (editor of *Light*, the publication of the London Spiritualist Alliance), and H. E. Hunt (past president of the

Marylebone Spiritualist Association and editor of *Service*) wanted to know Archbishop Lang's intentions concerning the publication of the report on spiritualism. "In the interests of Truth," the three individuals asked "whether the Report is—as they earnestly hope—to be made public, and whether it may soon be looked for?[26] For your signatories cannot believe that those facts will do other than form an impregnable base on which, even as in the earliest days of the Church, a living Christianity may ground itself, and today immensely widen its appeal." Drawing the primate's attention to the European war, the letter argued that "anything which can truly help the minds of men to take courage and comfort in the spiritual verities should be made patent and available to all." The response from Lambeth Palace repeated the official policy: the archbishop did not intend to publish the report. More study and investigation was required, and "premature publication was liable to give rise to misunderstanding."[27]

Spiritualist newspapers, which naturally wanted the report to be made public, expressed their dissatisfaction with the archbishop's refusal. The *Light* ran an editorial on 21 December criticizing Lang's reluctance to publish the report and also printed the letter which set out the archiepiscopal policy from Archbishop Lang to its editor. The paper argued that his reasons "cannot be regarded as satisfactory either by the prominent and influential members of the large Committee who drew up and signed the Report, or by the Church people and the Christian world for whose information the Report was intended."[28] The editor even suggested that the report might eventually be "altered" to weaken the content which "gives a large measure of understanding of psychic phenomena and the authenticity of communications with the world of spirit." Spiritualism, he argued, did not harbor any intention of becoming a rival religion, as some might wrongly suppose. Archbishop Lang should, therefore, view spiritualism as "providing a foundation of fact on which Churchmen could not only base their essential beliefs, but by which they would be able to assess the value of beliefs which have grown doubtful and for which new interpretations are needed." Seen in this context, the archbishop should have no reason to fear spiritualism. Two days later, the *Psychic News* published lengthy extracts from the joint letter from St. Clair Stobart, Lethem, and Hunt to the archbishop of Canterbury appealing for the publication of the report.[29] This paper also printed the negative response from the archbishop's secretary and the letter from Bishop Underhill, who pointed out that additional study and investigation into the subject was necessary. The paper did not express any opinion on Lang's decision to embargo the report on spiritualism.

The public interest in the committee's findings, not surprisingly, continued into the new year. On 15 January 1940, the *Daily Dispatch* of Manchester printed a story about the archbishop's report and the refusal of Archbishop Lang to publish its findings under the heading, "Bishops Suppress Report in Favour of Spiritualism."[30] The paper quoted Bishop Francis Underhill, who stated that "there was considerable divergence of views among members of the committee . . . [and] it was not thought wise to publish the report at the present." According to the Manchester paper, "Spiritualists are jubilant. They believe suppression of the report is clear evidence that the 'war' against spiritualism has crumbled." At the end of January 1940, Bishop Underhill informed Lambeth Palace that his post concerning the committee's report continued to increase.[31] He drew attention to the large number of newspaper clippings about the report which people had sent him, and included them in his letter to the archbishop. Archbishop Lang's secretary thanked the bishop for his concern and told him that the archbishop also had acquired a large collection of clippings dealing with the report. Lang, however, still refused to budge from his position on publication. "He does not think there is anything more that need be said at present," Bishop Underhill was informed, and Archbishop Lang believed that the "excitement will no doubt die down."[32]

Within a fortnight, Bishop Underhill was again in contact with the archbishop of Canterbury, and Underhill told Archbishop Lang about a recent letter he had received from an Anglican clergyman. He believed that this letter deserved serious consideration from the archbishop and remarked that it was typical of his recent correspondence from clerics who commented on the report and asked questions about its publication. With an eye to the past and the growth of spiritualism following the disasters of the Great War, Underhill believed that the current war would also produce an upsurge in the popularity of spiritualism. According to the bishop of Bath and Wells, "There is no doubt that the practice of Spiritualism is rapidly growing and if the war should enter on a more violent phase the many consequent deaths would make the problem a more pressing one than ever."[33] Underhill again spoke some harsh words against the lackluster and disappointing performance of the last Bishops' Meeting. The bishops, he maintained, did not give the report on spiritualism the time and consideration it rightly deserved. "The fact that the persons who signed the majority report did so was a remarkable one, yet the bishops seemed to have made up their minds rather rapidly not to accept it and hardly appeared to desire that there should be any further investigation by competent persons." He again mentioned the war in Europe: "particularly in this time . . . such investigation cannot safely be postponed."

Bishop Underhill refused to forget the alleged cavalier attitude of the Bishops' Meeting. "There is a general belief," he continued, "that a majority of the members of your Committee were to some extent impressed by the claims of Spiritualism or the Bishops would not have rejected their report." His correspondence seemed to indicate that many other interested persons also thought this was the case. Consequently, the "amount of truth contained in this suggestion seems to me to make the continued silence of the Church dangerous." Since Baron Palmstierna had already been allowed to see the report and another individual had petitioned for the same privilege, Bishop Underhill argued that the report should be made available to all those trustworthy individuals who had studied psychic phenomena for some time. Moreover, Underhill confessed that he would like "to have the report discussed again at a meeting of Bishops, in view of all that has happened since it was decided not to publish it, but I doubt whether your Grace would consider this course desirable." Underhill ended this long and despondent letter to Archbishop Lang on a personal note and expressed his feeling on the matter. The bishop assured Lang that he had not changed his own views on the worth and value of spiritualism. He also told Archbishop Lang how he handled people who sought his counsel on matters concerning spiritualism and its relation to the Anglican Church.

> I always advise those who consult me to be content with the teaching of the Church, but the four or five years of careful study I have given to the phenomena of spiritualism have convinced me that there ought to be further investigation of so perplexing and important a matter as soon as possible.

The reply to Bishop Underhill told him that Archbishop Lang would not grant permission to the second party who had approached him asking for permission to read the report. If the archbishop made an exception in this instance, Lang's secretary told the bishop, "it would be difficult to justify refusal in other certain cases."[34] The letter then addressed another subject Underhill had introduced, namely, the conduct of the last Bishops' Meeting and its reception of the report.

> His Grace recognised the force of what you say in your letter as to the attitude of the majority of the Bishops when the Report came before them at the Bishops' Meeting and he thinks that in view of what has since transpired it might be well if the Bishops had another opportunity of considering what steps, if any, ought to be taken to allay the suspicions aroused by the newspaper reports.

Archbishop Lang, Underhill was informed, planned personally to introduce the subject again at the next Bishops' Meeting, scheduled to take place in June 1940, under the title "Present Position with Regard to the Report of the Committee on Spiritualism."

Before the bishops could assemble to reconsider the findings of the committee on spiritualism, the controversy over the report continued to appear in the pages of two spiritualist newspapers, the *Light* and *Psychic News*. Some sensitive information about the report, it appears, had already been leaked to interested parties. Writing in the 4 January 1940 edition of the *Light*, Mrs. M. A. St. Clair Stobart noted that spiritualism was gaining some acceptance in ecclesiastical circles, and she pointed to the establishment of the archbishop's committee on the subject. The refusal to publish the findings, however, drew her wrath. "There is very little doubt that the Commission of enquiry into Spiritualism, consisting of influential people . . . was favourable to our cause, and we shall not rest until its results are made public."[35] Another edition of the same paper told its readers that "we must regretfully come to the conclusion that the Report is being suppressed because it favours the claims of Spiritualism."[36] The *Psychic News* also deplored the archbishop of Canterbury's policy of silence and pointed out that the "Church is mistaken if it thinks that it can prevent the spread of Spiritualism by a ban—a method that savours more of Rome than Canterbury."[37]

The 8 February 1940 edition of *Psychic News* contained a lengthy article written by Arthur Findlay, chairman of the International Institute for Psychical Research and critic of the church's apparent hostile attitude toward spiritualism,[38] entitled, "Why Bishops Suppressed Secret Report on Spiritualism."[39] He began by repeating the well-known fact that the bishops of the Church of England had decided against publishing the report on spiritualism. And he hinted that the findings of the committee probably saw spiritualism in a positive light. Findlay then took the reader on a journey throughout ecclesiastical history, and he condemned numerous past actions perpetrated by the Christian churches. According to his interpretation, "The whole history of the Church . . . reveals dishonesty, craftiness and cunning on the part of the priesthood, if anything occurred to affect the cherished beliefs on which they thrived." This attitude, he believed, also sadly and unfortunately doomed the fate of the report to silence, and he compared this policy of censorship by the Anglican bishops to the current Nazi suppression of truth. After describing the "history of the Christian priestcraft . . . [as] a sordid story," Findlay concluded by pointing out that their "latest effort to prevent the truth of Spiritualism being more widely known is only another proof that they are living up to their past tradition."

Throughout the month of February 1940, however, speculation and guesswork gave way to concrete facts as the findings of the archbishop's committee started to became public knowledge. By the end of the month, several newspapers articles confirmed that a "leakage" had indeed taken place. Bishop Underhill alerted Archbishop Lang and drew his attention to "a serious leakage of information about the Report of the Committee on Spiritualism" which the *Psychic News* carried on its front page.[40] Lambeth Palace replied to Bishop Underhill's letter and his concerns about the story in the *Psychic News* of 24 February, which was printed under the title, "Spiritualism Is Proved by the Church. Primate's Secret Committee Votes 9 to 3 in Favour!" The response told the bishop that Archbishop Lang had authorized his secretary to tell the press "that the statement is both unauthorized and inaccurate."[41] In the opinion of Archbishop Lang, it appeared "as though the Spiritualists were manoeuvring to force the archbishop to make the Report public."

The language of the *Psychic News* article seemed to bear out the archbishop's contention. The first sentence proudly proclaimed that "the Church of England, by nine votes to three, has decided that Spiritualism is true!"[42] "The nine were all the influential members of the 'Archbishop of Canterbury's Committee on

Spiritualism,'" it continued, and the "three, unimportant and unknown, merely 'reserved . . . opinion.'" The paper then told its readers that it had received this information from "someone who has seen the committee's secret report." The *Psychic News*, maintaining that "these historic findings have been hidden from the world, smothered by Orthodoxy," openly challenged Archbishop Lang to publish the report of the committee for all to read. The article retold the history of the committee and its purpose, and recounted the recent attempts on the part of some spiritualists to have its findings and conclusions made public. The question of publication and openness on the part of the church remained the controversial and emotional issue.

"If Spiritualism had been found untrue," the paper argued, "what would have happened then? Would the report have been suppressed?" The paper then gave several examples of alleged attempts on the part of the church to silence people who had looked favorably on the claims of spiritualism. The article also suggested that the Anglican Church feared the consequences, especially a drop in the numbers of those who attended Anglican services, which would follow if spiritualism came to be seen in a positive light. But the "suppression of the findings of a majority of a committee appointed by the Primate himself will not help to fill the churches," the newspaper maintained. The *Psychic News* ended the story by quoting from a talk given recently by Dr. W. R. Matthews, a member of the archbishop's committee. According to the paper, Matthews told the Society for Psychical Research that "one of the things discovered by the committee was that a number of people had found in mediumship, 'a confirmation of their Christian faith, and even a way from Agnosticism to belief.'" An editorial comment in the same issue expressed this idea more bluntly: "In Spiritualism religion has been removed from the realm of faith, hope and speculation into the region of demonstrable proof."

The demand for publication of the report continued to grow during the month of March. Using examples from history, such as Christianity's blind opposition to Galileo, Copernicus, and Bruno, the *Psychic News* pointed out that the current ban on publication was "in line with Orthodoxy's consistent opposition to invention, discovery and reform."[43] The paper demanded that the findings of the committee's report be made public and published. The lead article drew attention to the fact that several national papers had reported the policy of banning the report, but it also revealed some new facts about the deliberations and work of the committee. The paper told its readers that the committee heard witnesses, examined evidence, and that some members even attended séances. Moreover, the *Psychic News* also printed the names of those individuals, including Bishop Francis Underhill, who had signed the majority report, and identified the Rev. L. W. Grensted, whose wife possessed "psychic powers," as the person who drew up the report. After identifying several prominent Anglican churchmen who recognized positive aspects of spiritualism,[44] the paper concluded, "Loyalty to truth, wherever it leads, must be the paramount consideration of all Church leaders."

In the 9 March edition, the same paper reported that the signers of the majority report wanted their findings to be made public. This article repeated facts previously known about the committee, but the *Psychic News* now also published the main conclusions reached by the majority of the members, who saw spiritualism as a possible positive force in one's religious life. It again asked the routine question, "Would the report have been held up if Spiritualists had been found untrue?"[45] Another paper, the *Light*, printed an article which gave an indication of the policy which the friends and supporters of spiritualism planned to adopt, namely, a campaign to circulate a petition by which clergymen and other interested people or parties could express their feelings in favor of publishing the report. Publication of the report, it suggested, might even help or strengthen the church. If made public, the report would give Anglicans "some degree of guidance as to the validity of claims made for Spiritualism and some indication of the extent to which the basic teachings of the Church depend in the strength of the evidence for survival provided by Spiritualism."[46]

Mrs. M. A. St. Clair Stobart, no stranger to those Christians who saw the values of spiritualism, emerged as the organizer of this drive to force Archbishop Lang to make the report of the committee available for the public. St. Clair Stobart had been in touch with the archbishop since December 1939, and she wrote again to Archbishop Lang on 8 March and informed him that since the beginning of the new year she had received "communications from over two hundred clergy, expressing their views upon the desirability of its publication."[47] She quoted one letter which argued that the "clergy and the people in general have a right to receive such guidance as the authorities of the Church of England can give." The reply from the Archbishop Lang tried to assure St. Clair Stobart that the archbishop "is giving consideration to the suggestion that the question of making public the private and confidential document submitted to him and to his brother Bishops on the subject of Spiritualism should be reconsidered."[48] Lang's secretary pointed out that the archbishop needed to consult others on the matter. This could not be accomplished, however, until the end of June, and hoping to end this fruitless exchange of letters, he informed her that the archbishop would "be glad to be spared further correspondence on the subject" until then.

By this time, it became possible to identify the source who had leaked the information about the report and the conclusions of the committee. In March 1940, Bishop Francis Underhill told Archbishop Lang that "the information appearing in the press about the report on Spiritualism comes from Baron Erik Palmstierna," the individual whom Lang had allowed to see the report after an assurance of confidentiality.[49] The bishop reminded the archbishop of Canterbury that the statements appearing in the press were most accurate, and he consequently suggested a change in church policy dealing with the report. "Your

Grace may not agree with me," Underhill pointed out, "but I really think more harm is being done by letting the main points leak out bit by bit than by publishing it in full." Archbishop Lang replied to Underhill's letter and said that it did not surprise him to learn that Palmstierna had divulged the contents of the report, even after he had promised to keep the contents secret. Lang was "very disappointed to learn that he allowed his tongue to wag."[50] The archbishop saw some merit in Underhill's proposal to publish the text of the report in full, even though he disliked the appearance of yielding to the pressure exerted by the *Psychic News*. However, the archbishop reminded Bishop Underhill that the "decision to withhold the Report from publication was taken at a Bishops' Meeting and he must therefore wait until the next Bishops' Meeting takes place before coming to any decision." Bishop Underhill believed that Archbishop Lang had adopted the correct approach: "If the decision is not taken till June His Grace and the bishops will not seem to have been stampeded by the clamour of the spiritualists."[51]

Pressure on the archbishop to make public the contents of the report did not abate. Despite Lang's request to her not to disturb him, Mrs. M. A. St. Clair Stobart continued to press Archbishop Lang for action. On 14 March, she wrote to Lambeth Palace again and confessed that she understood the difficulties which the archbishop faced in regard to the publication of the report. But, St. Clair Stobart pointed out, "there has been so much leakage as to the contents of the Report, that official withholding is becoming rather futile."[52] She pleaded with Archbishop Lang to release the contents of the report as soon as possible "before the world has a chance to say that it was forced from him, and had only been withheld because the result was not in accordance with preconceived hopes." Moreover, "it would remove a wide-spread grievance and establish the fact that his Grace is not yielding to the public clamour, but responding to the great need felt by so many of his clergy for guidance on a subject which forms the basis of religion—namely, Life after Death." Reminding the archbishop of her position as chairman of the Confraternity, which represented numerous clerics who wanted guidance from their church leaders in the matter of spiritualism, she audaciously asked for a meeting with him to discuss the report.

The response from the Rev. Alan Don, the archbishop's private secretary, bluntly told Mrs. St. Clair Stobart that "the question of the publication of the private and confidential Report on Spiritualism will come up for further consideration in June" at the Bishops' Meeting.[53] Pointing out that the archbishop knew the arguments for and against publication quite well, the secretary informed her that the archbishop saw no need for a meeting on the subject. Lang asked St. Clair Stobart to use her "influence as far as possible to dampen down the clamour which has recently been filling certain sections of the Press." The letter concluded that "it will be much easier for the archbishop and his brother Bishops to give the subject due consideration if the Press would in the meantime leave the matter alone."

Archbishop Lang even appealed directly to the press to exercise some constraint in this matter. Speaking at a meeting of journalists at St. Bride's Church, Fleet Street, in March 1940, Lang took the opportunity to comment on his position in respect to the unpublished report on spiritualism, and he also expressed his views on the manner in which the country's papers reported his policy. Lang adopted a stern attitude and took the opportunity to remind the assembly of newspapermen that a "primary part of your business is to circulate news."[54] The *News Review* commented on Lang's address to the journalists, drawing attention to his comment, a "primary part of your business is to circulate news," and his stubborn refusal to publish the report dealing with spiritualism.[55] "Why doesn't he circulate the news of the report of his own committee? . . . If he won't give Fleet Street the news, how can he expect Fleet Street to print it?"

Despite this appeal for restraint from Archbishop Lang, the crusade for publication of the report continued to appear in the columns of the *Psychic News*. In the 16 March edition of the paper, there appeared extracts from Mrs. St. Clair Stobart's recent correspondence with Archbishop Lang which urged the publication of the report in the interest of truth and which also emphasized that a large number of Anglican clerics also wanted to know the contents of the report. A week later, the same paper told its readers that the archbishop of Canterbury planned to consult the Anglican bishops at their June meeting about possible publication of the report. No new information appeared in this article. However, people again viewed extracts of letters between Archbishop Lang and Mrs. St. Clair Stobart, read about the support for spiritualism from distinguished Anglican churchmen, and saw the news that the report would appear on the June agenda of the Bishops' Meeting.[56] Suggesting that Archbishop Lang was "himself psychic, though he prefers to speak of his 'mystical experiences,'" the paper asked its readers: "What lead will the Primate give to his bishops?"

Public comments by certain members of the archbishop's committee also appeared in the pages of the press, and consequently these statements also helped to keep the issue of the publication of the report alive. The master of the temple, Harold Anson, did not avoid the publicity associated with the controversy over the future of the report. In an interview for the *Psychic News*, Anson, who had openly "stated that Spiritualism is 'the scientific explanation of the Christian belief and faith in survival of life after death,'" defended the archbishop's decision not to publish the findings of the committee for the general public.[57] In an Easter sermon broadcast by the BBC, Anson spoke words which friends of spiritualism heard with the joy associated with the season: "I should *expect* life to be uninjured by death."[58] The *Psychic News* interpreted Anson's innocent remark in the sermon as an example of using "Spiritualism's evidence to support the resurrection of Jesus."[59] The *Light* gave a detailed report of the Easter sermon and pointed out that Canon Anson "demonstrated how effective is the use that can be made of psychic evidence for Survival in support of the basic teachings of the Christian religion."[60] Archbishop Lang eventually expressed his opinion on Anson's public statements. Responding to a letter from the canon, the archbishop cautioned him and suggested that "as a member of the Committee on Spiritualism you should hold your hand until the bishops have determined what course of action to adopt with regard to the Report."[61] The archbishop hoped that the June meeting of the Anglican bishops might finally resolve the question of publication.

Like other parties who longed to read the report, Mrs. St. Clair Stobart had to wait until the summer meeting. After being refused an interview with Archbishop Lang, she still wrote one last letter before the Bishops' Meeting. She told the archbishop's secretary that she understood the reasons behind Lang's refusal to grant an interview dealing with the question of the publication of the committee report.[62] St. Clair Stobart sympathized with Lang's reluctance because of the recent press reports and the unfavorable comments which some critics attached to his policy of secrecy. But, she queried, "what means is there left for exchange of views and ventilation of grievances between members of the public and those in authority?" Part of the problem might be due, she suggested, to the church's "attitude of aristocratic seclusion—a seclusion from which some of us are seeking to entice her out." The letter ended on an uncustomary note of sarcasm. St. Clair Stobart acknowledged that she would await the summer meeting when the bishops would decide the fate of the report and then thanked the secretary "for the courtesy with which you have acted as intermediary with the elusive archbishop."

As the summer months approached and the date for the Bishops' Meeting drew nearer, the press continued to carry stories about the report on spiritualism and the ban imposed by the archbishop of Canterbury. Most of the stories did not contain any new information, but these press reports kept the topic of spiritualism before the eyes of the public. The 13 April edition of the *Psychic News* again talked about the primate's address to the journalists and his admonition "to circulate news."[63] The paper also printed extracts of Mrs. St. Clair Stobart's letter of 4 April to Archbishop Lang and repeated the gist of earlier stories which reported the main conclusions of the committee. The *Light* also published the letters of Mrs. St. Clair Stobart and commented on an address given in January by one of the members of the committee, W. R. Matthews, the dean of St. Paul's. Talking about the committee's work, Dean Matthews noted that "strong difference of opinion was manifest in the Commission."[64] "What was perhaps unexpected," he continued, "was the evidence that a number of people had found in Psychical Research a confirmation of their Christian faith and even a way from agnosticism to belief." It would be the bishops at their June meeting, however, and not pressure from spiritualists or the press, who would decide the fate of the report. Should it be published? Should the ban of secrecy remain in force?

Notes

1. Lang to Underhill, 30 January 1939, Lang Papers, vol. 70, Lambeth Palace Library.
2. Underhill to Lang, 1 February 1939, Lang Papers, vol. 70, Lambeth Palace Library.
3. Archbishop's Committee on Spiritualism, *Report of the Committee to the Archbishop of Canterbury* (1939), Lang Papers, vol. 70, Lambeth Palace Library. The entire report was printed in its entirety for the first time in *Christian Parapsychologist* 3 (March 1979): 40-73. Sections of the report appeared earlier in the pages of *Psychic News* during 1947. The following references to the report comes from the March 1979 issue of the *Christian Parapsychologist*.
4. Preliminary, Archbishop's Committee on Spiritualism, 40-41.
5. Introductory Observations in Which All the Members of the Committee Concur, Archbishop's Committee on Spiritualism, 41-49.
6. The secretary of the Spiritualists' National Union told the committee that "these figures did not include attendance at the Marylebone Spiritualist Association, the Queen's Hall meetings, Spiritualist Community meetings at the Grotian Hall, or those at the House of Red Cloud or the 'Power' meetings at the Aeolian Hall." He thought that the membership of the churches affiliated to the union was in the neighbourhood of 15,000.
7. The report described the anonymous author as "a convinced Christian and a convinced believer in spiritualism." The types of psychical phenomena summarized included trace phenomena, direct voice, clairvoyance and clairaudience, automatic writing, materializations, healing, photographic evidence, psychometry, telekinesis, and impersonations.
8. The examples, in their entirety, concerning cremation read, "That cremation should not take place until after a lapse of four days, on account of the occasional delay in severing certain connections with the body" and "that with this precaution cremation makes things easier for the departed spirit as it gives a feeling of greater freedom."
9. Evidence, Archbishop's Committee on Spiritualism, 49-59.
10. For Dame Edith Lyttelton's personal experiences see Edith Lyttelton Diary, Chan I, 6/11, Churchill College Archives, Cambridge University, Cambridge. Her notes center around the psychic experiences of her husband, Alfred, who died in 1913. She also stressed the importance of religion and prayer in relation to her experiences of her dead husband.
11. Evidence, Archbishop's Committee on Spiritualism.
12. Conclusions of the Majority, Archbishop's Committee on Spiritualism, 60-66.
13. Minority Report, Archbishop's Committee on Spiritualism, 66-73.
14. The following items, among others, appeared on the agenda: The Church in Time of War (a major item of discussion), The Church's Educational Policy, The Church and Unemployment, Refugees, The Use of the Pulpit for Church Instruction, Episcopi Vagantes, The Ordination of Blindmen, The Ordination of Men Engaged in Social Work, The Proposed World Mission 1940-41, The Copying of Records as Requested by the Latter Day Saints, The Ninth Centenary of St. Willibrord, The Disposal of Unused Church Plate, The Constitution of the Provincial Council for Sunday Schools and Youth Movements, and The Council on the Christian Faith and the Common Life.

15. Bishops' Meeting, 1939-1944, BM 11, 28 June 1939, Lambeth Palace Library, Lambeth Palace. The minutes are also printed in *The Christian Parapsychologist* 8 (June 1990): 203-4.
16. Lang to Underhill, 26 July 1939, Lang Papers, vol. 70, Lambeth Palace Library.
17. Underhill to Lang, 28 July 1939, Lang Papers, vol. 70, Lambeth Palace Library.
18. Don to Underhill, 2 August 1939, Lang Papers, vol. 70, Lambeth Palace Library.
19. Palmstierna to Lang, 6 October 1939, Lang Papers, vol. 70, Lambeth Palace Library.
20. Lang to Underhill, 10 October 1939, Lang Papers, vol. 70, Lambeth Palace Library.
21. Lang to Palmstierna, 11 October 1939, Lang Papers, vol. 70, Lambeth Palace Library.
22. Palmstierna to Lang, 12 October 1939, Lang Papers, vol. 70, Lambeth Palace Library.
23. Lang to Underhill, 11 October 1939, Lang Papers, vol. 70, Lambeth Palace Library.
24. Underhill to Lang, 12 October 1939, Lang Papers, vol. 70, Lambeth Palace Library.
25. Don to Underhill, 7 December 1939, Lang Papers, vol. 70, Lambeth Palace Library.
26. M. A. St. Clair Stobart, Lethem, and Hunt to Lang, 9 December 1939, Lang Papers, vol. 70, Lambeth Palace Library.
27. Don to M. A. St. Clair Stobart, 11 December 1939, Lang Papers, vol. 70, Lambeth Palace Library.
28. *Light*, 21 December 1939.
29. *Psychic News* (London), 23 December 1939.
30. *Daily Dispatch* (Manchester), 15 January 1940.
31. Underhill to Don, 20 January 1940, Lang Papers, vol. 70, Lambeth Palace Library.
32. Don to Underhill, 23 January 1940, Lang Papers, vol. 70, Lambeth Palace Library.
33. Underhill to Lang, 31 January 1940, Lang Papers, vol. 70, Lambeth Palace Library.
34. Don to Underhill, 6 February 1940, Lang Papers, vol. 70, Lambeth Palace Library.
35. *Light*, 4 January 1940.
36. *Light*, 18 January 1940.
37. *Psychic News*, 27 January 1940.
38. J. Arthur Findlay attacked those clergy who ridiculed and criticized people drawn to spiritualism. J. Arthur Findlay, *The Rock of Truth or Spiritualism, the Coming World Religion* (London: Rider, 1933).
39. *Psychic News*, 8 February 1940. Other papers carried reports about the findings of the committee which emphasized the favorable report the majority of members gave to spiritualism and the reluctance of Archbishop Lang to publish the report. See

Daily Telegraph, 22 February 1940; *Daily Herald*, 23 February 1940; *Daily Sketch*, 23 February 1940; and *Sunday Dispatch*, 25 February 1940.

40. Underhill to Lang, February 1940, Lang Papers, vol. 70, Lambeth Palace Library. The letter is undated, but it was probably written on 22 February 1940.
41. Don to Underhill, 23 February 1940, Lang Papers, vol. 70, Lambeth Palace Library.
42. *Psychic News*, 24 February 1940.
43. *Psychic News*, 2 March 1940.
44. Some of the churchmen included two members of the committee (Dr. Matthews and Canon Anson), Bishop E. W. Barnes of Birmingham, Bishop Bertram Pollock of Norwich, and Bishop H. H. Henson of Durham. The paper also printed an extract from a recent statement made by the archbishop of York, William Temple: "The most important political questions of the day are the questions whether God exists and whether Man survives bodily death."
45. *Psychic News*, 9 March 1940.
46. *Light*, 14 March 1940.
47. M. A. St. Clair Stobart to Lang, 8 March 1940, Lang Papers, vol. 70, Lambeth Palace Library.
48. Don to M. A. St. Clair Stobart, 9 March 1940, Lang Papers, vol. 70, Lambeth Palace Library. The response from the archbishop's secretary eventually appeared in the 21 March edition of the *Light*.
49. Underhill to Lang, 11 March 1940, Lang Papers, vol. 70, Lambeth Palace Library.
50. Don to Underhill, 13 March 1940, Lang Papers, vol. 70, Lambeth Palace Library.
51. Underhill to Don, 15 March 1940, Lang Papers, vol. 70, Lambeth Palace Library.
52. M. A. St. Clair Stobart to Don, 14 March 1904, Lang Papers, vol. 70, Lambeth Palace Library.
53. Don to M. A. St. Clair Stobart, 21 March 1940, Lang Papers, vol. 70, Lambeth Palace Library.
54. *Psychic News*, 16 March 1940.
55. *News Review*, 14 March 1940.
56. *Psychic News*, 23 March 1940.
57. *Psychic News*, 16 March 1940. The same article also told its readers that Anglo-Catholicism, Roman Catholicism, and the Free Churches also held a low opinion of spiritualism.
58. *Psychic News*, 30 March 1940.
59. *Psychic News*, 6 April 1940.
60. *Light*, 4 April 1940.
61. Don to Anson, 26 April 1940, Lang Papers, vol. 70, Lambeth Palace Library.
62. M. A. St. Clair Stobart to Don, 4 April 1940, printed in *Light*, 11 April 1940, and *Psychic News*, 13 April 1940.
63. *Psychic News*, 13 April 1940.
64. *Light*, 11 April 1940.

Chapter Five

The 1940 Bishops' Meeting: Actions and Reactions

The relationship between war and spiritualism is not as obvious as the experience in England following the Great War suggests. In America, after the affair of the Fox sisters and the alleged supernatural "raps" which occurred in the state of New York during 1848, spiritualism grew in popularity throughout the country. "Scarcely another cultural phenomenon affected as many people or stimulated as much interest as did spiritualism in the ten years before the Civil War and, for that matter, through the subsequent decades of the nineteenth century."[1] Prior to the outbreak of the war in 1861, the leaders of America's churches recognized the dangers of spiritualism and took measures to combat it, but the number of men leaving to join the army on both sides took the strength out of the movement. But what role did the conflict in America have on the development of spiritualism? Did this war eventually contribute to a resurgence of spiritualism when the hostilities ended, or did events associated with the hostilities effectively weaken it?

R. Laurence Moore believes that the popularity of spiritualism did decline during the war years, but circumstances changed once the peace was signed in 1865. "After the Civil War," he argues, "the chart would show a recovery fed by the wish of many people to communicate with those who had perished during the war."[2] Consequently, a "vertible spiritual mania swept the country in the form of a modified ouija board called a planchette." Moore maintains that this recovery lasted until the 1870s, when scandals and the confession by Margaret Fox, that the "raps" were not supernatural but produced by the cracking of the toe joints, brought the movement into disrepute. Geoffrey Nelson, however, sees the decline of spiritualism taking place before the Civil War. Prior to the war, people had already become disillusioned with spiritualism due to the discovery of a number of fraudulent and dishonest mediums and the connection in the minds of many people between spiritualism and free love and socialism. In addition to the disruption caused by the loss of men to the military, Nelson offers another reason for its decreasing popularity. "Public activities seem to have ceased almost entirely during the war, and in the south [where spiritualism was widespread] the situation was worse than in the north, for Spiritualism was associated with the Anti-slavery movement."[3] In England, the Great War certainly did contribute to the growth of the spiritualist movement. Spiritualism did flourish during the 1920s and 1930s; however, things began to change when war broke out again. After this world war, spiritualism's appeal began to decline.

At the beginning of hostilities in 1939, spiritualism had been experiencing a growth in membership, but the war eventually crippled and weakened it. Spiritualism had prospered after the Great War, but the "movement was affected far more seriously by the Second World War and, in fact, has never recovered fully from the blow, for at no time since the war has Spiritualism attained the popularity or membership it had in the 'thirties."[4] Erroneous prophecies which predicted that war would never break out and the failure of prophecy to foresee events during the war years disillusioned many people, who began to lose faith in spiritualism "despite the fact that prophecy and fortune telling have always been condemned by reputable Spiritualists, who have taken care to point out that the 'departed' spirits cannot see the future but can only base their predictions on the same sort of evidence that is available to a 'living' person."[5] The blackout, the blitz, financial constraints caused by the war effort, and the shortage of men curtailed many activities of spiritualism and consequently weakened the movement. According to Geoffrey Nelson, spiritualism reached a low point in 1941. In that year, the Spiritualists' National Union reported an affiliation of only 313 churches with a membership of 10,250.[6] Because of a perceived risk to the nation's security, the police began to prosecute fortune-tellers and mediums, and this policy also hurt the spiritualist movement.[7] In spite of these adverse conditions and the declining strength of spiritualism, a campaign to publish the findings of the 1939 report on the relationship of spiritualism to Christianity continued throughout the 1940s.

A majority of the Archbishop's Committee on spiritualism had come to conclusions which seemed to find some positive aspects of spiritualism. Archbishop Lang, however, decided against making the findings of that committee public, citing the earlier decisions taken during the deliberations of the 1939 Bishops' Meeting which also wanted to keep the findings far from the public eye. But leaked information whetted the curiosity of some interested parties, and this led to numerous newspaper articles which demanded that Archbishop Lang should authorize the publication of the committee's findings. Moreover, a stream of letters on the subject began to arrive at Lambeth Palace; they also argued that the veil of secrecy should be lifted. Lang did not cave in but announced that the next Bishops' Meeting, scheduled for June 1940, would again study the report of the committee on spiritualism and the bishops would again take responsibility for any decisions concerning its publication.

The Bishops' Meeting considered the report of the Archbishop's Committee on spiritualism during its meeting held on Monday, 17 June 1940. The members had been asked earlier to bring their copies of the report to the meeting in order to facilitate the flow and the progress of the meeting. Bishop Francis Underhill, who had earlier agreed with the decision not to publish the report, "opened a long discussion by urging that the Report of the Committee on Spiritualism should be now published."[8] Underhill recognized that publication "would arouse much discussion, but in any case there had been a leakage and much capital would no doubt be made out of what had already leaked out unless the whole report was made public." The conclusions of the report would, he believe, satisfy both the spiritualists and those pious Christians who would certainly benefit from "information and guidance on the matter and who were at present being grossly misled by mediums and the like." The bishop of Bath and Wells ended his opening remarks by urging the assembly to reconsider the ban on publication and by telling his fellow bishops that "he personally had no interest in Spiritualism." Moreover, he did not think that "much reliable guidance would be likely to be forthcoming from those outside the Church who, in spite of 50 years of psychical research, still held very conflicting opinions on the whole subject."

The bishop of Winchester, C. F. Garbett, spoke next. He agreed that spiritualism had become an important and popular issue in some Anglican circles. Some Anglicans expressed a strong interest in the subject, but, nonetheless, he "did not think that the Report was worthy of being sent out in the name of the archbishop of Canterbury or of the Bishops as a whole." Bishop E. W. Barnes of Birmingham also spoke out against publication: "The Report would be taken to commit the Church of England and the Bishops, and would do more harm than good." He proposed instead a publication setting forth a statement of Christian doctrine on eternal life written by a small group of theologians. The archbishop of York, William Temple, believed that the report had value for the bishops as a guideline, "but if issued to the public it would be taken to have the commendation and approval of the Episcopate." And this, Temple quickly pointed out, "would do harm." R. G. Parsons of Southwark wanted the Bishops' Meeting to issue a statement which told the public that the contents of the report "leaked out through a breach of confidence and that it was never meant for publication." He also argued for a document which would address and clarify the Christian beliefs in eternal life.

The bishops of Litchfield, Norwich, Derby, Covenry, Lincoln, Wakefield, Guilford, and Truro also joined in the discussion before Archbishop Cosmo Gordon Lang brought the session to a close. The bishops did not want to change the policy which they had established earlier. The archbishop of Canterbury again thanked Bishop Underhill and his committee for the work they put into the report on spiritualism and "said that the general trend of the discussion appeared to point to the undesirability of publishing the Report in spite of the fact that a leakage had taken place. The Report was a private and confidential document," Lang reminded the bishops, and he had "never assumed that it would necessarily be published." When a vote was finally taken at the Bishops' Meeting, "a large majority were against publication" of the report on spiritualism.

One week after the bishops of the Anglican Church decided to continue the embargo on the report, Archbishop Lang wrote a "private and confidential" letter to Bishop Francis Underhill. Lang asked Bishop Underhill for help and advice about the statement that he would have to make announcing that the committee's report would not be published. The archbishop enclosed a draft statement and told Bishop Underhill that he knew "how disappointed you and the other members of your Committee must be, but I hope you will think that what I have said [in the draft statement] meets the case."[9] Archbishop Lang again expressed his gratitude to Bishop Underhill and ended on a positive note: "But I am sure that the Report will be of the greatest use to Bishops who are responsible for guiding the teaching of the Church in their relations with the clergy and others who may consult or write to them on this difficult matter."

The draft from Archbishop Lang, entitled "A Committee on Spiritualism," began by repeating the original charge to the committee, namely, "to investigate the subject of communications with discarnate spirits and the claims of Spiritualism in relation to the Christian Faith."[10] Lang emphasized strongly that the committee report was always meant to be private and confidential in nature, and he also mentioned that the members had not reached an unanimous conclusion. The statement from Lang then announced that the bishops of the Anglican Church at their recent June meeting decided that "it would not be advisable to publish the Report." On the positive side, however, the archbishop pointed out that the report did contain much valuable and important material on spiritualism and psychical phenomena. Nonetheless, the archbishop's draft concluded, "in respect of practical guidance to Christian people on a subject fraught with grave dangers it did not seem to be so clear or conclusive as to make its publication desirable." In reply, Bishop Underhill thanked Lang for sending him the statement and replied that he agreed with the wording of the draft.[11] Underhill also expressed his opinion that he did not believe it was necessary to consult the other members of the committee about the wording of the archbishop's draft statement.

But before Archbishop Lang issued the statement Lambeth Palace began to receive mail asking for information on the deliberations of the Bishops' Meetings. Not surprisingly, the chairman of the Confraternity of Clergy, Ministers, Laymen, and Spiritualists, Mrs. M. A. St. Clair Stobart, expressed her views to the archbishop. In the first place, she wanted to know the results of the discussions which took place during the June meeting of the Anglican bishops.

"And, if for any reason, the subject was not brought forward," she wrote, "may we respectfully hope that the Report will be published independently by the Archbishop, and not be indefinitely pigeonholed?"[12] Making explicit reference to the war currently being fought, she ended by telling Lang that a definite statement by the Anglican Church "on the subject of Life after Death . . . would be of special value in these death-dealing days." Lang's secretary, Alan Don, assured Mrs. St. Clair Stobart that the bishops had indeed discussed the question of publishing the report and had decided "that the Archbishop of Canterbury should issue to the Press a short statement to the effect that it was not considered desirable to make the Report public."[13] He also told her that the bishops recognized the importance and the necessity of issuing a statement on the subject of eternal life, and that several bishops had already begun to collaborate on the subject.

The official statement from Archbishop Lang dealing with the actions of the Bishops' Meeting appeared in the press on 5 July, and on the following day Lang received a request from the physicist, Robert John Strutt, fourth Baron Rayleigh, asking Lang for permission to see a copy of the report in confidence.[14] Archbishop Lang refused Lord Rayleigh's request: "The Report . . . was private and confidential," and the bishops at their recent meeting also decided that the report should not be published.[15] Moreover, he continued, the committee which had studied the relationship between spiritualism and the Christian faith had come to some conclusions which "did not seem sufficiently clear and helpful." Remembering his past mistake, Lang then told Rayleigh that previously he had "foolishly allowed a certain distinguished foreigner much interested in these matters to look at it [the report] under a pledge from him that he would regard it as strictly private." This individual failed to keep his word, and consequently sections of the report were leaked to the public. In the archbishop's estimation, some members of the committee also came up short in "observing the confidential character of the Report. I feel therefore that I dare not begin, even in your case where I know that confidence would be trusted, to make exceptions." The comments of W. R. Matthews, a member of the committee, must have angered the archbishop. In the Frederic W. H. Myers Lecture delivered in 1940, Canon Matthews made some remarks about the witnesses and the difference of opinion among the members, and referred to the delay in the publication of the committee's findings, suggesting "that they may have found their final resting place in the archiepiscopal pigeon holes, and not in the archiepiscopal mind."[16] Several other requests to see the report reached the archbishop's desk, but they did not express the outrage at the ban on publication which appeared in the pages of the spiritualist newspapers.[17]

The 11 July edition of the *Light* reported the policy of the archbishop of Canterbury not to publish the findings of the committee on spiritualism, and it also printed the official statement from Lambeth Palace which had recently appeared in *The Times* on 5 July 1940. The author of the article, Mercy

Phillimore, the secretary of the London Spiritualist Alliance and a witness before the committee, regretted that the majority report would remain private. Consequently, "it will not be available to give greater confidence, particularly to members of the Church who are also Spiritualists.[18] Spiritualists outside Church circles are less concerned with the opinion of the Church," she continued, and "it is the Church itself which stands to lose most by the decision." The Anglican Church had missed a golden opportunity to minister to the needs of people during times of personal crisis and anxiety caused by the war in Europe.

> It is a tragedy that in the present urgent need for spiritual guidance the Church should refuse to recognise a consensus of opinion based on ascertained fact which actually makes clearer and more intelligible to the reason of men the Christian dogmas taught by the Church, and which are frequently rejected by religiously-minded people who are without the key of understanding which Spiritualism can offer.

Numerous readers also contributed their thoughts and opinions on the decision of Archbishop Lang to enforce the ban on publication of the report. One interested person wrote a lengthy essay which argued that the beauty and the benefits of Anglican services and sacraments could be enhanced by means of spiritualism.[19] Baron Palmstierna, the "distinguished foreigner" who allegedly leaked the findings of the committee report, revealed to the press that at a recent meeting of spiritualists a message from the spirit world arrived which foretold the suppression of the report by the archbishop of Canterbury. "The Church will not have the courage to reveal to the world what they really feel and think about communications with us. Many of them have visions, but lack courage and are filled with self-consciousness."[20] Another communication, according to Baron Palmstierna, told the group "that it was doubtful that the Church authorities would be willing" to make the report public. On the other hand, one reader of *Light* defended the decision reached at the June Bishops' Meeting: "The bishops are trying to do their duty as they see it, and should not be charged with a crime."[21]

The *Psychic News* announced the church's decision to keep the findings of the committee from the public under the headline, "Bishops Smother Church Report on Spiritualism."[22] Quoting extracts from the archbishop of Canterbury's statement announcing that the report would remain private and confidential, the paper called this policy "clerical censorship." The report, it continued, "has been smothered by Orthodoxy, which true to its traditional policy is attempting to suppress any truth which conflicts with its antiquated theology." The newspaper's article argued that the report of the committee would have certainly been published if the conclusions had been critical of spiritualism and then gave a list of prominent prelates (York, Norwich, Chelmsford, Lincoln, and Liverpool) who had said favorable things about spiritualism in the past.

The paper's real condemnation of the embargo on the findings of the report, however, concerned the apparent lack of direction which Archbishop Lang's policy offered to clergymen, especially in light of the escalating hostilities on the Continent. It appeared to some that the Anglican Church would sadly repeat its failures to comfort the sorrowing and the bereaved. The memory of the last war still remained painfully clear in the minds of many Britons. "This guidance is now denied them, at a time when the ranks of the bereaved are being swollen because of the war," the paper pointed out, and it "is ironical that the Church should attempt to withhold from mourners, at a time when they most need it, the only means by which they can obtain real comfort." The Anglican Church had once again closed its eyes and turned its back to modern knowledge. But the lack of spiritual guidance or ecclesiastical direction especially concerned the *Psychic News*:

> In war-time, when religion should be able to give a magnificent lead, Orthodoxy pathetically scuttles itself. The refusal of the Primate backed by his diocesan bishops, to publish this historic document is one more nail in the coffin of Orthodoxy.

The following week's edition of the same paper continued to emphasize the theme that the Anglican Church had missed an opportunity to exercise leadership. Quoting "a well-known man who has seen the report," probably Baron Palmstierna, the lead article noted that "if the Church leaders had been bold enough to publish this epoch-making declaration it would have led to a religious renaissance, not only in this country but all over the Western world."[23] The article reported that "some of the Committee are disappointed—at least one is angry—that the fruits of their labours should be dismissed in an off-handed manner and then concealed from the world," and the paper argued that if the committee had produced a negative report "it is extremely doubtful whether it would have been suppressed." The Anglican Church made an enormous mistake by enforcing the ban of silence. "Very unwisely, the Primate and his bishops have decided to defend Orthodoxy rather than publish a document which would have been a turning point in the history of the Church."

A new man at Lambeth Palace did not mean a change in church policy concerning publication of the report. Cosmo Gordon Lang resigned as archbishop of Canterbury on 31 March 1942, and William Temple moved from York as his successor. Temple had already made a significant contribution to the debate raging over the official Anglican attitude toward the report on spiritualism. The 1940 Bishops' Meeting had suggested that the church undertake and sanction the publication of a pamphlet dealing with Christian beliefs on eternal life, and shortly before he moved south, William Temple wrote *The Christian Hope of Eternal Life*. He began this short work by drawing attention to the bereavement and sorrow associated with the war and the appeals and attractions of spiritualism. "At such a time as this it is inevitable that multitudes of people should turn their minds with new and often even agonising anxiety to the question of a future life," Temple pointed out, "and many turn to spiritualistic practices in hope of gaining the assurance which they so deeply desire."[24] The Christian doctrine of eternal life, on the other hand, offered the bereaved a "more secure and more inspiring confidence than any recourse to spiritualistic séances and the like."

The basis for the Christian belief, according to Temple, rested on the firm and strong faith in God. The tendency associated with spiritualism, which placed people at the center of reality, tended to create evil. One must escape from this "self-centredness, and our main spiritual need is to be delivered from this, and to learn to trust in God as the centre of life." If one, however, inverted this order and if one sought assurances "of survival of death independently of any faith in God, it may easily tend to intensify self-centredness." If one professed faith in God, one must necessarily entrust the souls of the departed to God's keeping. Moreover, Temple continued, "the nature of eternal life . . . cannot be grasped by us while on earth." People should also be conscious of the belief in the communion of saints. In Christian worship, "when we lift up our hearts to the Lord, forthwith it is with angels and archangels and with all the company of heaven that we laud and magnify God's glorious name."

Archbishop Temple then lashed out against some aspects of spiritualism. "How poor, in comparison with that rich experience," he pointed out, "is the dubious evidence provided by spiritualistic practices!" Temple told the reader that he recently had the opportunity to examine evidence associated with certain spiritualistic activities, and he came to the conclusion that there were many shortcomings which cast doubt on their veracity. Consequently, "this can be no more than a very insecure foundation for trust in a future life for ourselves or for those whom we love." For those bereaved Anglicans who believed that they had received some comfort or proof of life after death from spiritualism, Archbishop Temple maintained that "the foundation is precarious, and there is always the risk, at least, of stopping short at the stage of self-centred consolation." Only through self-surrender to "God made known in Christ" could one find the real secret of eternal life. He concluded his apologia with the final appeal: "It is primarily a call and challenge to accept the Gospel and so be made worthy to receive God's gift of fellowship with Himself; for eternal life, which is fellowship with God, is 'the gift of God in Christ Jesus our Lord.'"

On a pastoral level, Archbishop Temple did not abandon or ignore those Anglicans who wrote to him during the war and asked for his advice on questions dealing with spiritualism. In 1942, for example, a businessman "consulted the Archbishop (as 'a learned and discreet person') on the 'appearance' of his wife after her death and on some talk the two had had together."[25] The writer assured the archbishop that he had "never dabbled in spiritualism, knew very little about it, and don't like what I know." Responding in November 1942, Archbishop Temple informed the man that he had reached several conclusions about spiritualism throughout his life. In the first place, Temple drew a "sharp distinction between any experience which, like yours, is unsought, and anything resulting from resort to a medium or deliberate waiting for messages."[26]

Archbishop Temple then addressed the issue of life after death. "So far as I have considered physical phenomena, I know nothing that would persuade me to accept so great a conclusion as survival of death if I did not believe it on other grounds." But the archbishop pointed out that he was "strongly inclined to interpret some of the phenomena as actual communications." Noting the writer's experience of his wife, Temple told him that the evidence for appearances "is stronger" for those taking place at the moment of a death or in a dream, especially "of those who were very closely bound by love." The archbishop sounded like someone who believed in the claims of spiritualism: "With that background of thought I am led by the description of your own experience to believe that it was a perfectly real communion between you and your wife, in which she took the first step 'coming' to you." He followed up this statement by pointing out "that God did thus permit your wife to make known to you her love." The archbishop ended his letter and stressed that "all this rests on (1) faith in God and His care for us, (2) consequent faith in our survival of death and continued fellowship."

Archbishop Temple's personal views and the comfort he offered troubled Anglicans, however, did not placate all parties interested in spiritualism. Although the furor over the decision to enforce the ban on the publication of the report on spiritualism died down during Temple's brief tenure as primate, some correspondence on the topic did reach his desk. His written words on the Christian belief in eternal life did not answer the questions of many who wanted to see the conclusions of the committee's report themselves. Soon after Temple's appointment as the new archbishop of Canterbury, Maurice Barbanell, editor of *Psychic News*, wrote an open letter to the new primate about the report on spiritualism. "You are a courageous man," Barbanell began.[27] "You have already revealed that you are not afraid to change your opinion." The author then pointed out that "The publication of the report . . . would dispel the belief that the Church resorts to evasion and suppression rather than face up to Truth." Temple responded to Barbanell's challenge in a blunt manner.

> I took a foremost part in urging that the report should not be published. I did this because frankly I thought it a very ineffective piece of work and, quite irrespective of the tendency . . . in one direction or another, I thought it would be discreditable to the Church to produce so amateurish a statement on what is in any case a very important subject.

Barbanell answered and drew attention to the archbishop's contention that the report on spiritualism was an "amateurish statement" and "a very ineffective piece of work. The world needs spiritual comfort . . . We spiritualists are doing our best . . . to be of service," he continued. "If the Church refuses to permit co-operation, but insists on driving a wedge between us, that is not our fault." The reply from the archbishop of Canterbury remained the same: "As far as I can estimate my own judgment, I should have been opposed to print this report, whatever the upshot of it." Barbanell wrote several more letters hoping to reason with Archbishop Temple, but Temple refused to budge from his position. Others, however, also tried to force a change of the archiepiscopal mind.

In September 1942, Archbishop Temple received a copy of a letter from the Rev. E. G. Elcock who asked about the deliberations and outcomes of Archbishop Lang's committee on spiritualism. "It has been alleged to me," the letter stated, "that the report was with-held [sic] from publication, and, if this be so, I should be glad to know the real reason."[28] Archbishop Temple's chaplain thanked Canon R. E. Parsons, who had sent him the letter from Elcock, and informed him that "it was never intended that the report should be published."[29] After mentioning the unfortunate leakage of information, the archbishop's chaplain offered an explanation for the policy of silence adopted by the church: "If the report had been unanimous, one way or the other, the Committee might have decided to publish it, but this was not the case and it was strongly felt that to issue a majority report with a very strong minority report would merely have confused the public." The letter closed with another reminder that the committee never intended to publish its report on spiritualism.

Some members of the committee also wanted Archbishop Temple to ease the restriction on the contents of the report. In 1944, Harold Anson, one of the members of Lang's committee on spiritualism, approached the archbishop on behalf of Sir Ernest Bennett, M.P., and asked if Bennett could possibly see a copy of the committee's report "for purely confidential use."[30] Not surprisingly, a negative reply came from Lambeth Palace. "His Grace is very sorry not to accede to your request, but he has all along felt obliged to take the line that the Report on Spiritualism was a definitely confidential document between the Committee and the Bishops, and he does not feel that he could be a party to showing it to anyone."[31] This interest in the report, however, prompted Archbishop Temple to draft a memo to serve as a guideline for all future queries about the report on spiritualism and its publication:

> The Archbishop is anxious that the phenomena of the thing should be studied by scientific people; he thinks it is dangerous to get involved except as a scientific student until the laws governing these things have really been worked out. It is open to an enormous amount of deception—both self-deception and deception of other people.

[The] Report was never intended to be published nor was it drafted with that object.[32]

A few letters continued to trickle in which requested permission to examine the report, and the memo of January 1944 probably served as the standard refusal. One letter to the archbishop, however, sheds some light on Archbishop Temple's personal thoughts on spiritualism and its relationship to Christianity. In 1944, a letter reached the archbishop which asked him if it were appropriate for an Anglican priest to baptize a child whose parents and godparents professed a belief in spiritualism.[33] Moreover, the writer of the letter also asked "whether being a 'Spiritualist' does or does not mean also not professing Christianity." To the first question about the baptism Archbishop Temple replied that "it would not be right for a priest to baptize an infant if one of the parents was a Spiritualist."[34] Temple's position on the second question would have pleased many spiritualists: "There are some Spiritualists who profess and call themselves Christians, and the Church has never denounced Spiritualism."

If the letters directed to Archbishop William Temple's attention slowed down, some people who wanted the report published took their campaign to the pages of pamphlets. In 1942, after the resignation of Archbishop Lang, the Psychic Press brought out a booklet, *The Silence of Dr. Lang*.[35] This publication reprinted the history and the background of the archbishop's Committee on spiritualism, sections of letters to and from Lambeth Palace dealing with its possible publication, and extracts taken from the press expressing disbelief and dismay at the church's decision not to make public the report and its conclusions. The pages of this pamphlet contained nothing new or startling for the readers who had faithfully followed the controversy surrounding the publication of the report. But the author did claim that out of the archbishop of Canterbury's "refusal to publish the report there emerges a great triumph for spiritualism."[36] "Very unwisely," it concluded, "the Primate and his bishops decided to defend Orthodoxy rather than circulate a document which would have marked a turning point in Church history . . . by demonstrating that the psychic phenomena recorded in the Bible are being repeated today, [and] would give guidance to thousands of loyal members of the Church."[37]

In 1947, Maurice Barbanell, the editor of *Psychic News*, wrote the short booklet *Banned by the Church: The Secret Report on Spiritualism*. Again, the pages of this publication cover much of the same ground already reported by the newspapers about the committee and its conclusions. The author also pointed the finger of shame at the June 1940 Bishops' Meeting and the resolve of the bishops not to authorize publication of the report:

> You must remember that the verdict of the bishops was delivered in 1940, during one of the black periods of the war, when you would have thought the bishops of the official religion of this land might have given a magnificent

lead. Instead, as the Church has so often done in the past, it set its face against progress and anathematised a new truth.[38]

The author ended his pamphlet on a prophetic and positive note. "Truth cannot be suppressed for long," Barbanell pointed out, "Knowledge does spread and permeate."

In 1944, Margery Lawrence's book, *Ferry Over Jordan*, critiqued the shroud of secrecy which covered the deliberations of the archbishop's committee, including the failure to reveal the names of the members. "*But no public report has ever been made regarding that conclusion—which obviously implies that it was favourable to Spiritualism.*"[39] After dismissing the stereotyped claims which associated spiritualism with Satan and the forces of evil, she launched an attack against the integrity of the Anglican Church. "I have no use for anything that cannot face the truth; and the Churches cannot and *will* not face the truth we claim—which is that we can *prove* what they merely beg us to take on trust."[40] It appears that Mrs. M. A. St. Clair Stobart gave up her attempts to have the report made public, but she still continued to stress the close relationship between Christianity and spiritualism. In *The Open Secret*, which appeared in 1947, she demonstrated the similarities between spiritualism and the Christian Scriptures. "Spiritualism has been God's method," she declared and, moreover, "Spiritualism can save Christianity."[41] But the old relationship between bereavement and the appeal of spiritualism did not disappear from her arguments. "And though nothing can compensate us for the personal loss, or check the tears of sorrows when the parting comes," Mrs. St. Clair Stobart wrote, "the sting of death has gone, for we know that our beloved is living more gloriously than we."[42]

The report on spiritualism eventually reached the eyes of the public, but in the first instance not because of any ecclesiastical change of policy. The *Psychic News* published the text of the majority report in its 8 November 1947 edition. It appears that an unidentified and disgruntled member of Archbishop Lang's committee thought that interested people had a right to see the report and saw to it that a copy fell into the hands of the editor of the paper, Maurice Barbanell. Only after the embargo of forty years had elapsed, the *Christian Parapsychologist* printed the entire text of the report in March 1979. A recent edition of the same journal, in June 1991, noted that "as psychical research, spiritualism, and the attitude of the Churches to psychical enquiry have all altered so greatly in the last fifty years or more, the Underhill Report is now of little more than historical interest."[43] "Can we now bury it and, instead," the editor asked, "let the Churches' Fellowship for Psychical and Spiritual Studies alert the Christian world to the importance of the psychic dimension to human experience and the need for it to be integrated within orthodox Christian theology, spirituality, and practice?"

In his 1966 Frederic W. H. Myers Memorial Lecture, E. Garth Moore touched upon topics which had caught the attention of spiritualists and Christians between the two world wars. Like some of an earlier generation, Moore pointed out "that theologians have given but little encouragement to psychical researchers."[44] His comments about the relationship of Christianity to spiritualism, moreover, sounded similar to those spoken many times during the interwar period by those people who advocated closer study and an objective investigation of the two:

> In truth Psychical Research should be the meeting-point between the Natural Sciences and Theology. If each of the three were to show a proper respect for the others, doors might suddenly fly open which hitherto have been closed. I am sure that Theology has much to learn from both Psychology and Parapsychology. I am sure that Religion (which I do not confuse with Theology, despite their close relationship) has been considerably strengthened by Psychical Research.

The carnage of the Great War and the pastoral need to minister to the bereaved did certainly bring the question of the relationship of spiritualism and Christianity into sharp relief. This issue, which might appear dormant at times, will never totally disappear from theological discussions. As in the turmoil of the interwar period, it will continue to be the subject of research and study for generations.[45]

Notes

1. R. Laurence Moore, *In Search of White Crows: Spiritualism, Parapsychology, and American Cuture* (New York: Oxford University Press, 1977), 4.
2. Ibid., 64.
3. G. Nelson, *Spiritualism and Society*, 26.
4. Ibid., 162.
5. Ibid., 163.
6. Ibid., 164. In 1942, however, a slight increase in membership did occur.
7. The most famous case was that of Mrs. Helen Duncan. In 1944, she was charged "with pretending to communicate with deceased persons, to deceive and impose on certain of H. M. subjects." She was found guilty and sentenced to nine months' imprisonment. The Fraudulent Mediums Act of 1951 eventually recognized that not all mediums were witches or persons attempting to deceive the public. "This Act, which amended the Witchcraft Act 1735 and the Vagrancy Act 1824, in effect legalized the practice of mediumship in Spiritualist churches, and thus finally extended religious freedom to the Spiritualist movement." Ibid., 167.
8. "Report on the Committee on Spiritualism," Minutes of the Bishops' Meeting, 17 June 1940, Lambeth Palace Library.

9. Lang to Underhill, 24 June 1940, Lang Papers, vol. 70, Lambeth Palace Library.
10. "A Committee on Spiritualism," June 1940, Lang Papers, vol. 70, Lambeth Palace Library.
11. Underhill to Lang, 27 June 1940, Lang Papers, vol. 70, Lambeth Palace Library.
12. M. A. St. Clair Stobart to Lang, 1 July 1940, Lang Papers, vol. 70, Lambeth Palace Library.
13. Don to M. A. St. Clair Stobart, 3 July 1940, Lang Papers, vol. 70, Lambeth Palace Library.
14. Rayleigh to Lang, 6 July 1940, Lang Papers, vol. 70, Lambeth Palace Library.
15. Lang to Rayleigh, 8 July 1940, Lang Papers, vol. 70, Lambeth Palace Library.
16. W. R. Matthews, *Psychical Research and Theology* (London: Society for Psychical Research, 1940), 2. This was the Frederic W. H. Myers Lecture.
17. Harold Anson, one of the members of the archbishop's committee, acted diplomatically when it came to the contents of the report. In 1940, he received a request to write a book dealing with spiritualism, and because of his role as a committee member he asked Archbishop Lang for guidance. Lang's secretary told Anson that Archbishop Lang "sees no objection to your undertaking to write a book on the subject of Spiritualism provided that you do so under your own name and as a private individual." Drawing attention to Anson's knowledge of the contents of the report and the decision reached at the Bishops' Meeting not to publish the report, Lang suggested that he "refrain from actually quoting from the Report or mentioning its recommendations." Lang to Anson, 18 July 1940, Lang Papers, vol. 70, Lambeth Palace Library. In 1941, Anson's book was published, and he faithfully followed the suggestions from Archbishop Lang about refraining from making references to the report. This short book, *The Truth about Spiritualism*, covered a wide area of topics such as the modern evidence for survival, the techniques of a séance, physical phenomena, poltergeists, and evidence of survival. The last two chapters specifically addressed the relationship between religion and spiritualism. Anson expressed some criticism about the contention that spiritualism was a religion: "Spiritualism, considered as a religion, rests upon a misconception that messages given through mediums from the next stage of living are more likely to give us a fresh approach to God than messages given by men living in the flesh, and using their minds as a vehicle of divine truth." H. Anson, *The Truth about Spiritualism* (London: Student Christian Movement Press, 1941), 79.
18. *Light*, 11 July 1940.
19. Ibid.
20. *Light*, 18 July 1940.
21. *Light*, 25 July 1940.
22. *Psychic News*, 13 July 1940.
23. *Psychic News*, 20 July 1940.
24. W. Temple, *The Christian Hope of Eternal Life* (London: SPCK, 1942).
25. F. A. Iremonger, *William Temple: Archbishop of Canterbury*, 548.
26. Temple to ?, 7 November 1942, printed in F. A. Iremonger, *William Temple*, 548.
27. Printed in Maurice Barbanell, *Banned by the Church: The Secret Report on Spiritualism* (London: Spiritualist Press, 1947), 31. Excerpts from this correspondence are printed on pages 31-35.

28. Elcock to Parsons, 29 September 1943, W. Temple Papers, vol. 40, Lambeth Palace Library. Canon R. E. Parsons had forwarded this letter to Archbishop Temple.
29. Chaplain to Parsons, 30 September 1942, W. Temple Papers, vol. 40, Lambeth Palace Library.
30. Anson to Temple, 11 January 1944, W. Temple Papers, vol. 40, Lambeth Palace Library. Anson confessed that he could not find his copy of the report.
31. Chaplain to Anson, 14 January 1944, W. Temple Papers, vol. 40, Lambeth Palace Library.
32. Memo, January 1944, W. Temple Papers, vol. 40, Lambeth Palace Library.
33. Dymes to Temple, 4 June 1944, W. Temple Papers, vol. 40, Lambeth Palace Library.
34. Temple to Dymes, 8 June 1944, W. Temple Papers, vol. 40, Lambeth Palace Library.
35. *The Silence of Dr. Lang* (London: Psychic Press, 1942).
36. Ibid., 16-17.
37. Ibid., 17.
38. M. Barbanell, *Banned by the Church,* 24.
39. M. Lawrence, *Ferry Over Jordan* (London: Robert Hale, 1944), 20.
40. Ibid., 21.
41. M. A. St. Clair Stobart, *The Open Secret* (London: Psychic Press, 1947), 13.
42. Ibid., 24.
43. Editorial in *Christian Parapsychologist* 9 (May 1991): 39.
44. E. Garth Moore, *Survival: A Reconsideration: The Sixteenth Frederic W. H. Myers Memorial Lecture* (London: Society for Psychical Research, 1966), 12. See also E. Garth Moore, *Try the Spirits: Christianity and Psychical Research* (New York: Oxford University Press, 1977).
45. For a brief review of twentieth-century documents and reports dealing with the relationship between spiritualism and Christianity, see A. Haddow, "The Churches and Psychical Research: A Review of Some Twentieth-Century Official Documents," *Christian Parapsychologist* 3 (1980): 291-303.

Appendix One

Resolutions of the 1920 Lambeth Conference

Spiritualism, Christian Science, Theosophy

Resolution One (55). We affirm our conviction that the revelation of God in Christ Jesus is the supreme and sufficient message given to all mankind, whereby we may attain to eternal life. We recognize that modern movements of thought connected with Spiritualism, Christian Science, and Theosophy join with the Christian Church in protesting against a materialistic view of the universe and at some points emphasize partially neglected aspects of truth. At the same time, we feel bound to call attention to the fact that both in the underlying philosophy and in cults and practices which have arisen out of these movements, the teaching given or implied either ignores or explains away or contradicts the unique and central fact of human history, namely, the Incarnation of our Lord and Saviour Jesus Christ.

Resolution Two (56). We recognize that new phenomena of consciousness have been presented to us, which claim, and at the hands of competent psychologists have received, careful investigation, and, as far as possible, the application of scientific method. But such scientific researches have confessedly not reached an advanced stage, and we are supported by the best psychologists in warning our people against accepting as final theories which further knowledge may disprove, and still more against the indiscriminate and undisciplined exercise of psychic powers, and the habit of recourse to *séances*, "seers," and mediums.

Spiritualism

Resolution Three (57). The Conference, while prepared to expect and welcome new light from psychical research upon the powers and processes of the spirit of man, urges strongly that a larger place should be given in the teaching of the Church to the explanation of the true grounds of Christian belief in eternal life, and in immortality, and of the true content of belief in the Communion of Saints as involving real fellowship with the departed through the love of God in Christ Jesus.

Resolution Four (58). The Conference, while recognizing that the results of investigation have encouraged many people to find a spiritual meaning and purpose in human life and led them to believe in survival after death, sees grave dangers in the tendency to make a religion of spiritualism. The practice of spiritualism as a cult involves the subordination of the intelligence and the will to unknown forces or personalities and, to that extent, an abdication of the self-control to which God has called us. It tends to divert attention from the approach to God through the one Mediator, Jesus Christ, under the guidance of the Holy Spirit; to ignore the discipline of faith as the path of spiritual training; and to depreciate the divinely ordained channels of grace and truth revealed and given through Jesus Christ our Lord.

Appendix Two

Conclusions of the Majority

(A) In interpreting our evidence, it is important to take into account the theories, prevalent among the more experienced and careful Spiritualists, as to the nature and value of the alleged messages delivered through the agency of mediums. It is pointed out, on the evidence of the "communicators" themselves, that the communicators and guides are themselves at very different levels of spiritual development and of very partial knowledge, and that the "controls" of which they make use may often be very undeveloped personalities who are capable of this particular service because they are very closely linked with temporarily dissociated portions of the personality of the mediums concerned. There are thus at least three factors which would render messages, especially those of a high order of spiritual or metaphysical value, liable to disturbance, and which lead to the difficulties, generally recognized by Spiritualists, which the communicators would in any case find in transmitting messages which do not already lie within the general conditions of our knowledge. There is, however, nothing inherently self-contradictory, or necessarily improbable, in this account of the conditions involved in such communications. It is, however, no more than an hypothesis, incapable of scientific proof, nor does it assist us in determining the authenticity of the communications themselves. The verification of these, if it is possible at all, may rest upon ordinary scientific tests. To say this is not, however, to deny that the communications may sometimes be held to be convincing upon other than scientific grounds.

In any case it seems necessary to distinguish between the sense of contact with departed friends, or with "guides," and the assurance that messages have necessarily any high value because they come through this unusual channel.

It is perhaps of some importance to notice that there is general agreement in the communications that time has not the same rigid character as a "time-series" in the life that lies beyond death. This is, in any case, probable on other grounds, but it is of interest as indicating a possible reason why the communicators are frequently confused or mistaken as to exact indications of time. This may not be a failure in their own apprehension of the real significance of events, so much as in their power of conveying that apprehension in a form which can be adapted to the mentality of the medium and to the understanding of those to whom the message is directed.

(B) It is often urged as of great significance that Spiritualism in many cases re-affirms the highest convictions of religious people, and that it has brought many to a new assurance of the truth of teaching which had ceased to have any meaning for them. This is a point of some difficulty, since assurance seems to come along different and even conflicting lines. We cannot ignore the fact that at least one considerable Spiritualist organization is definitely anti-Christian in character. This divergence of testimony is explained by spiritualists as due to the continuance of spirits, at least for a period, within the system of beliefs which they have held in this life. It is held that even though the whole development of the personality is being raised from level to level, the attitudes to truth and goodness taken up in this life persist into the next, and that this somewhat divergent testimony to the truths of Christianity must be explained in this way. We should add that whatever be the value of this supposed confirmation of the truths of religion, Spiritualism does not seem to have added anything, except perhaps a practical emphasis, to our understanding of those truths. Many alleged communications seem, indeed, to fall below the highest Christian standards of understanding and spiritual insight, and indeed below the level of spiritual insight and mental capacity shown by the communicators while still in this life. While there is insistence upon the supremacy of love comparable with the New Testament assertion that "God is love," the accounts sometimes given of the mediatorial work of Christ frequently fall very far below the full teaching of the Christian Gospel, seeming to depend rather upon some power of working a miracle of materialisation (in the Resurrection appearances) than upon a radical and final acceptance of the burden of the guilt of man's sin, and a victory so wrought for us upon the cross.

Nevertheless, it is clearly true that the recognition of the nearness of our friends who have died, and of their progress in the spiritual life, and of their continuing concern for us, cannot do otherwise, for those who have experienced it, than add a new immediacy and richness to their belief in the Communion of Saints. There seems to be no reason at all why the Church should regard this vital and personal enrichment of one of her central doctrines with disfavour, so long as it does not distract Christians from their fundamental gladness that they may come, when they will, into the presence of their Lord and Master, Jesus Christ Himself, or weaken their sense that their fellowship is fellowship in Him.

(C) It is claimed by Spiritualists that the character of many events in the Christian revelation, as recorded in the Gospels, is precisely that of psychic phenomena, and that the evidence for the paranormal occurrences which Spiritualism has adduced strongly confirms the historicity of the Gospel records, in the sense that they also are records of paranormal occurrences, including instances, for example, of clairvoyance (in the story of Nathanael), and of materialisation (in the Feeding of the Five Thousand, and, above all, in the narratives of the Resurrection appearances). The miracles of healing are claimed as closely parallel to the healings performed through mediums. It is strongly urged that if we do not accept the evidence for modern psychic happenings, we should not, apart from long tradition, accept the Gospel records either.

It is certainly true that there are quite clear parallels between the miraculous events recorded in the Gospel and modern phenomena attested by spiritualists. And if we assert that the latter must be doubted because they have not yet proved capable of scientific statement and verification, we must add that the miracles, and the Resurrection itself, are not capable of such verification either. We must therefore ask what the proper Christian grounds of belief in these central truths of Christianity are.

The answer to this question is clearly that we believe upon a basis of faith, and not of demonstrable scientific knowledge. Our grounds for this faith are to be found either in a direct mystical assurance that Jesus of Nazareth, as we have received Him, is indeed God's Word to us, or, more broadly, in the apprehension of ethical and spiritual values. We do not accept the Gospels because they record wonders, but because they ring true to the deepest powers of spiritual apprehension which we possess.

But if this is so, we must clearly apply similar criteria to the claims of Spiritualism, and this means that while we regard some part of these claims as matter proper to the scientist, we regard some other parts as not properly capable of scientific verification or dispute, but, at the same time, as deserving the consideration of Christians upon grounds of another kind.

(D) It has been seen, in the account of the evidence submitted to our Committee, that so far as rigid scientific tests are concerned very little, if anything, remains both verifiable and inexplicable out of the whole mass of paranormal phenomena. Modern psychological knowledge has revealed a wide range of powers and of possible sources of misunderstanding in our subconscious or unconscious mind. When these are combined with the possibility of direct thought-transference, or telepathy, many of the communications delivered through mediums seem capable of explanation. We have to notice that one of our scientific witnesses declared that no good evidence for telepathy itself is yet forthcoming, but probably a majority of scientists would accept it as a fact without pretending to offer an explanation of it. If telepathy is denied, the evidence that these communications do come from discarnate spirits is greatly strengthened on the scientific side.

But the tests applied by scientists as such are in their very nature experimental, objective and impersonal. It is necessary to ask whether such tests do not in themselves invalidate an inquiry into values which are in essence personal and spiritual. The experiences which many people have found most convincing are of a kind which could hardly occur in the atmosphere of scientific investigation. They are sporadic, occasional and highly individual. They could not possibly be repeated, or submitted to statistical analysis. It is worth while to notice in this connection that in the ordinary affairs and beliefs of human life we do not ask for scientific verification of this kind. We accept many things as certain in the realm of personal relationships upon the basis of direct insight. When we say that we know our friends, we mean something very different from saying that we can give a scientific and verifiable account of them. But we are none the less sure of our knowledge. Similar certainties are to be found in the sphere of mystical experience.

It may well be that in this matter of the evidence for the survival of the human personality after death, we are dependent upon exactly this same kind of insight, and that scientific verification, though valuable where it can be obtained, is of secondary importance, and only partially relevant. And this is precisely the situation in which we find ourselves in our assurance of Christianity itself. "We walk by faith, and not by sight."

It is thus a weakness, rather than a strength, in the spiritualist position that it has been represented as resting upon scientific verification. If rigid scientific methods are applied it is probable that verification will never be attained.

We may sum up the position from the point of view of science as follows:

There is no satisfactory scientific evidence in favour of any paranormal physical phenomena (materialisations, apports, telekinesis etc.). All the available scientific evidence is against the occurrence of such phenomena. Further, the hypothesis of unconscious mental activity in the mind of the medium or sensitive is a strong alternative hypothesis to that of the action of a discarnate entity in cases of mental mediumship. Thus the strictly *scientific* verdict on the matter of personal survival can only be one of *non-proven*. Again, the whole question of extra-sensory perception is still a matter scientifically *sub judice*.

On the other hand, certain outstanding psychic experiences of individuals, including certain experiences with mediums, make a strong *prima facie* case for survival and for the possibility of spirit-communications, while philosophical, ethical and religious considerations may be held to weigh heavily on the same side.

When every possible explanation of these communications has been given, and all doubtful evidence set aside, it is very generally agreed that there remains some element as yet unexplained. We think that it is probable that the hypothesis that they proceed in some cases from discarnate spirits is the true one.

That so much can be said, even in so cautious a form, involves very important consequences, and makes necessary certain warnings. The following are the points upon which we wish to lay emphasis:

(A) It is abundantly clear, as spiritualists themselves admit, that an easy credulity in these matters opens the door to self-deception and to a very great amount of fraud. We were greatly impressed by the evidence of this which we received, and desire to place on record a most emphatic warning to those who might become interested in Spiritualism from motives of mere curiosity, or as a way of escaping from the responsibility of making their own decisions as Christians under the guidance of the Holy Spirit. It is legitimate for Christians who are scientifically qualified to make these matters a subject of scientific inquiry, though, as we have already said, such inquiry has its necessary limitations. But it is not legitimate, and it is unquestionably dangerous, to allow an interest in Spiritualism, at a low level of true spiritual value, to replace that deeper religion which rests fundamentally upon the right relation of the soul to God Himself.

(B) It is necessary to keep clearly in mind that none of the fundamental Christian obligations or values is in any way changed by our acceptance of the possibility of communication with discarnate spirits.

(C) Where these essential principles are borne in mind, those who have the assurance that they have been in touch with their departed friends may rightly accept the sense of enlargement and of unbroken fellowship which it brings.

(D) It is important to distinguish between assurance of this personal contact and assurance of the accuracy and authority of the messages received. As we have seen, and as many spiritualists admit, there is every probability that even authentic messages would be liable to distortion. There is very great danger of misdirection if such messages are accepted as giving authoritative guidance unless they are checked by our own human reason under the guidance of the Holy Spirit received through prayer. But there is no reason why we should not accept gladly the assurance that we are still in the closest contact with those who have been dear to us in this life, and who are going forward, as we seek to do ourselves, in the understanding and fulfilment of the purpose of God.

(E) We cannot avoid the impression that a great deal of Spiritualism as organised has its centre in man rather than in God, and is, indeed, materialistic in character. To this extent it is a substitute for religion, and is not, in itself, religious at all. We were impressed by the unsatisfactory answers received from practising Spiritualists to such questions as "Has your prayer life, your sense of God, been strengthened by your spiritualist experiences?" This explains in great part the hesitation of many Christians to have anything to do with it, and the strong opposition which they often feel towards it. But if Spiritualism does in fact make so strong an appeal to some, it is at least in part because the Church has not proclaimed and practised its faith with sufficient conviction. There is frequently little real fellowship even between the living, and the full and intimate reality of the Communion of Saints is often a dead letter. Spiritualism claims in fact to be making accessible a reality which the Church has proclaimed but of which it has seemed only to offer a shadow. That is, of course, only part of the truth. For many the appeal of Spiritualism rests upon much lower motives. It may stimulate curiosity in the bizarre. It may offer consolation upon terms which are too easy. It may afford men the opportunity of escaping the challenge of a faith which, when truly proclaimed, makes so absolute a claim upon men's lives that they will not face it but turn aside to some easier way.

(F) It is often held that the practice of Spiritualism is dangerous to the mental balance, as well as to the spiritual condition, of those who take part in it, and it is clearly true that there are cases where it has become obsessional in character. But it is very difficult to judge in these cases whether the uncritical and unwise type of temperament which does undoubtedly show itself in certain spiritualists is a result or a cause of their addiction to these practices. Psychologically it is probable that persons in a condition of mental disturbance, or lack of balance, would very naturally use the obvious opportunities afforded by Spiritualism as a means of expressing the repressed emotions which have caused their disorder. This indeed is true of Christianity itself, which frequently becomes an outlet, not only for cranks, but for persons who are definitely of unstable mentality.

It should be noticed that spiritualists themselves are very much alive to the danger to those who are already unstable, and even to those who are stable, where the motives are wrong and the precautions as to sincerity inadequate. Whatever else is clear in a matter where the evidence is difficult to interpret, it is certain that Spiritualism has every need of the high standards of Christianity and of its witness to a life which rests by faith upon God, and which is thereby freed from the conflicts of desire and of purpose to which all lives not so grounded are liable.

(G) The view has often been held, with some degree of Church authority, that psychic phenomena are real, but that they proceed from evil spirits. The possibility that spirits of a lower order may seek to influence us in this way cannot be excluded as inherently illogical or absurd, but it would be extremely unlikely if there were not also the possibility of contact with good spirits. The belief in angelic guardians or guides has been very general in Christianity. But in any case the Christian life is grounded upon God, and its fundamental activities are prayer and worship, which issue in loving service of mankind. A life so grounded has nothing to fear from evil powers or influences of any kind.

(H) The Church of England, for reasons of past controversy, has been altogether too cautious in its reference to the departed. Anglican prayers for the departed do not satisfy people's needs, because the prayers are so careful in their language that it is not always evident that the departed are being prayed for, as contrasted with the living. In general, we need much more freedom in our recognition of the living unity of the whole Church, in this world and in that which lies beyond death. But detailed suggestions on this point should be matters of dispute, and lie beyond the main purpose of this Report.

(I) If Spiritualism, with all aberrations set aside and with every care taken to present it humbly and accurately, contains a truth, it is important to see that truth not as a new religion but only as filling up certain gaps in our knowledge, so that where we already walked by faith, we may now have some measure of sight as well.

(J) It is in our opinion important that representatives of the Church should keep in touch with groups of intelligent persons who believe in Spiritualism. We must leave practical guidance in this matter to the Church itself.[1]

                      Francis Bath: & Well: P. E. Sandlands
                      W. R. Matthews   Gwendolen Stephenson
                      Harold Anson
                      L. W. Grensted
                      William Brown

Notes

1. The Committee do not recommend that any publicity be given to this note.

Appendix Three

Minority Report

We concur in Parts I, II and III of the foregoing Report but we are unable to assent to the conclusions contained in Part IV thereof, our opinion being as follows:—

1. Spiritualists claim that through paranormal psychical and physical phenomena they communicate with discarnate spirits and receive guidance. These communications are, they say, evidence of survival. But since these communications are received through paranormal psychical and physical phenomena, the hypothesis depends upon the validity of these phenomena. They have for a long time been subject to close scientific investigation, and scientists have provided us with the results of the latest research. They consider that the evidence does not show that paranormal phenomena exist. "Normal psychology and self-deception contain the whole thing, except in cases where fraud occurs . . ." (*Witness G*).

    It will be seen that those scientists who gave evidence before the Committee consider that the spiritualist hypothesis has not been proved; in fact there is no evidence which would convince a scientist or an open-minded layman that Spiritualists do communicate with discarnate spirits.

2. The alleged communications may not only be valueless but may also be misleading and therefore dangerous.

    (A) The alleged communications are for the most part trite and banal, either dealing with trivial and unimportant matters or adding nothing to the discussion of important subjects. No communication has been brought to our notice which has added anything to our knowledge of the Christian revelation. In many cases messages which are regarded by Spiritualists as important are commonplaces of

Christian experience and teaching. It is convenient at this point to refer to the messages which were received at a *séance* arranged by Witness H. We offer no explanation of the glass moving rapidly from letter to letter on the board and spelling out words, nor do we think it necessary to do so. We were disappointed with the content of the communications. There was nothing in them to suggest that they came from minds more enlightened than temporal ones: indeed the general level of the communications was lower than the average level of intelligence of those who took part in the *séance*. We agree that there was no possibility whatsoever of anyone who was touching the glass to direct it consciously towards any of the letters; there was, however, nothing in the messages to suggest that they were communications from discarnate spirits. The evidence of identification of the spirits who communicate through controls is far from satisfying, especially when it is remembered that spirits can, it is alleged, impersonate other spirits. Spiritualists themselves suggest that discarnate spirits are free to return to earth to see what is going on. If this happens they may well share their knowledge with each other, and thus destroy the value of any evidence as to identity.

(B) This brings us to the subject of the danger of receiving alleged spirit communications. We have had evidence of the lack of balance which spiritualist practices encourage in certain types of people. It is a possibility which may await anyone who turns to Spiritualism. Once it is granted that communications are received from discarnate spirits, there is a tendency to invest the messages with a special authority. The person who seeks and receives spirit guidance becomes his own judge of right or wrong. Authority for him lies in these communications which may, and as one witness specifically said, must override the ordinary canons of human judgment and common-sense. "Every man his own pope" is a fair description of the consequences of following spirit guidance. When spirit guidance comes into conflict with the authority of the Church, the Spiritualist is likely to prefer the former and ignore the latter. The power of choice is abandoned in favour of a message which cannot be checked. We have from our own observation of witnesses had ample evidence that spiritualist practices impair common-sense in the ordinary affairs of life and distort the ordinary standards of judgment. There are many Spiritualists who are apparently unable to make decisions on quite commonplace matters without resorting to guidance, so-called, obtained through a medium.

(C) As a result of spiritualist communications, there is a marked tendency among Spiritualists to despise the working of the mind. It is represented by the communication "the brain will kill the spirit." This probably accounts for the ignorance of many Spiritualists with regard to the modern developments of Christian thought. To encourage Spiritualism is to encourage also a growth of this obscurantist outlook. Mind and spirit, reason and faith, both have their place in the formation of Christian thought and doctrine. Spiritualists appear fearful lest too keen a use of the mind or of the critical faculties will invalidate their hypothesis.

(D) Spiritualists believe that the proof of man's survival and immortality obtained through communications will be of great help to the Christian religion and establish the faith of many now outside the Church. At first sight this view seems to have much in its favour, but examination shows that it is by no means so attractive as it first appears. It is highly improbable that the spiritualist hypothesis will ever receive that exact proof which scientists demand. Any proof that falls short of scientific standards would in fact be no proof at all and leave the Christian doctrines as they are at present— ultimately matters of faith. But even if experimental proof of survival were obtained, the Church would not necessarily be helped in its task and would almost certainly be impoverished. For, as the Archbishop of York points out in *Nature, Man and God*, "experimental proof of man's survival of death would bring the hope of immortality into the area of purely intellectual apprehension. It might, or it might not, encourage the belief that God exists; it would certainly, as I think, make very much harder the essential business of faith, which is the transference of the centre of interest and concern from self to God."

(E) We recall that locutions, revelation and visions have been experienced by the saints of the Church. As they sometimes resemble the spiritualist phenomena, we are obliged to comment on them. We are not called upon to investigate their genuineness nor to establish any standards by which they may be judged to be valid revelations of God. But we commend to those people who attach too great importance to these and similar phenomena the teaching of St. John of the Cross, as summarised by Dom John Chapman in his *Spiritual Letters*: "Don't waste time in discovering whether they are from God, or from yourself, or from the Devil—simply detach yourself from them; want God alone, and not His gifts."

3. These reasons persuade us that Spiritualism is not necessary to Christianity and has nothing to add to it. Taken together, the Apostles' and the Nicene Creed contain all that Spiritualism at its best seeks to preach:—

I believe in . . . the Communion of Saints; The Forgiveness of sins; The Resurrection of the body, And the life of the world to come.

We accept Von Hugel's estimate that "there is very little that is spiritual in Spiritualism." The Christian believes in immortality and in the Communion of Saints because he believes in God. Our objection to Spiritualism apart from the reasons we have already given, is that it reverses this order. The Spiritualist believes in God because he believes he has obtained experimental proof of survival and spirit communication. The consequences of this reversal are serious. The letter from Miss Evelyn Underhill deserves the closest study in this connection. Communication rather than God comes first in the spiritualist experiences. The spiritualist outlook, as Miss Underhill says, "is utilitarian and sub-Christian." The Spiritualists have little or nothing to say about the true end of religion, which is worship. Prayer to God is secondary to receiving communication from spirits. So much importance is placed upon the messages from discarnate spirits that the Spiritualist tends to overlook, if he does not altogether ignore, the Christian experience that in prayer and worship the Christian receives guidance from God Himself. The Christian, and the Anglican in particular, believes that he has, through prayer and sacrament, communication with the Godhead. With the Spiritualist, however, communication is not direct and is established only by means of intermediaries. It is not surprising that for the Spiritualist God becomes remote and inaccessible and the mediation of Christ a thing forgotten. The words "through Jesus Christ our Lord" cannot have the same meaning for the Spiritualist that they have for the Christian.

Spiritualists have no monopoly in believing in the continuance of our personalities after death, in communication which we know as the Communion of Saints and as guidance from the Holy Spirit, in immortality and in progress for the spirit in eternal life. The saints have had communications and visions, a number of them very well attested. But the Church has always been on its guard against allowing the phenomena to obscure their possible source—God. The Spiritualist lays great emphasis upon progress in the next world. So does the Church, but without the element of banality which marks the spiritualist picture of the hereafter. Spiritualism in trying to give a detailed account of the next world portrays an existence in which God is so remote that there seems for the instructed Christian but little reason to hope for it. There is an irreconcilable difference between the Church's teaching on the future life and the Spiritualist's account of an existence, very like our own, in which God is but dimly apprehended and where spirits yearn, not to see God, but to communicate with their relations and friends on earth. Acceptance of the spiritualist view of the future life would lead to diminished belief in the sovereignty of God and the redemptive power of Christ. In this conception God is but remotely concerned with all the activities of the future life and spirits are sometimes so earth-bound that, unsatisfied with the fullness of life beyond, they long to speak to the inhabitants of this world. The Church can hardly accept so material a statement of the future life.

4. Before considering what we think the Church's attitude towards Spiritualism ought to be, we think it relevant to refer briefly to the history of the movement, to which insufficient attention has, in our opinion, hitherto been paid. The movement in its modern form began in 1848, and we may well ask why, if some of the controls had been discarnate for thousands of years before then, they did not sooner succeed in establishing communication with people in this world. It was not until March 31st, 1848, that communications are alleged to have been received by two child mediums in America, Maggie and Katie Fox. Some forty years later, when both had become intemperate in their habits, Maggie, in the company of Katie, denounced Spiritualism as "absolute falsehood" and "the most wicked blasphemy known to the world." She later retracted this confession. But this beginning and the subsequent lives of the two mediums were a dubious foundation on which to build the spiritualist hypothesis and movement. Its subsequent history has indeed been chequered, and it should be borne in mind that it has been stated with good reason that "with the exception of Home there is hardly a prominent medium for physical manifestations against whom a good case has not been made out that he or she, at least on certain occasions, had recourse to unscrupulous trickery." Even Conan Doyle in *The Edge of the Unknown* admits that he underrated the corruption in the United States. The very state of mind in which most people come to be attracted by Spiritualism renders them unlikely and certainly unwilling to detect fraud. We think it undesirable in the extreme that the Church should give the least shadow of approval to a movement which is still being gravely abused by the unscrupulous.

5. Before the Church should consider giving any approval to the Spiritualist movement, it should examine very closely the components of that movement. They consist of separate groups, some of which profess to be Christians, but nevertheless teach pernicious doctrines; some are anti-Christian, some are religious but non-Christian, and others are queer mixtures of corruption and superstition. At one end of the scale are Anglican clergy who supplement their religious exercises with the practice of Spiritualism;

at the other end of the scale are the charlatans, who for a fee will go into a trance, or cast a horoscope, or give predictions based upon numerology. In the present condition of the Spiritualist movement to bless one is to bless all.

Nor is it easy to make distinctions, save from purely personal experience. There is no such thing as the religion of Spiritualism. There are instead a vast number of small groups under the guidance of a medium's spirit control. If a sweeping condemnation of the movement would be unjust to the honest and sincere spiritualists, a general or even modified approval would also be harmful. The Church should not attempt to have relations with the whole movement, and it should hesitate long before it selected a particular group for contact.

6. We are concerned at two marked tendencies in Spiritualism. First, it encourages a morbid curiosity on the part of many unscientific investigators. We regard this not only as mentally unhealthy, but morally dangerous. Secondly, it encourages an interest in the supernatural from the unworthiest motives. There are those who try to communicate with spirits in order to discover the future, for their own material profit. Both these tendencies lead to gross superstition, but the element of superstition is also introduced without them. There is a point where the Spiritualist movement mingles with the underworld of necromancy. Horoscopes, crystal gazing, and the like, are not dissociated from certain sections of the movement. No doubt these practices are repudiated by many Spiritualists, but it must not be forgotten that the Spiritualist hypothesis gives them a good measure of support. If it were in principle desirable that the Church should have contact with Spiritualism, we should feel bound to advise against any approach until the Spiritualist movement had set its house in order and purged itself of these dark works. Even so, and if this were done, that very denial of authority, which the Spiritualist hypothesis encourages, allows for a dangerous growth of superstition in individual practices.

7. We are not satisfied that the communications received proceed from discarnate spirits. In accounting for spiritualist phenomena, considerable allowances must be made for coincidence, mal-observation, honest self-deception, auto-suggestion and credulity and in particular for fraud and collusion among mediums. These elements will account for the vast majority of the phenomena which accompany spiritualist practices. A number of explanations has been made to account for what remains. We summarise the more important ones as follows:—

(A) Professor Wm. McDougall in *An Outline of Abnormal Psychology* considers that the least extravagant hypothesis for the interpretation of the facts is that the sub-conscious or secondary personalities of mediums possess wide reaching powers of telepathic reception. Some experts consider, however, that the telepathic hypothesis will not cover the facts.

(B) The compound theory is advanced by Professor C. D. Broad (*cf. The Mind and Its Place in Nature*). The theory is somewhat involved, but its principles are as follows: "Mind" is a compound of two factors, neither of which separately has the characteristic properties of a mind. "The psychic factor would be like some chemical element which has never been isolated; and the characteristics of a mind would depend jointly on those of the psychic factor and on those of the material organism with which it is united." The mind, on this theory, has properties which cannot be explained from either the body or the "non-body" part of human personality. It is to be noted, however, that following on Dr. Broad's theory of survival, what survives of the total personality after death is only a "psychic factor" or a mere "fragment".

(C) Cryptaesthesia, xenoglossy and lucidity have all been offered as explanations of psychic phenomena. But often the use of these terms raises more difficulties than it solves.

(D) Human powers of supernormal perception have not yet been fully investigated, and it is reasonable to suppose that they may provide a substantial, if not a complete, explanation of the phenomena. It is important to remember that certain of these powers are as extraordinary to most people as the phenomena of Spiritualism, although the former are supernormal and in no sense supernatural. Synaesthesia, for example, provokes as much amazement as second sight. We may ask, therefore, if the supposed connection of the Spiritualist phenomena with the future life has not invested them with a special degree of unusualness which, when they are compared to the supernormal powers of human perception, they do not deserve.

An interesting and important example of the way in which human powers of supernormal perception can be developed is described in *Preliminary Studies of a Vaudeville Telepathist* (S. G. Soal. University of London Council for Psychical research. 5s). Here it was shown that alleged telepathic powers in finding a hidden object were due to sharp observation of the footsteps of a person walking behind the subject and to observations of the involuntary head movements of his audience and their facial expressions. Skill in recognising playing cards could be accounted for by supposing that his acuteness of touch and alertness to sensory stimuli were exceptional. The experiments upon this artist are important because they prove that sensory perception may be cultivated to an extremely high degree. We see no reason why mediums should not possess or cultivate these same powers of perception. Unexplained, these powers would certainly mystify the sitter, who would regard them as supernatural. We consider that possession of these powers by mediums may explain a great many Spiritualist phenomena that are now regarded as psychic.

Exceptional muscular development in mediums may also account for some phenomena. It has been suggested, though not proved, that this development or an anatomical peculiarity has been used to produce alleged spirit rappings through movement of the joints or in other ways.

(E) Sensory hallucination is a possible explanation, but it is a phenomenon rare outside the *séance* room. On the other hand, it is in the *séance* room that the favourable conditions for this form of hallucination would exist.

(F) Subconscious or automatic co-operation on the part of sitters is held to account for the phenomena connected with *planchette*, tumbler moving and automatic writing. We consider that the *séance* which the Committee had with the friends of Witness H provides good evidence for this.

(G) Finally, we cannot ignore the fact that physics, physiology, psychology and biology have not reached the end of their researches. The trend of their advances has been to show that what one age regarded as a supernatural phenomena was rightly held to be explained in the next age by new discoveries. This has certainly been true in the history of Spiritualist phenomena. The process has not stopped, and those who accept the phenomena of this decade must not be disappointed if in time these are proved to be explicable by wholly natural laws.

8. In conclusion we believe that Churchpeople have drifted towards Spiritualism because the Church has not sufficiently emphasised:

(a) The value of praying for the dead;
(b) The doctrine of the Communion of Saints;
(c) The grounds for the Christian belief in eternal life;
(d) The value of the Eucharist as the meeting place for souls present and departed;
(e) A mystical side of Christianity which is within the reach of nearly every Christian;
(f) The truth that knowledge of and faith in God can be the only true consolation for mourners.

9. We recommend as follows:—

   (1) The Church should not seek to establish any relations with Spiritualism; the Church should regard it only as a field for scientific inquiry, the conduct of which is not normally a task for the clergy.
   (2) The practice of praying for the dead needs to be more widely commended.
   (3) An Office for the Dead is needed.
   (4) Anglican prayers for the dead do not satisfy people's needs, because the prayers are so cautious in their language that it is not always evident that the dead are being prayed for, as contrasted with the living.
   (5) Some well-informed literature about the possible dangers of Spiritualism is badly needed.
   (6) Better teaching is needed about the Communion of Saints.
   (7) Better teaching is needed about Eternal life and the grounds in experience for the Christian hope.

Guy Mayfield
Mildred Rawlinson
W. S. Wigglesworth

Bibliography

Manuscript Collections

Bishops' Meetings, 1932-1938. BM 10. Lambeth Palace Library. Lambeth Palace, London.
Bishops' Meeting, 1939-1944. BM 11. Lambeth Palace Library.
Lambeth Conference Papers, 1920. LC 135. Lambeth Palace Library.
Lang Papers. Vols. 70, 123. Lambeth Palace Library.
Lyttelton Diary. Chan I, 6/11. Churchill College Archives. Cambridge University, Cambridge.
Minutes. Archbishop's Committee on Spiritualism, 3 July 1938. Lang Papers. Vol. 70. Lambeth Palace Library.
Proceedings of the [Lambeth] Conference, 1 August 1908. LC 69. Lambeth Palace Library.
Proceedings of the [Lambeth] Conference, 5-7 July 1920. LC 105. Lambeth Palace Library.
Proceedings of the [Lambeth] Conference, 5 August 1920. LC 5/36.
W. Temple Papers. Vol. 40. Lambeth Palace Library.

Newspapers

The Church Family Newspaper (London); *Daily Chronicle* (London); *Daily Dispatch* (Manchester); *Daily Herald* (London); *Daily Sketch* (London); *Daily Telegraph* (London); *Light* (London); *News Review* (London); *Prediction* (London); *Psychic News* (London); *The Times*.

Printed Works

Anson, H. *The Truth about Spiritualism*. London: Student Christian Movement Press, 1941.
Archbishop's Committee on Spiritualism. Minutes. 3 July 1938. Lang Papers. Vol. 70. Lambeth Palace Library.

Archbishop's Committee on Spiritualism: Report of the Committee to the Archbishop of Canterbury (1939). *The Christian Parapsychologist* 3 (March 1979): 40-73.

Archbishop's Committee on Spiritualism. *Report of the Committee to the Archbishop of Canterbury* (1939). Lang Papers. Vol. 70. Lambeth Palace Library.

Barbanell, M. *Banned by the Church: The Secret Report on Spiritualism.* London: Spiritualist Press, 1947.

Barrow, L. *Independent Spirits: Spiritualism and English Plebeians, 1850-1910.* London: Routledge & Kegan Paul, 1986.

Bassett, J. *100 Years of National Spiritualism.* London: Headquarters Publishing, 1990.

Book of Common Prayer. Articles of Religion.

Boyd, J. *The New Spiritualism: Is It from Heaven or Hell? A Sober Examination of Sir Arthur Conan Doyle.* London: Pickering & Inglis, 1920.

Bradshaw, M., comp. *The War and Religion: A Preliminary Bibliography of Material in English Prior to January 1, 1919.* New York: Association Press, 1919.

Brandon, R. *The Spiritualists: The Passion for the Occult in the Nineteenth and Twentieth Centuries.* New York: Prometheus Books, 1984.

Brittain, V. *Testament of Youth.* London: Virgo Press, 1993.

Cairns, D. S., ed., *The Army and Religion: An Enquiry and Its Bearing upon the Religious Life of the Nation.* London: Macmillan, 1919.

Cannadine, D. "War and Death, Grief and Mourning in Modern Britain." In J. Whaley, ed., *Mirrors of Mortality: Studies in the Social History of Death.* New York: St. Martin's Press, 1981.

"The Christian Faith in Relation to Spiritualism, Christian Science and Theosophy." Proceedings of the Lambeth Conference, 5 August 1920. LC 5/36. Lambeth Palace Library.

Crockford's Clerical Directory.

Cuming, G. J. *A History of Anglican Liturgy.* London: Macmillan, 1969.

Davidson, R. "The Church's Opportunity." In *War and Christianity.* London: Jarrold & Sons, 1914.

———. Forward to *The National Mission of Repentance and Hope: Reports of the Archbishops' Committees of Inquiry.* London: SPCK, 1919.

———. "The Peace of God." In *The Testing of a Nation.* London: Macmillan, 1919.

De Brath, S. *Psychical Research, Science and Religion.* London: Methuen, 1925.

———. *The Religion of the Spirit.* London: Rider, 1927.

The Dictionary of National Biography.

Dixon, G. E. *Spiritualism: An Introduction.* Hull: Conrad Publishing, 1987.

Doctrine in the Church of England (1938): The Report of the Commission on Christian Doctrine Appointed by the Archbishops of Canterbury and York. London: SPCK, 1938.
Dougall, L. "The Natural Explanation of Spiritualist Phenomena." Lambeth Conference Papers, 1920. LC 135. Lambeth Palace.
Doyle, Sir Arthur Conan. *Pheneas Speaks: Direct Spirit Communications in the Family Circle.* London: Psychic Press, 1927.
———. *The Early Christian Church and Modern Spiritualism.* London: Psychic Bookshop and Library, 1925.
———. *The History of Spiritualism.* Vol. 2. London: Cassell, 1926.
———. *The New Revelation.* London: Hodder & Stoughton, 1918.
———. *An Open Letter to Those of My Generation.* London: Psychic Press, 1927.
———. *Psychic Experiences.* London: G. P. Putnam's Sons, 1925.
———. *The Vital Message.* London: Hodder & Stoughton, 1919.
Duffy, E. *The Stripping of the Altars: Traditional Religion in England c. 1400 – c. 1580.* New Haven: Yale University Press, 1992.
Editorial. *Christian Parapsychologist* 9 (1991): 38-39.
Edwards, O. D. *The Quest for Sherlock Holmes: A Biographical Study of Arthur Conan Doyle.* Edinburgh: Mainstream Publishing, 1983.
Findlay, J. Arthur. *The Rock of Truth or Spiritualism, the Coming World Religion.* London: Rider, 1933.
Forster, D. *Spiritualism and Life and Death: Addresses Delivered in Reply to Sir Arthur Conan Doyle by Mr James Boyd and Mr. J. T. Mawson.* London: Central Bible Trust Depot, 1920.
———. *The Vital Choice: Endor or Calvary? A Reply to Sir A. Conan Doyle's "The New Revelation."* London: Morgan & Scott, 1919.
Fussell, P. *The Great War and Modern Memory.* New York: Oxford University Press, 1975.
Gilbert, M. *The Great War: A Modern History.* New York: Henry Holt, 1994.
Graves, R. *Goodbye to All That.* London: Penguin Books, 1960.
Haddow, A. "The Churches and Psychical Research: A Review of Some Twentieth Century Official Documents." *Christian Parapsychologist* 3 (1980): 291-303.
Hastings, A. *A History of English Christianity, 1920 to 1985.* London: Fount Paperbacks, 1986.
Haynes, R. *The Society for Psychical Research, 1882-1982.* London: MacDonald, 1982.
Henson, H. H. *Retrospection of an Unimportant Life* Vol. 1. London: Oxford University Press, 1942.
Inge, W. R. *Lay Thoughts of a Dean.* New York: G. P. Putman's Sons, 1926.
———. "Perfect through Suffering." In *War and Christianity.* London: Jarrold, 1914.

———. "Risen with Christ." In *Christ and the World at War: Sermons Preached in War-Time*. London: James Clarke, 1917.
Inglis, B. *Science and Parascience: A History of the Paranormal, 1914-1939*. London: Hodder & Stoughton, 1969.
Iremonger, F. A. *William Temple Archbishop of Canterbury: His Life and Letters*. London: Oxford University Press, 1992.
Jalland, P. *Death in the Victorian Family*. Oxford: Oxford University Press, 1996.
Jasper, R. C. D. *The Development of the Anglican Liturgy, 1662-1980*. London: SPCK, 1989.
Jolly, W. P. *Sir Oliver Lodge*. London: Constable, 1974.
Jones, K. *Conan Doyle and the Spirits: The Spiritualist Career of Sir Arthur Conan Doyle*. Wellingborough, Northamptonshire: Aquarian Press, 1989.
Kent, J. *William Temple*. Cambridge: Cambridge University Press, 1992.
Kollar, R. "The Church of England and Joanna Southcott: The Revelation of Her Secret Writings in 1927." *Journal of Religion and Psychical Research* 22 (April 1999): 68-82.
———. "Prophecy, Anglicanism, and the Great War: The Archbishop of Canterbury and Joanna Southcott's Sealed Box." *Dutch Review of Church History* 78 (1998): 94-112.
Koven, S. "Remembering the Dismemberment: Crippled Children, Wounded Soldiers, and the Great War in Great Britain." *American Historical Review* 99 (October 1994): 1167-1202.
The Lambeth Conferences (1867-1930). London: SPCK, 1948.
Lawrence, M. *Ferry Over Jordan*. London: Robert Hale, 1944.
Le Fleming Shepherd, Marie. *Religion after the War: A Reply to the Rev. Chas. Tweedale, Vicar of Weston, Yorks*. London: Church Army Press, 1917.
Lockhart, J. G. *Cosmo Gordon Lang*. London: Hodder & Stoughton, 1949.
Lodge, O. "The Attitude of the Church to the Phenomena Known as Spiritualistic." *Hibbert Journal* 18 (1920): 259-74.
———. "Christianity and Spiritualism." In J. Marchant, ed., *Life after Death According to Christianity and Spiritualism*. London: Cassell, 1925.
———. "Ether, Matter, and the Soul." *Hibbert Journal* 17 (1919): 15-19.
———. Introduction to *Ancient Lights or the Bible, the Church, and Psychic Science: An Attempt to Restore the Ancient Light of the Bible and the Church*, by M. A. St. Clair Stobart. London: Kegan Paul, Trench, Truber, 1923.
———. *Past Years: An Autobiography*. London: Hodder & Stoughton, 1931.
———. *Raymond: Or Life and Death: With Examples of the Evidence for Survival of Memory and Affection after Death*. London: Methuen, 1916.
———. "The Scientific World and Dr. Mercier: A Reply." *Hibbert Journal* 16 (1917): 29-32.

Machen, A. *The Angels of the Mons: The Bowmen and Other Legends of the War*. New York: G. P. Putnam's Sons, 1915.

Marrin, A. "The Church of England in the First World War." Ph.D. diss., Columbia University, 1968.

———. *The Last Crusade: The Church Of England in the First World War*. Durham, N.C.: Duke University Press, 1974.

Mathews, B., ed. *Christ and the World at War: Sermons Preached in War-Time*. London: James Clark, 1917.

Matthews, P. *Christianity and Spiritualism*. Stoke on Trent: Key Press, 1998.

Matthews, W. R. *Psychical Research and Theology*. London: Society for Psychical Research, 1940.

Moore, E. G. *Survival: A Reconsideration: The Sixteenth Frederic W. H. Myers Memorial Lecture*. London: Society for Psychical Research, 1966.

———. *Try the Spirits: Christianity and Psychical Research*. New York: Oxford University Press, 1977.

Moore, R. Laurence. *In Search of White Crows: Spiritualism, Parapsychology, and American Culture*. New York: Oxford University Press, 1977.

Mosse, George L. *Fallen Soldiers: Reshaping the Memory of the World Wars*. New York: Oxford University Press, 1990.

Moynihan, M., ed. *God on Our Side*. London: Secker & Warburg, 1983.

Nelson, G. *Spiritualism and Society*. New York: Schocken, 1969.

Oaten, E. W. *"That Reminds Me": A Medley of Personal Psychic Experiences*. Manchester: Two Worlds Publishing, 1938.

The Official Report of the Church Congress held at Leicester on October 12th, 13th, 14th, 15th, 16th, and 17th 1919. London: Nisbet, 1919.

Oppenheim, J. *The Other World: Spiritualism and Psychical Research in England, 1850-1914*. Cambridge: Cambridge University Press, 1985.

Palmstierna, E. K. *Horizons of Immortality: A Quest for Reality*. London: Constable, 1937.

———. "'Horizons of Immortality' and the Subconscious Mind." Lang Papers. Vol. 70. Lambeth Palace Library.

Parker-Wakefield, M. *The Facts about Orthodox Religions and Spiritualism Explained*. London: Regency Press, 1995.

Perris, W. Walker. *The Wheat from the Chaff: An Introduction to the Study of Spiritualism and Its Relation to Christianity*. London: Regency Press, 1979.

Perry, M. *Psychic Studies: A Christian's View*. Wellingborough, Northamptonshire: Aquarian Press, 1984.

Perry, M., ed. *Spiritualism: The 1939 Report to the Archbishop of Canterbury*. Louth, Lincolnshire: The Churches' Fellowship for Psychical and Spiritual Studies, 1999.

Podmore, Frank. *Modern Spiritualism: A History and a Criticism*. 2 vols. London: Meuthen, 1902.

Prayer and the Departed: A Report of the Archbishop of the Archbishops' Commission on Christian Doctrine. London: SPCK, 1971.

Psychic Phenomena with Reference to the Christian Tradition. Lang Papers. Vol. 70. Lambeth Palace Library.

Report of the Committee Appointed to Consider and Report upon the Subject of Ministries of Healing: (a) the Unction of the Sick; (b) Faith Healing and "Christian Science." Lambeth Conference Papers. 1908. LC 78. Lambeth Palace Library.

Report of the Committee on "Supernormal Psychic Phenomena" to the General Assembly of the Church of Scotland. 26 May 1922. Lambeth Palace Library.

St. Clair Stobart, M. A. *Ancient Lights or the Bible, the Church, and Psychic Science: An Attempt to Restore the Ancient Lights of the Bible and the Church.* London: Kegan Paul, Trench, Trubner, 1923.

―――. *The Apocrypha Reviewed by a Spiritualist.* London: Kegan Paul, Trench, Trubner, 1930.

―――. *The Either—Or of Spiritualism.* London: Rider, 1928.

―――. *Miracles and Adventures: An Autobiography.* London: Rider, 1935.

―――. *The Open Secret.* London: Psychic Press, 1947.

―――. *The Prayer Book X-Rayed.* London: Psychic Press, 1939.

―――. *Psychic Bible Stories for Young and Old.* London: Wright & Brown, 1933.

―――. *Torchbearers of Spiritualism.* London: George Allen Unwin, 1925.

Salter, W. H. *The Society for Psychical Research: An Outline of Its History.* London: Society for Psychical Research, 1978.

The Silence of Dr. Lang. London: Psychic Press, 1942.

Spurr, F. C. "Christianity and Spiritualism." in J. Marchant, ed., *Life after Death according to Christianity and Spiritualism.* London: Cassell, 1925.

Stephenson, A. *Anglicanism and the Lambeth Conferences.* London: SPCK, 1978.

Stretter, B. H., et al. *Immortality: An Essay in Discovery.* New York: Macmillan, 1917.

Taylor, A. J. P. *English History, 1914-1945.* Oxford: Clarendon Press, 1965.

Temple, W. "All Saints' Day." In *Fellowship with God.* London: Macmillan, 1920.

―――. *The Christian Hope of Life Eternal.* London: SPCK, 1942.

―――. *Church and Nature: The Bishop Paddock Lectures for 1914-15.* London: Macmillan, 1915.

―――. "The Communion of Saints." In *Repton School Sermons: Studies in the Religion of the Incarnation.* London: Macmillan, 1913.

―――. "Death and Resurrection." In *Repton School Sermons: Studies in the Religion of the Incarnation.* London: Macmillan, 1913.

―――. *Mens Creatrix: An Essay.* London: Macmillan, 1949.

——. "More Than Conquerors." In *Fellowship with God*. London: Macmillan, 1920.

——. *Nature, Man and God, Being the Clifford Lectures Delivered in the University of Glasgow in the Academic Years, 1932-1933 and 1933-1934*. London: Macmillan, 1934.

——. "The Secret of Peace." In *Fellowship with God*. London: Macmillan, 1920.

——. "Triumphant Sacrifice." In *Fellowship with God*. London: Macmillan, 1920.

Thomas, K. *Religion and the Decline of Magic: Studies in Popular Belief in Sixteenth Century England*. London: Weidenfeld & Nicolson, 1971.

Tweedale, C. *Man's Survival after Death or the Other Side of Life in the Light of Human Experience and Modern Research*. London: Grant Richards, 1909.

——. *Present Day Spirit Phenomena and the Churches: The Modern Religious Position*. St. Louis: Progressive Thinker Publishing, 1933.

Whately Smith, W. *A Critique of the Phenomenal Basis of Spiritualism*. Lambeth Conference Papers, 1920. LC 135. Lambeth Palace Library.

Wilkinson, A. *The Church of England and the First World War*. London: SPCK, 1978.

——. *Dissent or Conform: War and Peace and the English Churches, 1900-1945*. London: SPCK, 1986.

Wilkinson, D. H. D. *A Christian Spotlight on Spiritualism*. London: Hillside Press, 1935.

Wilkinson, R. "'The War Has Made Me Think!' A Personal and Plain Statement of Fact." *London Magazine* 39 (1918): 118-20.

Winnington-Ingram, A. F. "Bearing the Cross." In *The Church in Time of War*. London: Wells Gardner, Darton, 1915.

——. "The Conditions of Victory." In *Christ and the World at War: Sermons Preached in War-Time*. London: James Clarke, 1917.

——. "Heaviness and Joy." In *The Church in Time of War*. London: Wells Gardner, Darton, 1915.

——. *Life for Ever and Ever*. London: Wells Gardner, 1915.

——. *Rays of Dawn*. Milwaukee: Morehouse Publishing, 1918.

——. "The Way Everlasting." In *The Church in Time of War*. London: Wells Gardner, Darton, 1915.

Winter, J. M. *The Great War and the British People*. Cambridge: Harvard University Press, 1986.

——. *Sites of Memory, Sites of Mourning*. Cambridge: Cambridge University Press, 1995.

——. "Spiritualism and the First World War." In R. W. Davis and R. J. Helmstadter, eds., *Religion and Irreligion in Victorian Society: Essays in Honor of R. K. Webb*. New York: Routledge, 1992.

The Worship of the Church: Being the Report of the Archbishops' Second Committee of Inquiry. In *The National Mission of Repentance and Hope: Reports of the Archbishops' Committees of Inquiry.* London: SPCK, 1919.

Index

Adamson, E., 81
Advisory Council on Spiritual Healing, 84
Angels of the Mons, 7
Anglican Church: Burial Office of, 39; declining membership of, 15, 109–10; eschatology of, 18, 21, 121–22; Office for the Dead, 122, 173; response to bereaved, x, xiii, 14, 15, 33, 36, 63, 65, 70, 77, 80, 85, 119, 144, 145, 151, 172; shortcomings of, x, 4–5, 14, 15, 24, 33, 36, 39, 47, 55, 57, 64–65, 66; worship experience in, 33–34, 168
Anglican Communion, 46, 61, 63
Anglo-Catholic party, 17
Anson, Harold, 87, 90, 92, 95, 98, 116, 125, 133–34, 137n44, 152n17, 163
anti-Christian spiritualists, 86, 158, 169
Archbishop's Committee on Spiritualism, ix–x, xiv, 107–37, 141, 142, 148–50, 152
astrology, 5
Atkinson, Justice, 115
automatic writing, 82, 172. *See also* automatism
automatism, 53, 62. *See also* automatic writing

Baily, Cyril, 90, 92
Baldwin, Stanley, 82
Barbanell, Maurice, 147–48, 149–50
Barnes, Ernest William, 89, 123, 137n44, 141
Beecher, Henry Ward, 44
Bell, G. K. A., 46
Bennett, Ernest, 148
bereavement, response to by the Anglican Church. *See* Anglican Church, response to bereaved
bereavement, and spiritualism. *See* spiritualism, bereavement and
Besant, Mrs. Annie, 67
Bird, L. W., 99, 100
Blavatsky, H. P., 67
Blatchford, Robert, 78
Boddy, A. A., 7
Bond, F. Bligh, 61, 74n62
Book of Common Prayer, 16, 24, 80
Brittain, Vera, 8
Broad, C. D., 171
Brown, William, 90, 91, 98, 116, 163
Brown, William (Witness F), 115
Burge, H. M., 47–48, 49–50, 54–58, 60, 102n18

Cannadine, David, 2, 8
Cecil, William, 60
Chapman, John, 167
Christian Psychic Society, 80

Christian Science, 46, 50, 51, 54, 55, 62, 63, 66, 89, 110, 155; as a cult, 55–56, 155
Christian Spiritualist Church Union, 80
Christianity, centrality of in spiritualism, 50, 51
Church Congress (1919), 37–38, 39–40
Colenso, John William, 46
communicating with spirits, 10, 12, 49, 51, 54, 64, 72n38, 81, 88, 96, 108, 109, 110, 112, 115, 118, 120, 121, 123, 142, 157–58, 160, 168, 170
communion of saints, 16, 23, 34, 53–54, 55, 57, 63, 65, 82, 117, 121, 156, 158, 162, 168; doctrine of, 15, 17, 18–21, 52, 71, 81, 89, 119, 122, 172, 173; hope in, 18, 146
Conan Doyle, Arthur, 11–15, 21, 28n73, 29n88, 34–36, 37, 40, 45, 57, 78, 169
Confraternity of Clergy, Ministers, Laymen, and Spiritualists, 23, 125, 132, 142
Copleston, E. A., 59

d'Aranyi, Miss, 96–97
Darwin, Charles, xi
Davidson, Randall, 3, 33, 34, 37, 40, 41, 42–44, 46, 47, 52, 54, 55, 56, 61, 62, 72n38, 79, 82–83
Dawbarn, Charles, 34–35
de Brath, Stanley, 43–44, 61, 62
de Candole, Henry, 92
Doctrine in the Church of England, 80–81
Don, Alan, 81, 132, 143
Dougell, L., 61
Doyle, Lady, 36, 37

Duffy, Eamon, 16
Duncan, Helen, 151n7
Durnford, Richard, 44

Eddy, Mary Baker, 66
Eden, G. R., 59
Elcock, E. G., 148
Elliott, G. Maurice, 82–83, 102n26
eschatology, of the Anglican Church, 21. See also Anglican Church, eschatology of

Fachiri, Mr. and Mrs., 96–97
faith, as center of Christianity, 120, 167
Findlay, Arthur, 129. See also International Institute for Psychical Research, Ltd.
Fodor, Nandor, 99, 116. See also International Institute for Psychical Research, Ltd.
Fox, Katie, 111, 169
Fox, Margaret, 111, 139, 169
Francis of Assisi, 14
Fraudulent Mediums Act of 1951, 151n7

Garbett, C. F., 123, 141
Gates, W. T., 44, 72n38
Gatty, Oliver, 116
General Assembly of the Church of Scotland, 69–70
Gnosticism, 110
Gnostics, 64
Gow, David, 61, 74n62
Great Box of Sealed Writings, 78–79. See also Panacea Society
Greater World Spiritualist League, 80
Grensted, L. W., 90, 91, 95, 98, 116, 130, 163
Guerry, W. A., 57

Halifax, Lord, 17
Hastings, Adrian, 15
Henn, H., 57–58
Henson, Herbert Hensley, 7, 46, 137n44
Hicks, F. C. N., 123
Hine, John Edward, 79
human personality, survival of after death, 110, 113, 118
Hunt, H. E., 125, 126

Ignatius of Llanthony, 44
Incarnation of the Lord, centrality of, 64
Inge, William Ralph, 5–6, 17–18, 38
Ingram, Kenneth, 92
International Institute for Psychical Research, Ltd., 99, 116, 129

Jesus Christ, as Mediator, 59, 60, 65, 71, 156, 168
Joan of Arc, 7
Jones, H. Gresford, 59

karma, and theosophy, 67
King, G. L., 59, 60, 74n59
Knox, E. A., 80

Lambeth Conference (1920), 22, 31n147, 33 ff; topics at, 46–47
Lang, Cosmo Gordon, ix, xiv, 44, 54, 79, 81–82, 83, 84, 86–88, 89–95, 98–101, 107–9, 112, 122, 123–24, 126–28, 130, 131, 132–34, 136n39, 140–42, 144, 145, 149, 152n17
Leicester Church Congress, 40–41
Leonard, Mrs. Osborne, 1, 9
Lethem, George, 125, 126
Lodge, Oliver, 1, 9–11, 35, 41, 61
Lomax, T. L., 39
London Spiritual Alliance, 110, 114, 144

Lyttleton, Edith, 115, 135n10

Machen, Arthur, 7
Macmillan, John Victor, 82–83
Magee, J. A. V., 39–41, 45
Maher, Paul, xv
materialism, and spiritualism, 7, 15, 23, 36. *See also* spiritualism, and materialism
Matthews, W. R., 92, 95, 96, 97, 98, 116, 130, 134, 137n44, 143, 163
Mayfield, Guy, 92, 98, 120, 173
McDougall, William, 170–71
medium, 64, 88, 89, 110, 111, 112, 113, 140, 147, 151n7, 152n17, 155, 157–58, 159, 160, 166, 169, 172
mediumship, 53
Moore, E. Garth, 151
Moore, R. Laurence, 139
Mozley, J. K., 90, 92
mysticism, 67

National Federation of Discharged and Demobilized Sailors and Soldiers, 34
National Laboratory of Psychical Research, 79
National Mission of Repentance and Hope, 33
National Peace Council, 78
necromancy, 5, 18, 39, 53, 69, 170
Nelson, Geoffrey, xi–xii, 78, 80, 139–40
Neo-Platonists, 64
Nowicki, Douglas R., xv

Oaten, E. W., 97, 115
occult, 67
Olcott, H. S., 67
Oppenheim, Janet, xi, xii
Oxford Movement, 16

pacifism, and spiritualism, 78
Palmstierna, Erik K., 94, 96–97, 98, 116, 125, 127, 131–32, 144
Panacea Society, 79. *See also* Great Box of Sealed Writings
pantheism, 67
Parsons, R. G., 141, 148
Perry, Michael, xiii, xiv, xv
Phelps, F. R., 52–54
Phillimore, Mercy, 110–11, 114–15, 143–44
Pollock, Bertram, 89, 137n44
prayers for the dead, 16–17, 34, 39, 80, 81, 119, 122, 163, 172, 173
predestination and election, doctrine of, 24
Price, Harry, 79
psychic phenomena, 69, 84, 85, 98, 112, 115–16, 120, 135n6, 162; and the early church, 22, 61, 117, 159; investigation of, 53, 56, 64, 67, 83, 86, 87, 89, 91, 97, 113, 118, 122–23, 165–66, 171–72; in sacred writings, xi, 10, 69, 114, 149, 159; similarity to Christian beliefs, 12, 114, 117; source of, 22, 86, 171; and spiritual gifts, 13, 69–70; types of, xiii, 69, 113, 115, 135n6, 159–60
purgatory, 81; Roman belief in, 16

Quest Club, 110, 114

Radford, L. B., 50–52
Raven, Charles, 90, 91, 92
Rawlinson, A. E. J., 90, 91, 98, 123
Rawlinson, Mildred, 120, 173
Reformers, 15–16, 39
Reid, William A., 69
reincarnation, and theosophy, 67
Richmond, Kenneth, 115
Robberds, W. J. F., 59
Romanism, 16, 17, 80

Ryle, Herbert Edward, 46

Sandlands, Paul E., 90, 91, 95, 98, 116, 163
Scripture: as basis for Christianity, 16, 53, 55; conflict with science, 85
séance, 14, 82, 83, 87, 96, 98, 130, 152n17, 155, 166, 172
Seven Principles of Spiritualism, 112
Shepherd, Mrs. M. le F., 31n152
Sheppard, Dick, 17
Soal, S. G., 171
Society for Psychical Research, xii–xiii, 8–9, 40, 42, 45, 49, 56, 60, 64, 70, 77, 79, 86, 87, 89, 91, 93, 111, 115, 130
Society of Communion, 22. *See also* Tweedale, Charles
sorcery, 69
Southcott, Joanna, 78–79
spiritual gifts, 13, 69–70
spiritualism: benefits to Christianity, xii, 21, 25, 110, 111, 114, 115, 144, 158; bereavement and, ix, 12, 14–15, 38, 58, 63, 77, 109, 115, 144, 146, 150; centrality of Christianity in, 50, 51; as a cult, 51, 52, 55–56, 57, 60, 64, 65, 89, 155, 156; dangers of, xii, 46, 48, 49, 50–51, 52–56, 57, 58, 61, 62, 74, 83, 87, 119, 120, 122, 142, 156, 166, 169–70; decline in popularity, 139–40; growth of popularity in, x, 5, 6, 8, 11, 17–18, 38, 61, 62, 63, 64, 71, 77, 78, 80, 107, 109, 139; and materialism, xii, 23, 36, 47–48, 55, 62, 63, 64, 71, 155; and pacifism, 78; position of Anglican Church on, xii, 51, 58, 61, 62, 64, 65, 68, 77, 85, 97, 99, 121, 128, 143,

150, 163, 173; psychological dangers of, 59–60, 65, 91, 162, 170; relationship to Christianity, xii, 10–11, 12, 13, 14, 23–24, 26, 28n73, 34, 47, 49, 55, 58, 60, 62, 63, 68, 71, 77, 79–80, 82, 84, 87, 107, 109–11, 113–14, 116–17, 140, 143, 149, 150–51; religious aspects of, 23, 52, 58, 60, 109–12, 114–15, 119, 131, 152n17, 156; scientific basis for, 43, 86–87, 118, 130, 157; scientific research and, 11, 49, 52, 56, 64, 91, 110, 113, 155, 159; as superstition, 17, 61, 170; supporting arguments for, 22, 37, 42–43, 44, 114, 159
spiritualist churches, xii, 85, 109, 112, 135n6, 140
Spiritualist Community, 125
Spiritualist Movement, 78
spiritualist organizations, xii, 8, 78, 80, 111–12, 135n6
spiritualists, anti-Christian, 86, 158, 169
Spiritualists National Federation (SNF), 28n51. *See also* Spiritualists' National Union (SNU)
Spiritualists' National Union (SNU), 9, 28n51, 62, 77, 80, 111–12, 135n6, 140
Spurgeon, Charles H., 44
St. Clair Stobart, Mrs. M. A., 23–25, 82–83, 125–26, 127–28, 131, 132–34, 142–43, 150
Stephenson, M. G., 46
Stephenson, Gwendolen, 92, 98, 116, 163
Strutt, Robert John, 143
suffering, views on, 3, 6
Swaffer, Hannen, 78
Swayne, W. S., 38, 39, 44–45

Talbot, E. S., 57–58
telepathy, 64, 159
Temple, William, 18–21, 52, 84, 86–87, 93–94, 102n18, 123, 137n44, 141, 145–49
Theosophical Society, 67, 68
theosophy, 46, 50, 51, 54, 55, 62, 63, 66, 67–68, 155; as a cult, 55–56, 155; karma and, 67; reincarnation and, 67
Thomas, Keith, xiv, 14
Tweedale, Charles, 22–23, 31n152, 61, 68–69. *See also* Society of Communion

Underhill, Evelyn, 90, 91–93, 109
Underhill, Francis, xv, 83–84, 86–91, 94–95, 97, 100–01, 102n29, 103n35, 107–09, 112, 116, 122–23, 126–28, 130, 131–32, 141–42

Vagrancy Act 1824, 151n7
vicarious atonement, doctrine of, 24

Waller, E. H. M., 55–56
Walpole, G. H. S., 56, 57
West-Watson, Campbell, 62
Weston, Frank, 46
Whately Smith, W., 42–43, 52
Whittingham, Walter Godfrey, 89
Wigglesworth, Walter S., 90, 95, 98–99, 100, 101, 107, 120, 173
Wild, H. L., 59
Wilkinson, D. H. D., 84, 103n34
Williams, Henry Herbert, 89
Winnington-Ingram, Arthur Foley, 4–5, 17, 34–35, 82, 88–89, 123
Winter, J. M., 6, 8
witchcraft, 5
Witchcraft Act 1735, 151n7
Woods, Frank Theodore, 38, 59, 73n59

About the Author

Rene Kollar is professor of history at Saint Vincent College and Saint Vincent Seminary, Latrobe, Pennsylvania. Professor Kollar received his Ph.D. from the University of Maryland in 1981. He is the author of *Westminster Cathedral: From Dream to Reality* (1987), *The Return of the Benedictines to London: A History of Ealing Abbey from 1896 to Independence* (1989), *Abbot Aelred Carlyle, Caldey Island, and the Anglo-Catholic Revival in England* (1995), *Aspects of the Revival of Monasticism in the West in the 19th and Early 20th Centuries* (1996), and numerous articles dealing with English ecclesiastical history.